The Popular Economy in Urban Latin America

The Popular Economy in Urban Latin America

Informality, Materiality, and Gender in Commerce

Edited by
Eveline Dürr
and Juliane Müller

LEXINGTON BOOKS
Lanham • Boulder • New York • London

Published by Lexington Books
An imprint of The Rowman & Littlefield Publishing Group, Inc.
4501 Forbes Boulevard, Suite 200, Lanham, Maryland 20706
www.rowman.com

6 Tinworth Street, London SE11 5AL, United Kingdom

British Library Cataloguing in Publication Information Available

Library of Congress Cataloging-in-Publication Data

Names: Durr, Eveline, editor. | Muller, Juliane, 1977- editor.
Title: The popular economy in urban Latin America : informality, materiality, and gender in commerce / edited by Eveline Durr and Juliane Muller.
Description: Lanham : Lexington Books, [2019] | Includes bibliographical references and index.
Identifiers: LCCN 2019007082 (print) | LCCN 2019008790 (ebook) | ISBN 9781498572408 (Electronic) | ISBN 9781498572392 (cloth)
Subjects: LCSH: Latin America—Economic conditions—1982- | Informal sector (Economics)—Latin America. | Urban economics—Social aspects.
Classification: LCC HC125 (ebook) | LCC HC125 .P6588 2019 (print) | DDC 330—dc23
LC record available at https://lccn.loc.gov/2019007082

Contents

List of Figures

Acknowledgments

The contributions to this book, except the chapter by Cristina Vega and Magali Marega, emerged from a symposium at the Ludwig-Maximilians-Universität München in 2016 entitled "Urban Economies: Grassroots Entrepreneurs and Neighbourhood Economies between Resilience and Innovation." This symposium was part of the editors' ongoing research projects in urban and economic anthropology, funded by the Deutsche Forschungsgemeinschaft (DFG) and the Ludwig-Maximilians-Universität München. We thank Luisa Marten and Hannah Roberson for their editorial assistance. We also thank Lexington Books, in particular Nicolette Amstutz and Jessica Thwaite, for their support throughout the publication process.

Introduction

(In)Formality, Materiality, and Gender in Latin American Cities

Juliane Müller and Eveline Dürr

Which actors, and with what *agencies*, are forming and transforming street markets and other place-based economies, and with what effects? What are the emerging lines of tension in these particular economies? Our book takes these questions as the starting point for a reframing of the current thinking in economic anthropology, sociology, and urban studies on popular economy and petty commerce. As the emblematic title of the seminal book edited by Gracia Clark, *Trader versus the State* (1988), reflects, it is this relationship that has been at the core of many studies of "informal" and street economies, especially in Latin America (Bhowmik 2010; Cross and Morales 2013; Evers and Seale 2015; Fernández-Kelly and Shefner 2008; Hansen, Little, and Milgram 2013; Wilson 2011). We argue that this classic dyadic relationship between vendors and the state needs to be complicated. We build on approaches that critically engage with the concept of informality and conceive of it as an ambiguous and politically contested term (Herrle and Fokdal 2011; Roy 2005, 2009; Roy and AlSayyad 2004). In cities, a range of actors with various agencies are involved in the functioning of popular trade. Consequently, informality is increasingly amorphous and polyvalent. Simultaneously, governmental and private-sector entities are pursuing diverse and often contradictory initiatives that combat and promote informality. In the process, a wide range of material, legal, and discursive devices—sometimes disputed—are transforming popular urban economies. We argue that reframing public space, urban markets, and commercial networks, as parts of broader socio-material entanglements within the context of changing political regimes and international investments, can help us to better understand these new aspects of contemporary worlds and possible futures of popular commerce. With this aim in mind, the book develops a cultural-economic perspective on the popular urban economy, foregrounding informality, materiality, and gender, based on ethnographic and archival research spanning more than three decades and several generations.

In Latin America, the proliferation of contact zones and the making of new connections has specific dimensions. It is the fastest urbanizing region in the Global South, as international organizations and the media never tire of announcing. This spurs anticipation of heightened levels of consumption. National and international corporations invest in housing, telecommunications, and mass retailing to target the purchasing power of the "rising middle-classes," phenomena we observe across the continent under both state-centric and liberal governments. Global brands specifically approach metropolitan areas in Latin America in their search for new outlets and "emerging markets." While international investment accelerates the privatization of public space, and the construction of shopping malls and hypermarkets add more challenges to popular commerce, these also produce novel interfaces and unexpected engagements between small-scale and big corporate actors. Moreover, East Asian investments are growing considerably throughout the region and redirecting popular commercial flows as, for instance, when Chinese-made commodities are imported to metropolitan centers by both native and Asian migrant merchants and further distributed through secondary cities and suburban marketplaces (Müller and Colloredo-Mansfeld 2018).

Popular urban economies in Latin American cities are becoming increasingly diverse and internally stratified as the landscape of opportunity widens but also becomes more fragmented. Today, popular commerce ranges from itinerant traders and traders with a formalized position on the sidewalk or in a street market, to shopkeepers, self-employed wholesalers, and importers who conduct business trips to China several times a year. It comprises shops and fairs that advertise through social media, and hawkers who own at best an outdated mobile phone. Technological change fosters new forms of interaction between traders, companies, and customers, and may create new imbalances in economic communities, when some individuals tap into new market niches and service offerings and are able to profit from the augmented national and international attention, whereas others fall behind. More experienced traders with established translocal connections, for instance, may withstand aversive policies, recreate commodity networks, and guarantee a stable basis of clients. Endurance amidst change can characterize some actors in urban economies and points to the "longue durée" of these gradually evolving processes. We argue that the manifold consequences of these developments should be understood by closely scrutinizing the many interfaces of traders with other actors and agencies. In this book, we not only concentrate on these issues, which are hardly addressed in the Latin American literature, but we also pay attention to the imaginaries associated with the "informal" and the materiality of grassroots commerce in the city. With this in mind, we follow more recent theoretical approaches in cultural economy and urban studies which call for popular commerce to be partly readdressed. Thinking on urban assemblages, diverse economies, and the cultural-economic approach, often drawing on post-structuralism and actor-network-theory (Amin and Thrift 2004; Çalışkan and Callon 2009, 2010; Farías and Blok 2016; Farías and Bender 2009; Gibson-Graham 2008), has the potential to provide new insights. In this edited collection—while remaining sensitive to history, gender, and urban politics—we aim to offer an ethnographically informed cultural and socio-material perspective on how popular economies and commerce thrive, transform, and persist in Latin American cities today.

POPULAR URBAN ECONOMY AND LATIN AMERICAN COMMERCE

In Latin American social sciences, "popular economy" is associated with the Peruvian scholars José Matos Mar (1984) and Aníbal Quijano (1998). The term has also been used since the early 1980s by Latin American economists and Chilean development scholars, influenced by the work of CEPAL (UN Economic Commission for Latin America and the Caribbean) headquartered in Santiago de Chile (Hillenkamp, Lapeyre, and Lemaître 2013). In the midst of economic and political instability, and of Marxist and structuralist debates on dependency, periphery, and modernity, this notion indicated a major shift in the analysis and political conception of Latin American petty traders and small family businesses in the world economy. Rather than being regarded as a residual feature of precapitalist modes of production, or as an impediment to "modern" economic development, artisanal economies and those based around small-scale trade have been seen as distinctively contemporary, reproductive, and (semi)autonomous, potentially with transformative power. These latter aspects have gained prominence since the mid-2000s, when the political shift to the left in the region coincided with the global financial crisis. The international economic turmoil has contributed to a felt urgency within economic anthropology, geography, and sociology to articulate alternatives to dominant free-market economics (Narotzky and Besnier 2014). In Latin America, this engaged research field resonated with emergent left-wing governments that have officially recognized a popular economy within economic plurality in Argentina, Bolivia, Brazil, Ecuador, and Venezuela (Coraggio 2013; Hillenkamp, Lapeyre, and Lemaitre 2013). Within these countries, pluralist economic thinking has been related to a fundamental questioning of mainstream economic theory (Gago, Cielo, and Gachet 2018), and the project of promoting indigenous and community economies. Such projects acknowledge reciprocal networks and particular cosmovisions, which are grounded in the notion of "buen vivir" (Escobar 2010, Gudynas 2011). Also, more applied approaches, such as "social and solidarity economy" (ESS), continue the thinking on popular economies (Coraggio 2013).

Less frequently addressed in the literature is the fact that economic policies in the region were also informed by resurgent nationalisms and top-down approaches that reintroduced economic orthodoxies and counteracted the heterodox opportunities of economic pluralism. As several chapters in this book highlight, equating the popular economy with a social and solidarity economy does not quite stand up to ethnographic scrutiny. Ethnographic studies offer a critical and potentially counterintuitive contribution to approaches that—while opening the discursive and imaginative space of the possible—tend to re-instantiate conceptual boundaries between capitalist and community economies (Gibson-Graham 1996, 2008; Lane and Wood 2009). While we are sympathetic toward empirical research on distributive practices and institutional arrangements that spread surplus value, to look for them among popular traders might be a challenge. Whereas artisan cooperatives, associations of petty producers, and social enterprises, funded by international institutions and NGOs, follow principles of solidarity and redistribution more closely (Hillenkamp 2014), the reciprocity, mutuality, and collaboration found in urban popular economies across Latin America may play out differently than anticipated by these models (Antrosio and Colloredo-Mansfeld 2015; Nelms 2015). Moreover, the long tradition of livelihood studies and feminist Marxism reminds us that the community, the household, and kinship relations are all, potentially, part of capitalist value production (Bear, Ho, Tsing, and Yanagisako 2015; Gago, Cielo, and Gachet 2018). This critical stand does not foreclose the possibility of semiautonomous spaces and the resilience of popular economic practices, and these may be especially pertinent when it comes to understanding gender as key analytical category of popular trade (Vega and Marega, this book).

(IN)FORMALITY

It is hard to overlook the fact that informality is losing its shape. Giant internet and technology companies, who are evading both value-added taxes on their transnationally traded and promoted items and services, and labor regulations for their dispersed workforce, are not behaving so differently from those so-called informal economic actors, a term which is still associated with marginalized populations in the Global South and epitomized by street trade. As Keith Hart (2012) reiterated in the aftermath of the post-2008 financial crisis, the informalization of labor worldwide is widely acknowledged to have its roots in liberalization and deregulation policies that have been ongoing since the 1980s. However, in this book, we are interested not so much in informality as a ubiquitous phenomenon and grand narrative of neoliberal globalization, but in the constant oscillation between liberalization and state intervention in Latin America, concomitant changes in the politics of informality, and its impact on popular commerce in cities. In our analysis, we do not understand the informal economy as that which is unregulated by the state, nor do we conceptualize the "informal" and the "formal" as a pair of contrasting tendencies. Rather, we understand formality and informality as being simultaneously produced through legal-political, material, and discursive processes and multiple agencies in the city. In this, we take up the notion of informality as an "urban organizing logic" (Roy 2005), and a contested concept in negotiations over power, legitimacy, resources, and value (Herrle and Fokdal 2011; McFarlane 2012). In other words, we see informality not as something outside, beyond, or opposed to the state, but produced by the state and other powerful actors, and circulated and disputed among various stakeholders. This implies that "the formal-informal distinction is a multifaceted resource for naming, managing, governing, producing, and even critiquing contemporary cities" (McFarlane 2012, 89). We borrow these perspectives from critical urban thinking and studies on informal settlements (for an overview see Alfaro d'Alençon et al. 2018) to stress the shifting configurations of actors and agents involved in the co-constitution of economic (in)formalities in Latin American cities. We believe that crossing borders between bodies of research—in particular between urban planning, governance, and approaches centered on labor and economic activities—allows for the reframing and advancing of the debate on street and popular commerce in Latin America that has long centered on political economy, social structure, and the political struggles of traders versus the state, as mentioned above (Roy and AlSayyad 2004).

Today, economic informality is not generally condemned, but it is, at once, both selectively repressed and stimulated. As a political instrument, "informality" continues to criminalize traders and their activities, legitimizing top-down interventions in certain neighborhoods and commercial areas. As targets of "financial inclusion," "informal" market actors are seen to possess "hidden" assets and potentialities (Mörtenböck and Mooshammer 2015). As a marketing tool for (social) entrepreneurialism and slum upgrading, the informal has been framed as flexible, disruptive, and non-bureaucratic for at least three decades, not only by liberal economists (De Soto 1989), but also by global architects and artistic curators (Roy 2011; SLUM lab 2015). Since the 1980s, informality has become an internationally circulating buzzword used to point to either creativity or precarity, to capitalist accumulation or urban survival. This book sets out to unbundle the situated disputes and frictions that necessarily arise around such a polymorphous concept that accommodates diverse practices, multiple understandings, and contrasting interests.

Disputes around the meanings and boundaries of informality are addressed in several chapters. In Brazil, Bolivia, and Ecuador, the political changes from a neoliberal to a state-interventionist model have meant a shift from celebrating the competitive advantage and creative potential of informal economies, to condemning tax evasion and "anti-patriotic" practices. In Rafael Correa's Ecuador, a top-down approach to economic sovereignty, combined with ideas on popular economies as social and solidarity based, has tended to dismiss the distinctive place-based economies shaped by both competition and cooperation, as Colloredo-Mansfeld shows in his contribution. This chapter illustrates that competition is a highly controversial notion: it is not only at the heart of controversies on popular economies, but is also implicitly present in anthropological theories of the 1990s on globalization and cultural difference.

The research featured in this book, such as in the chapters by Mörtenböck and Mooshammer on Brazil, Göltenboth on Cuba,[1] and Colloredo-Mansfeld on Ecuador, reveals that disputes often do not break out into open conflicts, but rather emerge as "frictions" (Tsing 2004)—curious and at once disturbing misunderstandings among the people involved. It is through these frictions that urban popular economies are co-produced and maintained. Otavalo producers and traders in the North of Ecuador cannot but interpret business analyst Michael Porter's graphs on competitive advantages according to their own experiences, creating a distinctive apparel industry and commercial towns. In Belo Horizonte's "Hippie fair" Brazil (Mörtenböck and Mooshammer, this book), the controversy over whether it is an arts-and-crafts market to be protected as cultural patrimony, or a place for the exchange of Chinese-made cheap and counterfeit merchandise, seems constitutive for its ongoing existence. The artist's space of Muraleando in Havana, Cuba, is imagined as social space and solidary economy while actually maintained by mercantile strategies. These examples show that informality has gained new momentum as a vernacular discourse and contested concept in everyday use. As an index of difference between peoples and practices, the informal-formal binary expresses expectations and hopes of legality and citizenship on the one hand (Lazar 2012), and imaginaries of noncapitalist practice and vital creativity on the other. As "informality" is a notion that informs boundary-marking policies and policing around certain kinds of commercial transactions, spaces, and goods, it acquires material dimensions that have yet to be explored in more detail.

MATERIALITY

Given the eminent material quality of the goods moved in popular circuits of import, wholesale, and retail trade, it is surprising how little attention has been paid to materiality in research on urban informality and popular economy in Latin America. The same is true for infrastructure and the built environment as material expressions of particular commercial worlds. This seems to be a consequence of the research focus on the relationship between traders and the state and political economy approaches that have long dominated sociological and political debates.

To address this lacuna, we want to ask what an emphasis on materiality might offer for a better understanding of urban popular commerce. Obviously, materiality hints at the things and products being exchanged. Whether these are cloths from an indigenous weaving tradition or made in China and imported, or whether they are individual artworks or electronic devices produced by big corporations, makes a difference to traders and customers. There is an embodied material dimension to commerce as traders handle, bundle, unbundle, store, pack, move, and unpack goods with different physical qualities. Further, value is created through the encounters between traders and customers whose identities are formed in relation to goods they prefer to find in street markets. In this sense, the things of popular commerce matter (Miller 1998). In different ways and to various degrees they matter for traders' tasks and responsibilities, and for consumers, municipal authorities, and urban planners. They matter as annoyances, as disconcerting overflows into spaces not planned as marketplaces. The products of popular commerce are voluptuous, vulgar, appealing, and repellent in their sheer visibility and omnipresence. They seem to epitomize the unlimited growth in commodity production under capitalism as lower-strata consumers increase their material possessions. In a way, traders' merchandise is—like households' everyday objects—too obviously "there," out on the streets and pavements to be "seen" and analyzed (Miller 2005, 5). Urban popular commerce foregrounds the most visible dimension of materiality: the stuff and the commodities, but also the rubbish and remains arranged and left behind on paved sidewalks and streets, in stalls, shops, and warehouses.

While a humanist focus on materiality scrutinizes the constitutive role that "things" play in individuals' lives and the various ways in which things and people are related (cf. Miller 2005), posthumanist approaches tend to reconceptualize the very nature of things and their characteristics, that is, the status of "things" (Latour 2005) and "materials" in general (Ingold 2007). These approaches point to the ambivalent and sometime capricious ways of being of "things" and stress the relevance of interrelated forces in the production of life-worlds, and as we contend, of urban places that are "never ready-made, but always in formation" (McFarlane 2012, 101). Again, borrowings from urban studies with a focus on place-making in informal settlements as an interrelated process of material form and social practice are potentially productive here (Lombard 2014). For instance, in Latin America, popular urban commerce stands in a long tradition of periodic rural and rural-urban fairs where producers, many of whom are native women, sell staples and fresh produce from the ground, and of warehouse structures which sustain these flows of merchandise. Attempts by state actors and international forces to appropriate these material structures, or to redevelop urban space according to global and corporate templates such as the shopping mall, are powerful material and ideological interventions into more bottom-up forms of infrastructure and architecture (Mörtenböck and Mooshammer 2015). In this sense, what is classified as an informal market or as street trade is in fact often part of a "historical sequence of related phenomena," a variation of physical structures of local and regional economies (Mooshammer 2015, 25).

An approach in which materiality and economy are prominently brought together is actor-network-theory (ANT). Within this broad field that scrutinizes the entanglement of human and nonhuman agencies, the objective of ANT economics is to go beyond social-network and institutional analyses of markets to address the pragmatic impact of "heterogeneous constituents: rules and regulations; technical devices; metrological systems; logistical infrastructure; texts, discourses and narratives; technical and scientific knowledge; [human] competences and skills" (Çalışkan and Callon 2010, 3). Influenced by Science and Technology Studies, the research focus of ANT economics has been the "distribution" of calculative agencies in technology-intense industries, global finance, and world markets, as well as managerial and expert contexts (Çalışkan 2010; Callon, Millo, and Muniesa 2007). Two chapters in this book (Vereta-Nahoum and Müller) make use of the focus on market devices to analyze the material and regulatory interventions of state representatives and private enterprises in popular commerce and urban marketplaces. While hinting at novel insights gained by applying the perspective to urban popular economy, they also bring new dimensions to the fore: socio-material *agencements* beyond calculative functions, incomplete processes, and reversals of market devices, as well as their political nature (Vereta-Nahoum, this book). In this vein, they relate to approaches that link the material world to social and political domains, exploring multiple agencies and marketplaces as urban assemblages (Farías and Bender 2009).

By considering some traders, goods, and spaces in the planning process, and excluding others, urban planners produce formality as well as informality, which could be seen—analogously to Roy's urbanizing logic—as a mode of market-making in the city. Vereta-Nahoum's chapter illuminates how multiple state agents deploy material and regulatory devices to define a "proper" trading space with "legitimate" actors and products. These are processes of differentiation that precede the deployment of calculative agencies. Likewise, Müller, in her chapter on La Paz, Bolivia, looks at how multinational electronics corporations, while very much part of local socioeconomic worlds in terms of networks and face-to-face relations, assert power over popular commerce through the usage of technological devices and material incentives. Corporate employees use incentives and marketing instruments, rather than coercion, to induce traders to sell original brand-name appliances. Thus the "proper" market they envision and bring about differs significantly from that of the urban planners described in Vereta-Nahoum's chapter. Müller argues that although multinational corporations' practices in popular commerce heighten inequalities among traders, they also contribute to the ongoing attractiveness and persistence of popular wholesale and retail areas in the city.

Several chapters in this book show that the nexus between materiality and power is especially salient when it comes to urban development plans that often leave little room for street commerce and open markets. As Vega and Marega describe, urban planning in one neighborhood brings about material transformation in others, as popular traders create their own spaces at the crossroads of rural-urban transport networks and in otherwise transited areas. Those actors who are no longer recognized search for new (informal) opportunities elsewhere.

Moreover, the political nature of popular urban commerce includes sensory material dimensions, such as the smell of rotting garbage and cardboard, or the shining modernism of electronics. The informal as a particular aesthetic of goods and spaces may be framed as chaotic and "messy," or as creative and constructive, from the perspective of Western, middle-class, and bourgeois standards of governing urban space and commerce (Chalana and Hou 2016; Ghertner 2015; Vodopivec and Dürr forthcoming).

GENDER

The chapters in part III and the epilogue illustrate the trajectories, livelihoods, and opportunities of women traders within the world of popular commerce, which in many parts of the world has been, and continues to be, overwhelmingly female. The fact that women are over-represented in street economies and other trading activities reflects ongoing structural disadvantages with regard to education, domestic work, and labor-market access, but is also in part native to Latin American commerce over the longue durée. Highland indigenous women of Quechua and Aymara descent epitomize marketplace trade and commercial mobility across the Altiplano plateau (Babb, this book).

But how do female and male social roles in urban popular economy constitute each other? As the chapters in this section highlight, popular commerce is situated at the intersection of various institutions: the household and extended family, as well as public life and political organization. Traders move their family lives onto the street and into their shops. Their children become socialized into the trade from a very early age, not only because they assist their parents, but also because they do homework in the market and spend a lot of free time playing and sprawling around stalls and piles of merchandise. This dissolution of the boundaries between private and public space, and the use of public space as an extension of the household and the material base of the trading business, has in some contexts facilitated the political leadership of women, as described in the epilogue. Whereas the political agency of women in popular trade is starting to be acknowledged, research is still scarce on how male traders—out of necessity or ambition for upward mobility, whether married or as single heads of households—assume trading and provisioning tasks long seen as exclusive female domains. The contributions in this book, while attentive to the presence and roles of men, concentrate on women and advance the respective research traditions and approaches.

In order to understand the historical formation of subjectivities in the Andes, "complex networks of commerce and exchange" have to be taken into account (Arnold et al. 2009, 25ff; see also Larson, Harris, and Tandeter 1995). As Florence E. Babb explores in her chapter, the category of the *chola* emerges through urban encounters and economic transactions across racialized lines. In contemporary Peru, gender, racialized conceptions of social actors, and ethnicity continue to function as forms of difference in what Babb terms "braided" inequalities. Her feminist intersectional analysis highlights how structural differences are reproduced in articulation with one another. These differences emerge out of everyday practices and encounters in the city, but are also dependent on historical inequalities rooted in colonialism and on current global hierarchical discourses and institutions—and thus point beyond the local to broader contexts (Babb 2018; Mollett 2017).

Vega and Marega show in their contribution to this book that an intersectional analysis of difference and structural inequality should not lose sight of women's capacities for (semi)autonomous action. After a review of the shifting debate from informal to popular economy in Latin American social sciences, they stress, as does Babb, the gendered nature of popular commerce and the prominence of women within it. With an emphasis on reproduction and ordinary economic life (Narotzky 1997), they identify an eminent female character to networks, practical knowledge, and spatial appropriation, all features associated with the popular economy. In fact, the figure of the "cuentapropista"—a self-employed, independent trader, related more closely to the household, neighborhood, and union than to a firm or other capitalist institution—is most likely a woman. Whereas gender continues to be a pertinent axis of analysis in studies of urban market trade (Milgram 2008; Scarborough 2010), it is surprisingly underdeveloped in work on Latin American popular economies, from the early studies of José Matos Mar and Aníbal Quijano to the present, except in the more applied development-studies research which features a comprehensive literature on gender (Hillenkamp 2014; Hillenkamp, Lapeyre, and Lemaître 2013; Miles and Buechler 1997). This is all the more striking as research on rural-urban trade and mobility in Latin American cities gained momentum through a focus on women (Babb 1998 [1989]; Buechler 1978; Seligmann 1989, 1993). One potentially fruitful way to reintroduce gender into the analysis of the popular economy is to engage with decolonial theories (Babb 2018) and feminist analysis influenced by Marxism and poststructuralism (Vega and Marega, this book). Today, heads of households and women traders with an independent income continue to create semiautonomous spaces of selling, caring, and provisioning in the midst of much hardship.

In the epilogue, Carlos Alba Vega tracks the lives of four generations of traders and union leaders in Mexico City. Since three of the four protagonists are women, these generations highlight the reproduction over the longue durée of a "female dynasty" in popular commerce. The text—woven together out of interview materials and the long-term fieldwork of Carlos Alba Vega—offers a unique glimpse into the self-understanding of female traders, strategies of union leadership, and vernacular terms of popular commerce in twentieth-century Mexico. The women depicted knew—and know—how to make their street business grow, unite thousands of traders, and negotiate with municipal and national politicians. There is a lack of knowledge about female popular commerce in Mexico and elsewhere in Latin America over the historical longue durée. Referring once again to the Andes, indigenous women in the sixteenth- and seventeenth-century silver city of Potosí were extending credit across ethnic boundaries and commercializing food, raw silver, *chicha* (maize beer), cloths, wax, and coca leaves (Mangan 2005, 128ff.). Thus, we call for bringing gender back into the center of the debate on urban popular economy and commerce in Latin American and Caribbean cities.

THE INDIVIDUAL CONTRIBUTIONS TO THIS BOOK

Rudi Colloredo-Mansfeld opens the book's first section on "informality" and shifting politics with a chapter on competition as a culturally and politically structured mode of interaction. Critiquing ideas that simplify competition as an individualistic pursuit of profit, he reviews prominent business and anthropological theory from the 1990s to identify the ways that cooperating and competing reinforce each other and, in doing so, become a crucial way of establishing the distinctive urban identities of Andean provincial cities. The material presented in his chapter comes from long-term ethnographic fieldwork in three Ecuadorian towns, Tulcán, Atuntaqui, and Otavalo. Colloredo-Mansfeld shows that family-run businesses frequently subscribed to ideals of cooperating with competitors to solve problems, but these efforts at cooperation were not sustained as the government became hostile toward some important practices of popular economies, including the import of inexpensive Chinese-made goods and the prevailing informality of economic transactions.

Peter Mörtenböck and Helge Mooshammer explore the accelerating hybridization of formal and informal economic practices underway at one of Latin America's largest open-air markets, Belo Horizonte's "Hippie Fair," officially called the Feira de Arte, Artesanato e Produtores de Variedades da Avenida Afonso Pena. Belying its uniform and ordered appearance, the fair's multi-actor structure highlights the proliferation of formal-informal linkages that affect not only street vendors, manufacturers, and administrative bodies, but also large segments of the city's population. The authors argue that two decades of globalization, in conjunction with the recent economic crisis and emerging forms of self-organized economies, have substantially altered the relationship between the informal and formal sectors, both conceptually and practically. They show the importance and ambivalence of the ongoing spatial transformation of informal markets in generating new economic climates that, in some cases, create alternative socioeconomic places, and in others, an expansion of capitalist markets.

Natalie Göltenboth addresses the processes underpinning the touristification and commodification of an artist community space in Havana, Cuba, in the aftermath of the "período especial" since 2002. The artist space Muraleando began with a series of workshops for children, developed into a center of popular art and art education, and today serves as a destination for US tourists in search of an "authentic" socialist Cuba. Göltenboth analyzes Muraleando as a meeting point of diverse, even contrasting imaginaries that are involved in the creation of an urban microeconomy. She shows how the entanglement of capitalist strategies and social ideals, embedded in the special economic and political situation of the island, cuts across common ideas of neoliberal market economies and their social(ist) counterparts in Latin America.

André Vereta-Nahoum's chapter introduces the second part of this book. He reconstructs the history and conflictive operation of a vast marketplace comprising thousands of stalls selling inexpensive mass-produced clothes in central São Paulo, the Feira da Madrugada (Night Market). Analyzing legislative debates, executive policies, and newspaper articles discussing the area, the chapter traces various views about the place of this market in the urban economy and the succession of devices that have attempted to know, constitute, and regulate the proper agents of trade, its practices, and the spatial organization of the area. In conversation with recent literatures in urban economies and market devices, Vereta-Nahoum follows market making as a process of contested place-making in the global city. He argues that devices work to constitute this marketplace as much through their regulatory and material aspects as through their creative deployment and subversion by traders.

Juliane Müller's analysis follows encounters between East Asian multinational corporations (MNCs) and Bolivian traders at two marketplaces in La Paz, Bolivia. MNC staff tap into popular commerce as they interact and cooperate with traders on a daily basis, and acknowledge undeclared goods as original brands with official warranties. Drawing on long-term fieldwork, Müller analyzes these encounters as interfaces of technology, knowledge, and power. East Asian manufacturers apply market devices (professional merchandising, marketing, and retail chain management) in order to remake popular commerce over time. Instead of reclaiming the implementation of commercial law and official norms, they have set out to "formalize" Bolivian popular trade through marketizing.

Florence E. Babb's contribution opens the third section, which focuses on gender, space, and inequality. She turns to her long-term Andean research and recent work in Lima, Peru, to reconsider the experiences of Quechua women and men who are negotiating their identities in the urban economy. Dress, language, music, cuisine, and other cultural forms are among the practices that may either be eroded or retained in the migration process. She focuses on Polvos Azules, a marketplace where thousands of Andean migrants transplanted into the city find space to sell all manner of goods. At a time when Peruvians are reckoning with both deep-seated racism and a desire to manifest interculturality, Babb examines persistent exclusionary practices and the responses of Lima's labor migrants in negotiating gender and ethnic subjectivities. She shows that an intersectional approach that includes gender and race/ethnicity enables a better understanding of differences in livelihood experiences. An intersectional feminist approach can shed light on complex social realities and the challenges of everyday experience among the popular classes that recent discussion on informality and urban popular sectors has tended to overlook.

Cristina Vega and Magali Marega likewise analyze movements and strategies of female retail vendors in Quito, Ecuador, from a critical gender perspective. They argue that a sense of female relational autonomy at work and high levels of spatial mobility have enabled the women to reproduce their families by bringing into play knowledge practices, links, and networks characteristic of the popular economy. In the Ecuadorean capital of Quito, rural-urban migrations, non-formal work, the occupation of space in the streets, and trade are part of the constituent dynamics of the modernizing city and have been reconfigured in a constant play of disputes and negotiations. During the national and municipal government of Revolución Ciudadana, the regulation of street trade and the creation of new subcentralities coincided with the displacement of small-scale traders to suburban areas with laxer regulations. Vega and Marega argue that popular appropriations and valuations of space, as well as women's practices of cooperation, kinship, and community building, are essential to understanding the dynamics of trade in Latin American neighborhoods and cities today.

In an evocative epilogue, Carlos Alba Vega offers an oral history account of one of the most prominent female leaders of a traders' union in Latin America, if not the world. Guillermina Rico and her daughter Silvia look back on fifty years of political advocacy and collective organization among street vendors. Their trajectories give us a unique insight into unexpected female leadership in changing, yet enduring, popular economies.

NOTE

1. While Cuba is actually located in the Caribbean, we felt that including "Caribbean" in the title of this book would not have been appropriate as Spanish-speaking Cuba is our only example from this culturally, linguistically, and historically diverse region.

BIBLIOGRAPHY

Alfaro d'Alençon, Paola, Harry Smith, Eva Álvarez de Andrés, Cecilia Cabrera, Josefine Fokdal, Melanie Lombard, Anna Mazzolini, Enrico Michelutti, Luisa Moretto, and Amandine Spire. "Interrogating Informality: Conceptualisations, Practices and Policies in the Light of the New Urban Agenda." *Habitat International* 75 (2018): 59–66.

Amin, Ash, and Nigel Thrift. *The Blackwell Cultural Economy Reader*. Malden, MA: Blackwell Publishing, 2004.

Antrosio, Jason, and Rudi Colloredo-Mansfeld. *Fast, Easy, and In Cash. Artisan Hardship and Hope in the Global Economy*. Chicago: University of Chicago Press, 2015.

Arnold, Denise Y., Rosana Barragán, David Llanos, Carmen B. Loza, and Carmen Soliz. *¿Indígenas u obreros?: la construcción política de identidades en el Altiplano Boliviano.* La Paz: Fundación UNIR, 2009.

Babb, Florence E. *Women's Place in the Andes: Engaging Decolonial Feminist Anthropology*. Oakland: University of California Press, 2018.

———. *Between Field and Cooking Pot: Political Economy of Marketwomen in Peru*. Austin: University of Texas Press, (1989) 1998.

Bear, Laura, Ho, Karen, Tsing, Anna and Sylvia Yanagisako. Gens: "A Feminist Manifesto for the Study of Capitalism." *Theorizing the Contemporary. Cultural Anthropology website, March 30, 2015*. https://culanth.org/fieldsights/652-gens-a-feminist-manifesto-for-the-study-of-capitalism.

Bhowmik, Sharit K., ed. *Street Vendors in the Global Urban Economy*. New Delhi: Routledge, 2010.

Buechler, Judith-Maria. "The Dynamics of the Market in La Paz, Bolivia." *Urban Anthropology* 7, no. 4 (1978): 343–60.

Çalişkan, Kory. *Market Threads: How Cotton Farmers and Traders Create a Global Commodity*. Princeton, NJ: Princeton University Press, 2010.

Çalışkan, Koray, and Michel Callon. "Economization, Part 1: Shifting Attention from the Economy towards Processes of Economization." *Economy and Society* 38, no. 3 (2009): 369–98.

———. "Economization, Part 2: A Research Programme for the Studies of Markets." *Economy and Society* 39, no. 1 (2010): 1–32.

Callon, Michel, Yuval Millo, and Fabian Muniesa, eds. *Market Devices*. Malden, MA: Blackwell Publishing, 2007.

Chalana, Manish, and Jeffrey Hou. *Messy Urbanism: Understanding the "Other" Cities of Asia*. Hong Kong: Hong Kong University Press, 2016.

Clark, Gracia, ed. *Traders Versus the State: Anthropological Approaches to Unofficial Economies*. Boulder, CO: Westview Press, 1988.

Colloredo-Mansfeld, Rudi, and Jason Antrosio. "Economic Clusters or Cultural Commons? The Limits of Competition-Driven Development in the Ecuadorian Andes." *Latin American Research Review* 44, no. 1 (2009): 132–57.

Coraggio, José Luis. "La presencia de la Economía Social y Solidaria y su institucionalización en América Latina." *Umbrales. Revista del Postgrado en Ciencias del Desarrollo* 26 (2013): 83–114.

Cross, John and Alfonso Morales, eds. *Street Entrepreneurs: People, Place, and Politics in Local and Global Perspective*. London: Routledge, 2013.

De Soto, Hernán. *The Other Path: The Invisible Revolution in the Third World*. New York: Harpers & Row, 1989.

Escobar, Arturo. "Latin America at a Crossroads: Alternative Modernizations, Post-liberalism, or Post-development?" *Cultural Studies* 24, no. 1 (2010): 1–65.

Evers, Clifton, and Kirsten Seale, eds. *Informal Urban Street Markets*. London: Routledge, 2015.

Farías, Ignacio, and Anders Blok. *Urban Cosmopolitics: Agencements, Assemblies, Atmospheres*. London: Routledge, 2016.

Farías, Ignacio, and Thomas Bender. *Urban Assemblages: How Actor-Network Theory Changes Urban Studies*. London: Routledge, 2009.

Fernández-Kelly, Patricia, and Jon Shefner, eds. *Out of the Shadows: Political Action and the Informal Economy in Latin America*. University Park, PA: Penn State University Press, 2008.

Gago, Verónica, Cristina Cielo and Francisco Gachet, eds. Economía popular: entre la informalidad y la reproducción ampliada. Presentación del dossier. *ÍCONOS. Revista de Ciencias Sociales* 62 (2018): 11–20.

Ghertner, D. Asher. *Rule by Aesthetics: World-Class City Making in Delhi*. Oxford: Oxford University Press, 2015.

Gibson-Graham, J. K. *The End of Capitalism (As We Knew It): A Feminist Critique of Political Economy*. Minneapolis: University of Minnesota Press, 1996.

———. "Diverse Economies: Performative Practices for 'Other Worlds.'" *Progress in Human Geography* 35, no. 2 (2008): 613–32.

Gudeman, Stephen. *Economy's Tension: The Dialectics of Community and Market*. New York: Berghahn Books, 2011.

Gudynas, Eduardo. "Buen Vivir: Today's Tomorrow." *Development* 54, no. 4 (2011): 441–47.

Hansen, Karen Tranberg, Walter E. Little, and B. Lynne Milgram, eds. *Street Economies in the Urban Global South*. Sante Fe, NM: SAR Press, 2013.

Hart, Keith. "Between Bureaucracy and the People. A Political History of Informality." Working Paper No. 2008/27. Copenhagen: Danish Institute for International Studies, 2008.

———. "How the Informal Economy Took Over the World." *The Memory Bank*, Last modified October 17, 2012. thememorybank.co.uk/2012/10/17/the-informalization-of-the-world-economy/.

Herrle, Peter, and Josephine Fokdal. "Beyond the Urban Informality Discourse: Negotiating Power, Legitimacy and Resources." *Geographische Zeitschrift* 99, no. 1 (2011): 3–15.

Hillenkamp, Isabelle. *La economía solidaria en Bolivia. Entre mercado y democracia*. La Paz: CIDES-UMSA/IRD, 2014.

Hillenkamp, Isabelle, Frédéric Lapeyre, and Andreia Lemaître, eds. *Securing Livelihoods: Informal Economy Practices and Institutions*. Oxford: Oxford University Press, 2013.

Ingold, Tim. "Materials against Materiality." *Archaeological Dialogues* 14, no. 1 (2007): 1–16.

Itzigsohn, José. "Neoliberalism, Markets, and Informal Grassroots Economies." In *Out of the Shadows: Political Action and the Informal Economy in Latin America*, edited by Patricia Fernández-Kelly and Jon Shefner, 81–96. University Park, PA: Penn State University Press, 2008.

Lane, Christel, and Geoffrey T. Wood. "Capitalist Diversity and Diversity within Capitalism." *Economy and Society* 38, no. 4 (2009): 531–51.

Larson, Brooke, Olivia Harris, and Enrique Tandeter, eds. *Ethnicity, Markets, and Migration in the Andes: At the Crossroads of History and Anthropology*. Durham, NC: Duke University Press, 1995.

Latour, Bruno. *Reassembling the Social: An Introduction to Actor-Network-Theory*. Oxford: Oxford University Press, 2005.

Lazar, Sian. "A Desire to Formalize Work? Comparing Trade Unions Strategies in Argentina and Bolivia." *Anthropology of Work Review* 23, no. 1 (2012): 15–25.

Lombard, Melanie. "Constructing Ordinary Places: Place-Making in Urban Informal Settlements in Mexico." *Progress in Planning* 94 (2014): 1–53.

Mangan, Jane E. *Trading Roles: Gender, Ethnicity, and the Urban Economy in Colonial Potosí*. Durham, NC: Duke University Press, 2005.

Matos Mar, José. *Desborde popular y crisis del Estado*. Lima: Instituto de Estudios Peruanos, 1984.

McFarlane, Colin. "Rethinking Informality: Politics, Crisis, and the City." *Planning Theory & Practice* 13, no. 1 (2012): 89-108.
Miles, Ann and Hans Buechler, eds. *Women and Economic Change: Andean Perspectives*. Society for Latin American Anthropology Publication Series 14, 1997.
Milgram, Lynne B. "Activating Frontier Livelihoods: Women and the Transnational Secondhand Clothing Trade between Hong Kong and the Philippines." *Urban Anthropology* 37, no. 1 (2008): 5-47.
Miller, Daniel, ed. *Materiality*. Durham, NC: Duke University Press, 2005.
———. "Why Some Things Matter." In: *Material Cultures: Why Some Things Matter*, edited by Daniel Miller, 3-21. Chicago: University of Chicago Press, 1997.
Mörtenböck, Peter, and Helge Mooshammer, eds. *Informal Market Worlds: The Architecture of Economic Pressure—ATLAS*. Rotterdam: nai010 publishers, 2015.
Mollett, Sharlene. "Irreconcilable Differences? A Postcolonial Intersectional Reading of Gender, Development and Human Rights in Latin America. *Gender, Place & Culture* 24, no. 1 (2017): 1–17.
Mooshammer, Helge. "Other Markets: Sites and Processes of Economic Pressure." In *Informal Market Worlds: The Architecture of Economic Pressure—READER*, edited by Peter Mörtenböck and Helge Mooshammer, 17–32. Rotterdam: nai010 publishers, 2015.
Müller, Juliane. "Place-Based (In)Formalization: A Bolivian Marketplace for Consumer Electronics and Global Brands." *Latin American Research Review* 52, no. 3 (2017): 1–13.
Müller, Juliane, and Rudi Colloredo-Mansfeld. "Dossier: Entrepreneurship, Artisans, and Traders. The Remaking of China-Latin American Economies." *Journal for Latin American and Caribbean Anthropology* 23, no. 1 (2018): 9-93.
Narotzky, Susana. *New Directions in Economic Anthropology*. London: Pluto Press, 1997.
Narotzky, Susana, and Nico Besnier. "Crisis, Value, Hope: Rethinking the Economy." *Current Anthropology* 55, no. S9 (2014): 4–16.
Nelms, Taylor C. "'The Problem of Delimitation': Parataxis, Bureaucracy, and Ecuador's Popular and Solidarity Economy." *Journal of the Royal Anthropological Institute* 21 (2015): 106–26.
Portes, Alejandro, and Richard Schauffler. "Competing Perspectives on the Latin American Informal Sector." *Population and Development Review* 19, no. 1 (1993): 33–60.
Quijano, Aníbal. *La economía popular y sus caminos en América Latina*. Lima: Mosca Azul Editores, 1998.
Roy, Ananya. "Urban Informality: Towards an Epistemology of Planning." *Journal of the American Planning Association* 71, no. 2 (2005): 147–58.
———. "Why India Cannot Plan Its Cities: Informality, Insurgence, and the Idiom of Urbanization." *Planning Theory* 8, no. 1 (2009): 76–87.
Roy, Ananya, and Nezar AlSayyad, eds. *Urban Informality: Transnational Perspectives from the Middle East, Latin America, and South Asia*. Lanham, MD: Lexington Books, 2004.
Seligmann, Linda J. "To Be in Between: The Cholas as Market Women." *Comparative Studies in Society and History* 31, no. 4 (1989): 694–721.

———. "Between Worlds of Exchange: Ethnicity among Peruvian Market Women." *Cultural Anthropology* 8, no. 2 (1993): 187–213.

SLUM lab. *Si/No: The Architecture of Urban-Think Tank.* ETH Zürich D-ARCH, Museum of Architecture of TU Munich, 2015.

Tsing, Anna. *Friction: An Ethnography of Global Connection*. Princeton, NJ: Princeton University Press, 2004.

Vodopivec, Barbara, and Eveline Dürr. "Barrio Bravo Transformed: Tourism, Cultural Politics and Image Making in Mexico City." *Journal of Latin American and Caribbean Anthropology*. Forthcoming.

Wilson, Tamar Diana, ed. "Approaches to Informal Economies." Special Issue, *Urban Anthropology* 40, no. 3–4 (2011).

Part I

(IN)FORMALITY

Chapter One

Culture, Competition, and Urban Identities in Ecuadorian Popular Economies

Rudi Colloredo-Mansfeld

In 2016, two of Ecuador's well-known popular economies were unraveling. In their collapse, they seemed to reveal an enduring truth about capitalism, competition, and urban space. One of these economies was in Tulcán, in the northern Andes and a long-time hub of cross-border dealing with Colombia. Beginning in the 1970s, merchants and traders arrived from throughout the Ecuadorian highlands in order to sell to Colombians. In the early 2000s, the market suffered when Ecuador adopted the US dollar as its national currency. In the mid-2000s, a rise in businesses selling Chinese imports had given the market a new lease on life. Beginning in 2015, though, global forces have again conspired against the city's trade. Ecuador significantly raised tariffs on Chinese goods. Meanwhile the Colombian peso continued to lose value against the US dollar. The trade bonanza abruptly shifted to Ipiales, Colombia. Colombians stayed home to shop; Ecuadorians traveled by the thousands to Ipiales; and more than five hundred of Tulcán's small retailers and wholesalers went out of business in 2016 (Benalcazar 2016).

The second troubled town was Atuntaqui, a center of textile businesses that had more than 450 small and medium-size family businesses producing sweaters, pajamas, and other casual clothes. Starting in 2001, local manufacturers secured significant backing from the MICIP (*Ministerio Industria Comercio y Pesca* or Ministry of Industry, External Trade, and Fisheries) to upgrade production. Businesses invested in new showrooms, revitalized commercial avenues, and worked together to jointly market their town as a center of fashion. They formed a Chamber of Commerce whose trade show began to attract over one hundred thousand visitors by 2006. However, starting in 2009, intermittent tariffs on imported clothes opened up new opportunities to sell large orders to national clothing retailers in Ecuador. Atuntaqui's family brands withdrew from their shared promotions. Before long, the recently established chamber struggled to organize their exhibition, and by 2016 it had ceased all programming. Businesses were once again operating in isolation, behind the high walls of family compounds. The retail district went quiet.

These faltering provincial cities can be read in terms of an old critique of capitalism: the brutal pressures of competition, temporarily stayed, must forcefully return. If Atuntaqui manufacturers united in a moment of crisis, once the crisis was passed, they reverted to a raw individualism. The lesson from Tulcán is also clear. Hundreds of traders in a border town creatively exploited an international opportunity. However, small operators do not control economic policy, but merely respond to it. Rules of trade fit the interests of those in power—and rules change as those interests shift. For writers such as Gibson-Graham (1996, 263), clear thinking about competition reveals the "naked and visible monster" of capitalism for what it is: driven by accumulation, unpredictable, and hostile to human community.

In this chapter, I want to challenge this bare-bones reading of competition. Indeed, anthropology is long overdue for far more thoughtful engagement with the topic. A deeply relational act, competition promotes cultural, actions that anthropologists have long studied: cultivating position, creating difference, fashioning meaningful commodities, and inscribing boundaries (Bourdieu 1993; Lash and Urry 1994). The reverse is also true. By studying competition, we can reintegrate the showiness of local culture—the arresting details of specific identities and public lives—with the force of capital. To compete successfully, men and women must signal economic strength, make deals where there is a chance for gain, and build up social, cultural and economic capital that will ensure continuity and legitimacy (Aldrich and Fiol 2007). These contests reveal an enduring *structural tie* among economic actors, a dependency on each other to secure acceptability even as they contest each other for earnings (Antrosio and Colloredo-Mansfeld 2015). Overlaying the daily, market hustle is an uncertain field of mediation, a domain in which people can insist on a common interest as well as the private ones.

Such issues point to an important dynamic of urban spaces. The vitality of provincial Andean cities is inseparable from the unresolved tensions among competition and commonality that mark the family enterprises of small-town economies. Stephen Gudeman (2016) has written extensively about the battle between self-interest and mutuality in the economy. His discussions foreground the house as the place where joint action, pooled resources, and long-term perspective allow mutuality to flourish. In contrast, the firms of global commerce channel people toward the narrow calculus of self-interest. Provincial cities with large numbers of family enterprises represent an intermediate economic space between these two ideal types. "The fate of the family firm is a special case" when it comes to competition, Carrier (1997, 21) observes in his thoughtful critique of the market model. In contrast to both the house and the firm, urban economies in Latin American entail businesses, run out of homes, interwoven in neighborly relations, and tied into distant client networks. Commercial rivalry spreads from houses to workshops to streetscapes, and from family operations to civic activity (Colloredo-Mansfeld 2002).

To be sure, trades can enter into destructive modes of competition. At times, powerful operators devastate the once stable enterprises of a whole town. However, traders often see these moments as pathological. It is precisely here, in conflicts when entrepreneurs legitimize some acts as fair competition and sets limits on insupportable alternatives—"disloyal competition"—that commerce becomes melded with civic life (Rosen 2016). People move beyond private interest in a deal to promote a public purpose with which they identify.

Along with revealing critical urban processes, an anthropologically sophisticated understanding of competition will help delineate important political transitions. In Latin America, that means being able to identify with far more precision what has changed with the post-neoliberal politics that have emerged in the last decade. Rejecting a market-centered orthodoxy that had prevailed across much of the region since the 1980s, new governments in Bolivia, Venezuela, Ecuador, and Brazil in the 2000s committed to promoting social equity, not just economic expansion, and fought for renewed national authority over trade (Leiva 2008). At the same time, even leftist governments accepted globalization, counted on expanding export earnings, and had a proclivity for extractivist-supported government spending (Grugel and Riggirozzi 2012; Kennemore and Weeks 2011). In what way have such changes remade practices within the multigenerational commercial districts that were built during neoliberalism? If a left-leaning state sees little civic virtue in economic competition, the pressures of the market have hardly let up. Understanding the form and weight of commercial rivalries teaches about the real breadth of the socialism of Rafael Correa, president of Ecuador from 2007 to 2017.

This chapter starts with an ethnographic overview of three interlinked market towns in Ecuador's northern highlands. I then develop the discussion of the cultural work that competition does by critically engaging ideas that emerge in the unexpected convergences among well-known anthropologists and widely read business economists that emerged in theorizing about globalization. I use these ideas to assess the neoliberal moment of northern Andean popular trades, exploring government-sponsored competitiveness training programs in the early 2000s. I am especially interested in the varied civic purposes of competition consultants, business operators, and politicians found in these projects. The chapter subsequently moves to a "post-competition" moment and the disarray in two different commercial districts that followed a more active government defense of national trade. In tracing these Andean competitiveness programs, I show the cultural possibilities of competition, including a surprising promise of mutuality that is ultimately revealed when the state withdrew from trying to promote it.

The work reported here draws on focused ethnographic research conducted over the course of six months of fieldwork from 2001 to 2005, with additional, annual follow-up visits between 2009 and 2016. In the towns of Otavalo and Atuntaqui, our research team, directed by two anthropologists and including Ecuadorian research assistants earning university degrees in business and architecture, partnered with an artisan union in Otavalo and the Chamber of Commerce in Atuntaqui. In each town, surveys were done with segments of the larger textile sectors, documenting firm size, capital investments, and products. Supplemental work focused on design and innovation across different market niches (see Antrosio and Colloredo-Mansfeld 2015 for more details on methods). This chapter draws on extensive observations of trade association meetings.

NORTHERN ANDEAN POPULAR ECONOMIES

Throughout Latin America, urban, popular markets mix wildly diverse goods: Chinese electronics, native peasant-grown crops, global brands, nationally made consumer products, and artisanal commodities. While these products ship to all corners of the region, individual cities and their markets develop distinctive commercial districts with local personality. In northern Ecuador, three stand out.

Otavalo, a market town straddling the Pan-American Highway eighty kilometers north of Quito, is internationally identified with a distinctive indigenous, Quichua-speaking ethnic group and their craft industries (Buitrón 1947; Colloredo-Mansfeld 1999; Meisch 2002; Rubio Orbe 1956). In the 1980s, Otavaleño families moved beyond their own treadle-loom products, seeking out thousands of rural women to knit sweaters and creating a pipeline of products for sales through family members living abroad. By 1993, a dozen shipping companies operated out of the small town. A distinctly Andean form of "low-end globalization" (Mathews and Alba Vega 2012) had been launched, with growing expatriate communities in Amsterdam, Barcelona, New York, and Santiago de Chile.

The turn to machinery in Otavalo was indirectly helped by the industrial textile infrastructure already in place in Atuntaqui, a center of apparel production that is located a short bus trip to the north along the Pan-American Highway. For most of the twentieth century, Atuntaqui's civic and economic life revolved around a single, large textile plant set up by two Spanish investors in the 1920s. In the 1960s, the factory went into a steep decline. For years, retired workers had invested in their own workshops, buying electric looms and producing shawls, ponchos, and other woolens. With the collapse of the big facility, these artisanal operations stepped up production.

Atuntaqui's goods rarely found their way outside of Ecuador. The one exception was through Tulcán, the capital of Carchi Province and less than ten kilometers from the Colombian border. Buoyed by the currency advantage of the relatively weak Ecuadorian sucre in relation to the Colombian peso, intermediaries in Tulcán stocked stores with a wide range of Ecuadorian merchandise from gas stoves to toothpaste. Atuntaqui's sweaters became a reliable offering. By the 1970s, so many Otavaleños had moved to Tulcán to pursue cross-border trade, particularly with Atuntaqui's products, that they had formed a formal Carchi-based trade association.

For small, provincial cities, Otavalo, Atuntaqui, and Tulcán have surprisingly cosmopolitan histories of development, international sales, and investment. By the 1990s, the economy of each place had a distinctive specialization—indigenous products, casual apparel, and trading. Such trade expertise had reinforced customs and cultural identities unique to each place. At the same time, as competition grew at home, operators gained a willingness to travel further, take on more risks, and find a way to make a success of international connections (Antrosio and Colloredo-Mansfeld 2015). By the early 2000s, the state began to take seriously the desires of these businesses to succeed in national and international deals. In a direct, though long-routed way, prescriptions born in the 1980s for US president Ronald Reagan's economic team made their way into popular training workshops set up for Andean weavers.

COMPETITION AS A VIRTUE: GLOBALIZATION, DIFFERENCE, AND SPACES OF ENCOUNTER

The rise of competitiveness as the focus of economic policy tracked the decline of mass production and national industries (Lash and Urry 1987; Harvey 1989; Piore and Sabel 1984). As neoliberal economic policy took hold in the United States, Great Britain, Mexico, Chile, and elsewhere, states abandoned the protection of industries. Instead, urged by business economists such as Harvard Business School's Michael Porter (Porter 1998; 1998 [1990]), governments developed policies around competitive advantage. In simple terms, competition focuses on what is required of an individual operation to gain an edge. In contrast, competitive advantage involves a group of interrelated businesses and the underlying factors that enhance the commercial contests unfolding among all of them (Wolfe and Lucas 2005; Drabenstott, Novack, and Weiler 2004). For those embracing competitive advantage, the proper focus of industrial policy was no longer the nation. Rather, it was the subnational level and the clusters of businesses where one finds the crucible of rivalry and innovation.

In the 1990s, there was an interesting convergence in the writings of Porter and the anthropologist Arjun Appadurai, whose essays on international cultural flows became the starting point for anthropological discussions of globalization. Both writers were concerned with the intimacy and pressures of new global connectivity. Anthropologist and economist alike came to focus on situated difference as the essence of culture and of competitive strategy. Thus, Porter writes in 1996, "Competitive strategy is about being different. It means deliberately choosing a different set of activities to deliver a unique mix of value" (Porter 1998 [1996], 45). In the same year, Appadurai writes, "The most valuable feature of the concept of culture is the concept of difference, a contrastive rather than a substantive property of certain things" (Appadurai 1996, 12). To track how meaningful cultural differences will prevail amid the forces of globalization, Appadurai offers a retelling of classic theories of rites of passage, initiations, and other rituals of community life. Rather than seeing them as the esoteric collective life of premodern peoples, Appadurai argues that such rites solve the ever-present human problem of defining what "local" is and defending it against an expansive outside world. In the 1990s, competition became the distinctive and valued rite of that defense of place to survive in a hostile world. By the end of the 2000s, the Comaroffs (2009) made this convergence of the business and the cultural explicit with their volume *Ethnicity, Inc.* which detailed the ways culture itself became subject to the technologies of copyrights and trademarks, winding up for some people as yet another branded product.

The connections between the latest business theories in vogue at Harvard of the 1980s and the development policies of the Andean countries in the 2000s were overt. In 2001, representatives from MICIP built a training program around Chilean competitiveness manuals that were in turn based on Porter's ideas. The guides specifically focused on the "Diamond of Competitiveness"—a graphical device to teach business strategy. As a starting point for discussion, it signaled two key propositions: (1) to develop a business plan, start with the setting in which the commercial rivalry unfolds, and (2) to position one's firm, leverage relations, not just with supporting industry but other agencies as well. In Otavalo, Atuntaqui, and elsewhere, officials recruited local business to workshops on these ideas, programs that were known as PACA, an acronym that organizers left untranslated from English: Participatory Appraisal of Competitive Advantage. If nothing else, the training program was an indoctrination in the idea that individuals had to work together and build the shared circumstances to achieve the prosperity of an individual business. As one PACA manual put it, "PACA tries not only to analyze the economic potential, but also the potential for collective action. It was developed in a setting where organizational weakness and lack of interaction between institutions are commonplace" (Meyer-Stamer 2003, 9).

In the course of PACA, Ministry officials led local business leaders from trade associations through an intensive class in Porter's ideas. With trainers in place, they invited artisans and family manufacturers to join a daylong effort to identify sources of strength for their businesses and potential commercial partners that could enhance quality or lower costs. With cards and colored markers, producers listed the names of suppliers, of rivals, and of government agencies and tried to locate them on Porter's diamond that was outlined on a large bulletin board (see figure 1.1). In a second stage, PACA facilitators left the town of Otavalo and went to rural schools where they recruited knitters, weavers, and the manual workforce of the craft industry to go through the same program.

Most saw little value in Porter's ideas. Theirs was a market with many producers creating similar products for tourists, foreigners who had little understanding of the intricacies of weaving. Without the ability to brand, trademark, or copyright, no Otavaleño artist could defend a distinctive set of products. Only when it came to collective action did the participants in the workshop see the importance of this new approach to competition. An official with the municipal government took pains to explain the links between competing, organizing, and development. She noted,

> [the municipality was committed to] new paradigms of sustainable development. We are not just here to say, "How cool, how great this new process is." Instead, we are going to see it through, certain that in this moment we need to organize ourselves. Many times and especially in the artisan sector, we say "No, we are not organized." But in this particular circumstance we have a lot of competition with the Peruvians. So what are we doing as producers to solve the problems? The answer is PACA.

This message about organizing competitors hit home. Leaders of the UNAIMCO (*La Unión de Artesanos Indígenas del Mercado Centenario de Otavalo*), the largest artisan indigenous artisan association in Ecuador, identified "disloyal competition" as a threat far greater than the rising costs that had come with the dollarization of the economy. They faulted their own membership for a lack of innovation, rampant copying, and overproduction

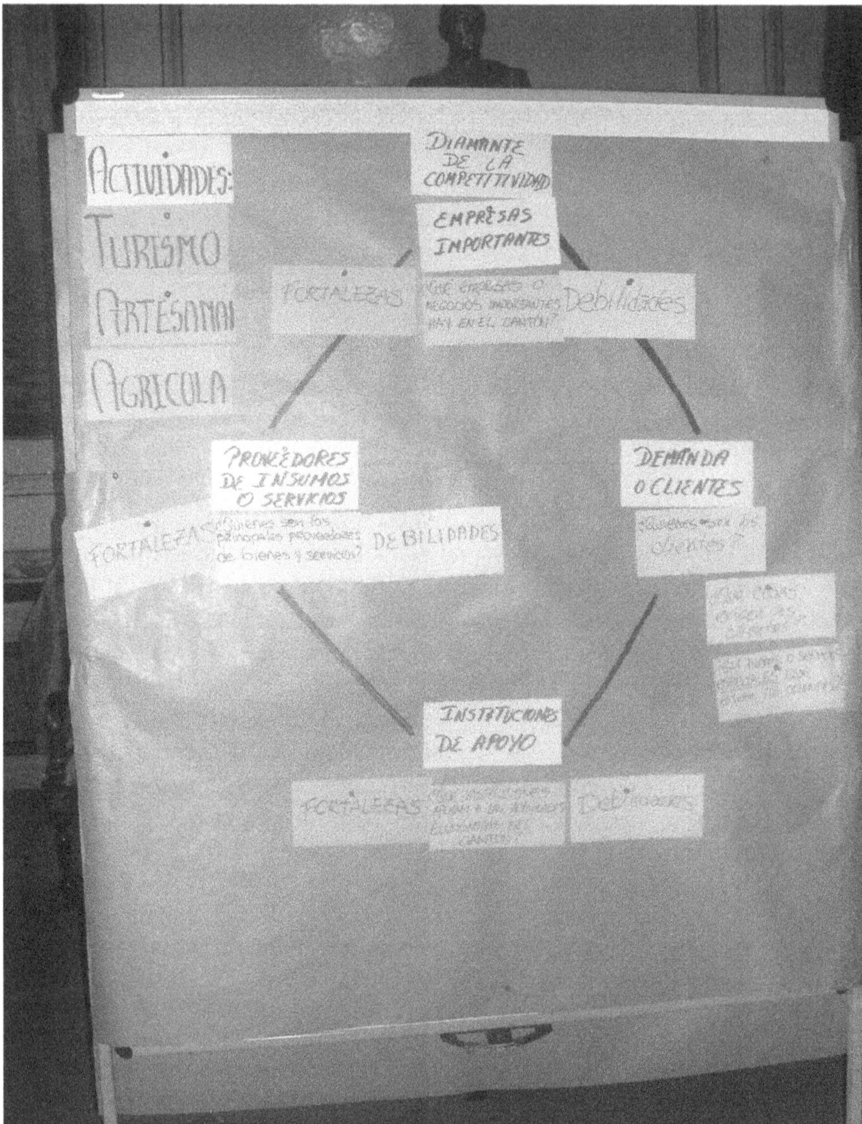

Figure 1.1. Competitiveness training activity: applying Porter's diamond of competitiveness to Otavalo artisan economy, Otavalo, June 2, 2005.
Rudi Colloredo-Mansfeld

of a limited set of tired designs. The public call to link fair competition and sustainable development rang true to him. So did the insistence on producers working closely with suppliers. In the months immediately after the dollarization, sweater knitters started a boycott of the yarn factories for their erratic new pricing policies. During a meeting that drew over three hundred members of the union, a sweater maker stood up in the auditorium and addressed the factory owners on stage, saying,

> One must think about the impoverished hand knitters. If Ecuador wants to get ahead, we all need to get together. You [wool yarn factory owners] need to make sacrifices. We artisans must also make sacrifices. Only in this way can we get out of this trouble. I ask of the UNAIMCO leaders to work directly with the factory owners to look at numbers and data [to find a solution to improve quality].

PACA taught people that competing can also mean cooperating with other business operators. There was civic virtue, a common good to be had, when people set aside their individualism.

The most urgent worry for UNAIMCO market vendors was the foreign threat that the municipal official mentioned: in the early 2000s, the market was on the verge of being taken over by Peruvians. In fact, Peruvian crafts initially came to be sold locally by Otavaleño traders who moved between Lima and Otavalo. By 2005, though, between eighteen and twenty shops that specialized in Peruvian crafts operated around the Plaza de Ponchos, the majority owned by Peruvian migrants. Ecuadorian importers and vendors in Otavalo's market who had pioneered the traffic in Peruvian wares lost their market. One Otavaleño reseller observed, "In the plaza the majority sell Peruvian things. Yes, [the Otavaleños] are now frightened, but they created their own problem, 'if you raise ravens, they will peck out your eyes.'"

The response of artisan leaders, however, was not to drive the Peruvians out but to try to rally their membership to compete with them. The new president of the UNAIMCO asked, "How can we expel them when Ecuador has signed agreements with GATT and bilateral agreements with Peru and Colombia?" For him the problem was not at home, but for Otavaleño traders elsewhere, he said in 2001,

> The problem is that Ecuadorians cannot sell as easily abroad as others can here. The Ecuadorian government just lets people in and does not do anything. But Ecuadorians cannot sell elsewhere. UNAIMCO has letters sent from the Colombian border where customs officials have confiscated goods. The foreign ministry must be involved to make sure Ecuadorians have a fair opportunity.

In July 2001, representatives from the Ministry of Foreign Trade came to Otavalo to discuss measures to improve the competitiveness of artisan goods, and the possibility of establishing an internationally recognized trademark for their crafts. However, the UNAIMCO leadership took advantage of their time with the ministry officials, to push not for protection of their goods, but for an expansion of trade with Peru and Bolivia. They wanted the free importation of woolen yarn. One of the UNAIMCO officers referred back to the wool boycott and negotiations, "We got the price stability, but we did not get an improvement in quality. We need to free the importation of raw material in order to improve the quality."

Due to ongoing complaints from their membership, in July 2001 UNAIMCO organized a meeting among Peruvians, municipal officials, and union members who had challenged the legality of Peruvian stores (based on presumed tax violations). The treasurer, the oldest member of the leadership and one who spoke exclusively in Quichua during meetings, once again linked cooperation and competition:

> There are always different problems in the market. Some people do not want to be integrated into UNAIMCO. We artisans want to live freely, don't we? We do not want to live under some group. People are not well integrated. They do not live well organized. In that way we have problems. Now we are trying to adjust, fix problems of competition, now we must become united because of the need. What is the point of everyone living for his one side? Now thinking about it, everyone should live well organized. Why? To take care of our market, isn't that right?

Repeatedly in the early 2000s, Otavalo's manufacturers and merchants revealed a remarkable acceptance of globalization and competition. They projected an idealized economic world as an outcome of having the opportunity to compete: manufacturers would get the best raw material at the best price from anywhere; Ecuadorian goods would cross borders unimpeded; the national government would open markets across South America. Certainly, they sought limits on their rivals. They saw the town's market plaza as distinctly theirs—both economically and culturally. However, this was not to be the boundary of their work. Rather, they had a multi-national view of Colombians, Ecuadorians, Peruvians, and Bolivians contending in a wider economic community.

THE CITY AS CLUSTER: ORTHODOX COMPETITIVE ADVANTAGE

Neoliberal policy in Ecuador, as in other nations, came to have a distinct, urban mode of action. As Brenner and Theodore write, "cities have become increasingly important geographical targets and institutional laboratories for a variety of neoliberal policy experiments" (Brenner and Theodore 2002, 368). They go on to list place-marketing, empowerment zones, urban development corporations, and business incubator projects, among others. North of Otavalo, Atuntaqui epitomized urban-focused, market-centered development (see figure 1.2). The city's T-shirt and sweater makers received substantial financial support from the national government's Ministry of Foreign Trade and Competitiveness. Targeted with six different programs of quality improvement in the early 2000s, these producers worked intimately to create, in their compact grid of commercial streets, an industrial "cluster" (again, using the English word and again employing a concept popularized by Porter). As manufacturing operations adopted the latest industrial sewing machines, an urgent program was introduced to address the skilled labor shortage. In trying to unite textile businesses and technical high schools, paid consultants articulated a wider vision of a city that integrated itself institutionally and technically in order to compete.

In a tense meeting, a member of the chamber complained to the government consultants, "The skills at the high school are very basic. The machines

Figure 1.2. Joint marketing program, Atuntaqui, February 2006.
Rudi Colloredo-Mansfeld

are dated. [The graduates] arrive at their jobs at the work shop and then they race back out, afraid of the sound of the new industrial sewing machines." Consultants turned the operator's negative commentary about workers into another opportunity to promote the importance of joint action across the cluster. The representative of the ministry said, "If there was a space of encounter [an organized coming together of everyone], one would be in position to solve these problems caused by the new machinery. In this space of encounter, one can arrange all the benefits and duties of all the participants." The president of the Chamber of Commerce doubted the plan. He said,

> If we come together in this system of encounter and we lay out what we are doing at this moment, we then say, OK, ladies and gentlemen, from this moment we are now going to work in this new way. We are going to change the method of work because it is good for you and it is good for us. The workers then resist, "We are going to strike. Period." We need to work with the reality of our businesses. A person who is practically trained and in addition educated with civic values, this person goes along with changes more quickly—the business operator, the workers and the indirect workforce alike.

For this businessman, a space of encounter alone would not lead to a modern workforce. Rather, change is possible when those involved see that change itself is part of meeting one's civic duties.

Porter's ideas took a decade to arrive in Otavalo and Atuntaqui, provincial cities where generations of family businesses have competed with each other ceaselessly. Gaining widespread traction, the ideas of cluster development offered a way to work within such competitiveness. Indeed, caught up in realizing their hopes for an urban concentration of interacting firms, state officials ended up celebrating provincial businesses operators largely as who they were. Indeed, too often state-led urban revitalization and economic redevelopment pursues the logic of erasure. Family workshops, street vending, and small entrepreneurial ventures are the market equivalent of disorder "to be swept out of the metropolis" (Anand 2017, 66). Yet during this pro-competition period, the state approached artisans and merchants in their everyday economic role: as perpetual competitors. They granted a legitimacy to careers that normally are disdained for their informality. This place-based approach fit well with the market-driven sociality that so many people lived day-to-day in small cities where businesses are operated by neighbors. Furthermore, this kind of collaborative competitiveness reinforced an urban multiculturalism that had been emergent in 1990s Latin America (Hale 2005). Each town needed not just a trade, but an identity and an edge to get ahead in the market. Competing, place-making, and community building merged in an almost devout commitment to market-centered development.

SOURING ON COMPETITION: THE POST-NEOLIBERAL TURN TO SOLIDARITY ECONOMIES

At some point in the 1990s, the pursuit of competitiveness went from being one civic virtue among many (i.e., stability, ethical rectitude, rational management) to the prime virtue and an inescapable duty. Theories of competition themselves began to emphasize a kind of "no-way-out" nature of destructive innovation and the pressures it brought to bear. In 1997, Harvard Business School professor Clayton Christensen published the *Innovator's Dilemma: When New Technologies Cause Great Firms to Fail* (Christensen 1997), warning that even a highly successful and well-run business was at risk of losing out to an upstart with an inferior product. As with his Harvard Business School colleague, Michael Porter, before him, Christiansen offered a powerful narrative that called people to action not just in the business world, but in the public, educational, and healthcare sectors. And the resulting ceaseless emphasis on competitiveness became a monotonous, and ubiquitous, policy. This is neoliberalism as Bourdieu described it (1998, 35): "an unfettered capitalism without any disguise but rationalized, pushed to the limit of its economic efficacy by the introduction of modern forms of domination, such as 'business administration' . . . market research and advertising."

In Latin America, this neoliberal fever broke in the mid-2000s. Led by left-leaning governments in Bolivia, Venezuela, and Ecuador, Latin America has seen the rise of a new social compact in which the state, not the market, is the institution responsible for social welfare. Still committed to capitalism and globalization, the new administrations nonetheless offer a vision of national economies that combines economic sovereignty, resource extractivism, and more forceful trade and industrial policy. In Ecuador, President Rafael Correa, who served from 2007 until 2017, oriented his larger economic policy toward reinscribing economic boundaries within national ones (de la Torre 2013).

Correa still embraced the vibrant productivity of artisanal manufacturers and family businesses. But in his vision, he followed new conceptions of the "popular and solidarity economy" (*economía popular y solidaria*) in which profit and commerce ceded ground to social purposes (Nelms 2015). Allied with the thinking of Gibson-Graham (2005), Wright (2010), and others, Correa insisted that the popular economy operated according "to the common good and concepts based not in egoism, not in individualism, not in competition, but rather in principles much closer to our reality, our tradition, like the principle of solidarity" (cited in Nelms 2015, 110). The state's new duty lay in reaching out to these actors and supporting them with financing, training, and regulation. In this way, the popular economy would achieve public recognition.

In practice, this downgrading of competitiveness had the unintended consequence of rekindling the destructive and isolating market rivalry that was meant to end with the turn away from neoliberalism. Since 2007, businesses have tried to find their way in marketplaces that have had the terms of trade rewritten by the state and the footings of business reshaped by Chinese-made commodities. As they move away from cluster development programs, market actors have found themselves with an impoverished discourse for finding social purpose in their deal making. They have little leverage for promoting cooperation along with competition. As in the heyday of neoliberalism, the daily contest for sales can still be tracked in Otavalo, Atuntaqui, and Tulcán. However, the state has rejected informal economic transactions and penalized cheap imports. The thousands of families who live from both have moved back into the shadows of their towns' official life.

In Otavalo, the historic indigenous craft trade fractured. The town's artisan manufacturers and the diasporic traders went their separate ways. Woolen products that had driven the artisan boom faded. Families repurposed power looms for the making of hammocks and entrepreneurs began to make a variety of beach bags out of hammock material. The Quichua identity of these products largely disappeared as manufacturers stamped the bags with silhouettes of palm trees, Bob Marley, and marijuana leaves. At the same time, in the wake of the dollarization, inexpensive Chinese apparel became the most sought-after merchandise by the Otavaleño merchants.

Selling inexpensive Chinese apparel acquired in open wholesale markets is about as undifferentiated an occupation as one can find in a Latin American popular market. Yet, even here—perhaps especially here—vendors fought for an edge (Müller and Colloredo-Mansfeld 2018). As the Chinese trade matured in the 2000s, merchants tried to build inventories of specific goods that not only sell well, but whose colors, quantities, styles, or designs positioned a seller in relation to others. In this economy, cheapness was not just a matter of thrift, but a point of pride and pleasure on the part of buyers and sellers.

José Santillan is an apparel merchant who was born just outside of Otavalo but has worked for twenty-five years in Tulcán. He had been able to make it work during the 2000s. Once Correa's government began to use tariffs to target inexpensive apparel, low-cost toys, and other cheap commodities that saturate provincial marketplaces, José's risks, losses, and bad deals began to mount up. It was never an easy business. To begin with, it was costly to get into the trade. Chinese manufacturers produced such a variety of styles and sizes that resellers had to buy an extensive inventory to have basic offerings in each niche. A smaller operator can choose to just get "a little of everything," José said. However, Chinese resellers came to compete with them directly in the same markets and successful Otavaleños had to quickly scale up their inventories. José responded by the end of the 2000s, largely by combining cheap Chinese cardigans with sweaters from Atuntaqui.

In 2013, one of his largest deals went badly wrong. A longtime client from Colombia took possession of a very large order. This client then immediately shut down his store and disappeared, owing José nearly 60,000 US dollars. José tried to recover the goods, traveling on a tip to a town in Colombia where he thought the client had moved. He got nowhere. Having lost all his inventory, savings, and, as a consequence, access to credit, José and his wife Mercedes had no choice but to start from scratch with the most affordable product they could sell—simple fleece blankets made of Chinese material. These items were everywhere in Tulcán. Three Otavaleño brothers imported containers of them from the free-trade zone of north Chile. Chinese families also ran shops in Tulcán that offered bales of one hundred blankets at rock bottom prices. Across the border in Colombia, Ipiales had scores of shops selling similar items.

Unable to buy in the quantity of his rivals, José sought to customize his inventory, selecting items that might be rare within the wide array that importers brought in. It is here that the lack of connection with his Chinese suppliers had begun to anger José in 2015, more than fifteen years since he had started to work with them. The issue was not credit. He said that the problem was a lack of courtesy. "They are half angry with you all the time. You have to buy from them so you put up with it. You come in make your purchase and get out," José said. They would not engage in the kind of bargaining that José does with his Ecuadorian suppliers. He searched for exclusive merchandise that might complement his distinctive style. Failing to match the selection of his rivals in town or the prices of the Colombians, he fell back to promoting the traditional Otavaleño reputation for skilled handiwork.

Their economic downward spiral had a distinctive social component that reflected the retrenchment of economic inclusion in Correa's Ecuador. As an informal trader, José had no recourse when he was robbed of his inventory. As a dealer in Chinese imports, he had no government program that could help create a "space of encounter" in which Chinese traders and indigenous Ecuadorians could come together. A decade earlier Otavaleños were faced with another foreign trading power—the Peruvians—and had the backing of artisan associations and municipal market authorities to try to mutually solve their problems. Left on his own to work things out with the Chinese, José lacked the economic or social capital needed. His store became one more shuttered shop front in an emptying commercial district.

On the face of it, the changes that came to Atuntaqui were more optimistic than those of Tulcán. The adoption of protectionist measures against Chinese-made clothing opened mass-market sales opportunities that had always been out of reach. Family firms began to give up on the brands they had worked with government consultants to carefully craft. Instead, once they secured huge orders from national chain stores, these businesses willingly sewed the labels of the chain stores into their products. And as manufacturers lost interest in creating their own identity, many withdrew their financial support from the joint marketing that had brought life to the commercial district. The annual trade show lost its exhibitors and its budget.

As sales multiplied, so did labor abuses. Workers filed complaints. The state responded with frequent inspections of Atuntaqui's factories. New regulations were issued, raising wages, establishing work-site medical benefits, and improving safety. After years of abuse, businesses entered into long-term agreements with state inspectors to pay off extensive fines.

One business owner, Jorge Vega, explained to me in 2011 how he got into trouble with the state: "with production, you do not have to have everything regulated in a clothing workshop—the businesses have always cut corners. The big businesses, they save five cents out of every dollar in revenue to pay labor fines and complaints brought by workers." He had had thirty-eight labor cases brought against him during the high-tariff boom months in 2008 and 2009. He did not worry so much about the complaints themselves, just the timing. The tariffs had been reduced and he lost his big clients who again purchased imports. Thus, he did not have the revenue to pay the rest of his fines.

Ultimately, Jorge laid off 75 percent of his workers, leaving less than twenty employees. He also shut his five franchised stores, four of which were in small cities in Ecuador's coastal region. I asked if he felt he was getting squeezed out by the large, national chains. He did not see it that way, but rather as a market restructuring: "The economic model is forcing mid-size firms to become small firms. The small firms are disappearing. The big ones have the capital and they keep growing."

The small firms did not really disappear, though. They were there in 2011 and have grown in number through 2015. Yet, they are invisible to both the buying public and labor inspectors alike. For example, when Jorge laid off his workers, he complied with labor laws and paid them between 6,000 and 10,000 US dollars each in severance costs. Some agreed to take their payout in the form of industrial sewing equipment. Most of these workers then established themselves as independent operators producing for Jorge. These subcontracts saved Jorge significant labor costs.

Jorge did not think many other firms had trimmed their workforce as radically as he and his wife had. However, evidence from the Chamber of

Commerce suggests such subcontracting was widespread. In 2014 and 2015 the Chamber of Commerce struggled to finance the annual trade show, as the larger firms no longer stepped up to underwrite the fashion shows and musical performances. Membership in the chamber dropped, even as one officer of the chamber estimated that the number of small-scale clothing assembly operations had climbed to between three hundred and four hundred businesses by 2015. Indeed, subcontractors fundamentally remade Atuntaqui. The town was quickly shifting away from being an independent hub of fashion with streets lined with bright, branded retail operations. Instead, it became a city of piecework production with hundreds of operations employing fewer than ten workers each.

For men and women in the popular markets of provincial cities, post-neoliberal Ecuador has been one in which street-level capitalism has become more monstrous and more naked, to use Gibson-Graham's (1996) adjectives. Traders who had committed to expanding their businesses and adopting modern business methods now lacked the public economic spaces that consultants once tried to cultivate in Otavalo and Atuntaqui that could bring people together to work through their disagreements. Only in 2016, with the complete collapse of sales in Tulcán, did vendors and municipal authorities unite to demand help from the central government. The help that did arrive came in the form of limited tax relief and loan consolidation. The state saw its purposes in staving off personal financial collapse, but no longer in seeing entrepreneurs through to achieving a workable business. As these enterprises shrink, retail landscapes wither, trade associations struggle to maintain membership, and civic projects get set aside. Having dropped its engagement with the hustle of competition, the state has let multiple strands of urban connectivity snap and unravel.

CONCLUSIONS

The 1990s moment of globalization sparked a surprising convergence between an anthropologist's theories of culture and an economist's arguments about industrial organization. In each conceptualization, difference and locality conferred durable characteristics that held up far beyond the context of their origin. Two decades later, the thinking of geographers Gibson-Graham and another economist, Ecuador's president Rafael Correa, intersected in a radically alternative way of thinking about the economy. They granted legitimacy to the informal and unrecorded transactions of provisioning a home and caring for others, seeking to resocialize economic relations and invest in the productive possibilities of communal ties. In the 1990s, "local" was powerfully generative of difference, texture, and meaning amid a global popular consumer culture. By the 2010s, "local" was a deep reservoir of community, buffeted by surface storms of capitalism but with strong currents that flowed apart. In these opposing views, "competition" is the critical concept. Ordering/productive in the earlier scheme, it is cast as atomizing/destructive in the other.

With the end of the Cold War in the 1990s, the purposes and rhetoric of competition intensified, especially as the IMF, the WTO, and other entities and financial powers proposed ever more orthodox pro-market policies for countries such as Ecuador whose finances had faltered. Whether it occurred for a single enterprise or a national economy, a moment of hardship was a revelation of the failure of competitiveness. States became partners in offering a remedy. Yet, even when committed to action, the state was there not so much to rescue a particular enterprise or trade but to become a broker of its citizen's talents and products in a world economy. Such a trade-centered view of state action fit into the widespread atrophy of social welfare spending. Importantly, though, it aligned state ministries with the everyday aspirations of family businesses—to have a durable edge in the market. The irony of the social and solidarity economy-based policy making that came later is that, in rejecting competition as antisocial, officials blinded themselves to the primary space of encounter for those working in urban popular economies.

These tradespeople gave distinctive character to provincial cities precisely through their hustling for work and sales. The pursuit of competitiveness became a surprisingly wide and inclusive force in shaping the character of urban life. In a generic way, competing for trade created cities as places of contact, recognition, and calibration among vendors and producers. Investments in commercial position—displayed inventories, branded stores, staffing market stalls—sustained the possibility of mutual intelligibility. Each public display encoded a shared place-based way of going about business in economies that knew fewer national boundaries. The day-to-day business decisions collectively materialized the look and feel of a place. Under both neoliberal and post-neoliberal administrations, cities served as test sites for economic policy. As troubles mounted up for informal vendors through swings in tariff policy, exchange rate pressures, and shifts in flows of Asian-made goods, the government intervened. Across Otavalo, Atuntaqui, and Tulcán, political responses amplified the deviations in the fortunes of different towns. One city's loss of protection from imported goods became another's gain in international products and retail commerce. Streetscapes, plazas, and marketplaces layered with faded brands and updated store fronts signaled the sequences of good times and economic busts that towns experienced.

In urban popular markets, men and women have few or no economic options outside of the daily selling they aspire to. They must compete;

their competition builds their social and civic world. Regularly over the past decades, that world has lost political legitimacy from above, whether due to government attacks on informality or to the ideological devaluation of commerce and competing. Rejected for the way they compete, men and women in urban popular markets become all the more exposed to the crises that ever-changing economic policy sends their way. And yet it is among those that they compete most fiercely against that they find allies with whom to defend their trade, hometown, and promising next steps for their work.

BIBLIOGRAPHY

Aldrich, Howard E., and C. Marlene Fiol. "Fools Rush In? The Institutional Context of Industry Creation." In *Entrepreneurship: Concepts, Theory and Perspective*, edited by Álvaro Cuervo, Domingo Ribeiro, and Salvador Roig, 105–27. Berlin, Heidelberg: Springer Berlin Heidelberg, 2007.

Anand, Nikhil. *Hydraulic City: Water and the Infrastructures of Citizenship in Mumbai*. Durham: Duke University Press, 2017.

Antrosio, Jason, and Rudi Colloredo-Mansfeld. *Fast, Easy, and in Cash: Artisan Hardship and Hope in a Global Economy*. Chicago: University of Chicago Press, 2015.

Appadurai, Arjun. *Modernity at Large: Cultural Dimensions of Globalization*. Minneapolis: University of Minnesota Press, 1996.

Benalcazar, Washington. "Tulcán está en crisis, tras 20 años de bonanza." *El Comercio*, June 13, 2016. http://www.elcomercio.com/actualidad/tulcan-crisis-bonanza-ecuador-comercio.html.

Bourdieu, Pierre. *The Field of Cultural Production: Essays on Art and Literature*. New York: Columbia University Press, 1993.

———. "The Myth of 'Globalization' and the European Welfare State." In *Acts of Resistance: Against the Tyranny of the Market*, 29–44. New York: The New Press, 1998.

Brenner, Neil, and Nik Theodore. "Cities and the Geographies of 'Actually Existing Neoliberalism.'" *Antipode* 34, no. 3 (2002): 349–79.

Buitrón, Aníbal. "Situación económica y social del indio Otavaleño." *America Indígena* 7 (1947): 45–67.

Carrier, James. "Introduction." In *Meanings of the Market: The Free Market in Western Culture*, edited by James Carrier, 1-68. Oxford: Berg Publishers, 1997.

Christensen, Clayton. *The Innovator's Dilemma: When New Technologies Cause Great Firms to Fail*. Cambridge, MA: Harvard Business Review Press, 1997.

Colloredo-Mansfeld, Rudi. *The Native Leisure Class: Consumption and Cultural Creativity in the Andes*. Chicago: Chicago University Press, 1999.

———. "An Ethnography of Neoliberalism: Understanding Competition in Artisan Economies." *Current Anthropology* 43, no. 1 (2002): 113–37.

Comaroff, John L., and Jean Comaroff. *Ethnicity, Inc*. Chicago: University of Chicago Press, 2009.

de la Torre, Carlos. "Technocratic Populism in Ecuador." *Journal of Democracy* 24, no. 3 (2013): 33–46.

Drabenstott, Mark, Nancy Novack, and Stephen Weiler. "New Governance for a New Rural Economy: Reinventing Public and Private Institutions—A Conference Summary." In *New Governanace for a New Rural Economy: Reinventing Public and Private Institutions*, 1–7. Kansas City: Federal Reserve Bank of Kansas City, 2004.

Gibson-Graham, J. K. *The End of Capitalism (As We Knew It): A Feminist Critique of Political Economy*. Minneapolis: University of Minnesota Press, 1996.

———. "Surplus Possibilities: Postdevelopment and Community Economies." *Singapore Journal of Tropical Geography* 26 (2005): 4–26.

Gudeman, Stephen. *Anthropology and Economy*. New York: Cambridge University Press, 2016.

Grugel, Jean, and Pía Riggirozzi. "Post-Neoliberalism in Latin America: Rebuilding and Reclaiming the State after Crisis." *Development and Change* 43, no. 1 (2012): 1–21.

Hale, Charles. "Neoliberal Multiculturalism: The Remaking of Cultural Rights and Racial Dominance in Central America." *PoLAR: Political and Legal Anthropology Review* 28, no. 1 (2005): 10–28.

Harvey, David. *The Condition of Postmodernity*. Oxford: Basil Blackwell, 1989.

Kennemore, Amy, and Gregory Weeks. "Twenty-First Century Socialism? The Elusive Search for a Post-Neoliberal Development Model in Bolivia and Ecuador." *Bulletin of Latin American Research* 30, no. 3 (2011): 267–81.

Lash, Scott, and John Urry. *The End of Organized Capitalism*. Madison: University of Wisconsin Press, 1987.

———. *Economies of Signs and Space*. London; Thousand Oaks, CA: Sage, 1994.

Leiva, Fernando Ignacio. *Latin American Neostructuralism: The Contradictions of Post-Neoliberal Development*. Minneapolis: University of Minnesota Press, 2008.

Mathews, Gordon, and Carlos Alba Vega. "Introduction: What Is Globalization from Below?" In *Globalization from Below: The World's Other Economy*, edited by Gordon Mathews, Gustavo Lins Ribiero, and Carlos Alba Vega, 1–16. New York: Routledge, 2012.

Meyer-Stamer, Jörg. "Participatory Appraisal of Competitive Advantage (PACA): Launching Local Economic Development Initiatives." Mesopartner Working Paper January 2003. http://www.value-chains.org/dyn/bds/docs/377/PACA%20 Meyer-Stamer.pdf.

Meisch, Lynn. *Andean Entrepreneurs: Otavalo Merchants and Musicians in the Global Arena*. Austin: University of Texas Press, 2002.

Müller, Juliane, and Rudi Colloredo-Mansfeld. "Introduction: Popular Economies and the Remaking of China-Latin America Relations." *Journal of Latin America and Caribbean Anthropology* 23, no. 1 (2018): 9–17.

Nelms, Taylor. "'The Problem of Delimitation': Parataxis, Bureaucracy, and Ecuador's Popular and Solidarity Economy." *Journal of the Royal Anthropological Institute* 21, no. 1 (2015): 106–26.

Piore, Michael, and Charles Sabel. *The Second Industrial Divide*. New York: Basic Books, 1984.

Porter, Michael. "Clusters and the New Economics of Competition." *Harvard Business Review* November–December (1998): 77–90.

———. "What Is Strategy?" In *On Competition*, 39–73. Boston: Harvard Business School Press, 1998 [1996].

———. *The Competitive Advantage of Nations*. New York: The Free Press, 1998 [1990].

Rosen, Tracey A. "Toward an Anthropology of Competition? Some Preliminary Observations on the Value of 'Unfair Competition' in Greece." Paper presented at the Biennial Meeting of the Society for Cultural Anthropology, Ithaca, New York, May 13–14, 2016.

Rubio Orbe, Gonzalo. *Punyaro, estudio de antropologia social y cultural de una communidad indigena y mestiza*. Quito: Casa de la Cultura Ecuatoriana, 1956.

Wolfe, David A., and Matthew Lucas. *Global Networks and Local Linkages: The Paradox of Cluster Development in an Open Economy*. Ithaca, NY: McGill-Queen's University Press and School of Policy Studies, Queen's University, 2005.

Wright, E. O. *Envisioning Real Utopias*. New York: Verso, 2010.

Chapter Two

The Art of Crafting Formal-Informal Linkages

On the Enduring Appeal of Belo Horizonte's Hippie Fair

Peter Mörtenböck and Helge Mooshammer

While informal markets arguably have a long history as arenas of economic self-help of one kind or another, in recent times there has been a noticeable shift when it comes to the ways political and administrative authorities deal with these spatialized networks of bottom-up entrepreneurialism. The publication in 1973 of an article by anthropologist and self-taught economist Keith Hart on the high level of completely unregistered economic activity in the slums of the Ghanaian capital of Accra (Hart 1973) was instrumental in introducing the notion of an "informal sector" into debates among development professionals. In the following decades, the majority of policy responses to such informality were geared toward a single strategy of "integration," that is, making these activities conform to the requirements and regulations of the dominant economic order. Although Keith Hart's own approach had been more open-minded and the principal impetus of his studies had been to "draw attention to activities that had previously been invisible to the bureaucratic gaze" rather than to coin a concept, the "informal economy" has subsequently become "a keyword helping to organize a segment of the academic and policy-making bureaucracy" (Hart 2015). This bureaucratic absorption of the concept of the informal economy, which has led to often forcefully enacted measures to combat informal economic activities on the ground, has largely been based on the assumption that—as a flagship report by the World Bank on Latin America and the Caribbean in 2007 still put it—informality is counterproductive when it comes to enabling investment climates and thus acts as "a drag on growth" (Perry et al. 2007, 22).

Increasingly, though, governments around the world are signing up to the idea that the source of a new and perhaps different kind of growth may lie precisely in "informal"—that is, self-initiated and deeply socially structured—milieus that foster bottom-up explorations of novel entrepreneurial activities. An unholy marriage between, on the one hand, the fallout of the global financial crisis of 2007–2008, which has led to severe austerity measures and massive cutbacks in social services in many parts of the world, and on the other, the allure of beguiling success stories of informally born startups that turn into global market disruptors seemingly overnight has generated a new willingness to abandon old administrative patterns geared toward forcing everyone to conform to the prevalent economic paradigm and to open up the policy toolbox to novel ways of instigating new forms of economic organization. From the initiation of a range of comprehensive and multifaceted programs aimed at consolidating the business foundation of family entrepreneurs active in the popular economy[1] to the promotion of all sorts of themed and carefully orchestrated pop-up market places, we are seeing a whole new wave of support for low-key "informal" places of exchange. Physical urban markets are no longer only understood as odd economic remnants tolerated because they function as valves for pressures from the lower end of the economic pyramid, but are being increasingly embraced as incubators of change and future prospects.

One of the largest street markets in Latin America, officially registered as the Feira de Arte, Artesanato e Produtores de Variedades da Avenida Afonso Pensa (Arts, Crafts and Variety Products Fair on Avenida Afonso Pena), but colloquially known as the Hippie Fair (Feira Hippie), takes place every Sunday in the center of Belo Horizonte, the capital of the Brazilian state of Minas Gerais. The history of its social, economic, and spatio-urban transformation over the last half century is indicative of wider changes in how urban markets are understood and sheds light on how the global economic and political volatility of the last decade has generated new cultural and political pressures to (re)capture the energy of marketplaces as sites of more easily accessible economic opportunities, as well as of encounters with the new and unknown, potentially harboring new sources of prosperity and generally improving the quality of urban life. From its inconspicuous beginnings as a marginal space of 1960s countercultural experience, Belo Horizonte's Feira Hippie has grown into a major distribution point for the global shadow trade in cheap mass-produced knickknacks and knockoffs. The current tensions around the market's official arts-and-crafts orientation and the regulatory commitment to local authenticity, which stand in stark contrast to the actual display of overwhelmingly low-quality, throwaway goods, highlight not only the divergence of interests between local middle-class residents and the city's poor, who come to the centrally located market from a ring of peripheral favelas primarily as a way of having a cheap day out, but also the broader question of how the path to future economic development is to be delineated. In this respect, the story of the Feira Hippie and the changing fate of its organizers, traders, and customers, which is playing out in the cultural narrative, political framing, and architectural set-up of the market, is also a story about the clash between the idea of an economy of free-flowing global trade and local protectionism, between subscribing to consumer demands and cultivating authentic craftsmanship, and between enforcing hegemonic market interests and embarking on new models of formal-informal linkages.

INCORPORATING INFORMALITY

Informal markets often arise on the fault lines inscribed by global alliances of money and power: wars and humanitarian crises, national and infrastructural borders, the worldwide trade in waste, and the marginal spaces of urban transformation (Mörtenböck and Mooshammer 2015). They act as globalization's safety valve while also providing livelihoods for millions of people trading in the streets of cities around the world. Informal markets represent a globally distributed yet often stigmatized economic practice that is orientated toward concrete opportunities and whose local differences cannot be understood from either a uniform overall perspective or a purely local one. This practice is rather the expression of an economic setting in which forces of differing dimensions and ranges converge and create new market conventions. Seen in this way, different types of informality can be understood as characteristic patterns of transaction through which different spaces and economies are brought together (Roy 2005, 148).

Today, informal marketplaces are not only experiencing increasing pressure from state and corporate actors, but also a change in the orientation of this pressure. The last two decades of globalization, in conjunction with the recent economic crisis and emerging forms of self-organized, peer-to-peer economies, have substantially altered the relationship between the informal and formal sector, both conceptually and practically. This change has been reflected in a revised understanding of the informal economy as an alternative, multifaceted mode of economic governance outside state regulation. It is also reflected in the recent rise of self-employment and increasing state support for start-ups, micro-businesses, social entrepreneurship, and peer-to-peer industries in countries of the Global North as well as the Global South.

The ongoing spatial transformation of informal markets is not only indicative of these macro-economic changes. It is also playing an instrumental role in the generation of new economic climates—signifying, in some cases, generative activity based on alternative knowledge and use of city services and land, and alternative livelihood strategies (Evers and Seale 2015), and in others, an expansion of the market economy's reach into new territories, particularly within the framework of markets run by the poor in developing countries (Roy 2010). In this respect, informal markets are important sites of negotiation where new forms of interaction (shaped by technological and organizational changes) between state and non-state actors pursuing different political and economic interests are explored.

In light of these developments, this text examines distinct incorporations of informality in the urban economic realm—both in the sense of absorbing the economic capacities of informal activities into the formal realm, and in the sense of adopting informal methods in carrying out activities in the formal urban economy. While for reasons of argumentative strategy we use the terms "formal" and "informal" as distinct categories in this text, it is important to point out that there is no clear-cut binary of "formal" and "informal" economic conduct. Both terms reflect particular roles assigned within a continuous economic fabric. Although often characterized by uneven power relations, the distinction between "formal" and "informal" is not necessarily synonymous with the disparity between the wealthy and the poor. There is "informality from above," just as there is "informality from below" (Ribeiro 2006); there is "elite informality," just as there is "subaltern informality" (Roy 2005, 147). And there are degrees of planning, order, deliberations, and protocols involved in informal markets, just as there are in formal markets. Against this background, the term "integration" often masks a range of extra-market processes, ideologically biased goals, and purpose-driven interventions that are central to the ongoing creation of a global market and economic standardization (Humphrey and Skvirskaja 2012). For these reasons it is necessary to look not only at the direct and overt strategies of transforming informal marketplaces but also at the political and social undercurrents linked with the struggle to control these sites and to benefit from their economic informality.

In order to address the accelerating hybridization of formal and informal economic practices in the pursuit of new market opportunities, we will focus here on the transformations underway at one of Latin America's largest open-air markets, Belo Horizonte's "Hippie Fair." Belying its uniform and ordered appearance, the fair's multi-actor structure highlights the proliferation of formal-informal linkages that affect not only street vendors, manufacturers, and administrative bodies, but also millions of people who use this inner-city space as an opportunity to engage in all kinds of exchange. Many people come here regularly to spend their Sunday meeting friends, listening to samba music, hunting for bargains, strolling around, chatting with vendors, and enjoying cheap food and drinks. If one is looking for economic informality, it can be found at the Hippie Fair in many different variants: as entrepreneurial or survivalist strategy, as support structure, as business innovator, as time-saver, or as stopgap solution. With its almost seamless transition between informal and formal economic practices, the fair has effectively turned a busy traffic corridor into a safe and much-frequented inner-city place of encounter between many different segments of the population.

From a neoliberal perspective as well as in the perception of many formal-sector actors, the most attractive achievement of informal marketplaces is the creation of new market environments—places for trade and commerce—that can offer opportunities for economic growth. However, policy approaches to the integration of the economic potential of informal marketplaces differ widely, ranging from market closures and relocations to structural upgrades and the transformation of informal markets into closely regulated shopping environments, regardless of their role as a crucial lifeline for millions of people at the bottom of the economic pyramid (Mörtenböck and Mooshammer 2015). While in the past, informality has often been seen as an inferior condition associated with low productivity—as a "drag on growth"—reviews of contemporary policy practices are pointing toward a revised understanding of the relationship between the formal and informal sectors in terms of participants and modi operandi, as well as emergent strategies of resistance.[2] What is at stake in this change is not just a different way of dealing with the informal sector, but—through the proliferation of formal-informal linkages—a paradigm shift affecting many contemporary systems of socioeconomic stratification.

With the informal economy estimated to account for more than half of all nonagricultural activities in large parts of the world (International Labour Organization 2013), we are seeing increased interest across the political spectrum in accessing the potential of the informal economy by integrating its entrepreneurial energies, assets, and networks into wider economic circuits.[3] Attesting to this growing interest, the development of many informal marketplaces across Latin America has been characterized by a variety of attempts at integration. Besides juridical (trade licenses, rights of use, etc.), financial (access to credit, poverty alleviation, etc.), and organizational measures (access to piped water, electricity supply, agreements with informal workers' unions, etc.), such attempts often revolve around spatial organization and range from the forced removal and relocation of informal markets to urban fringes or the dispersal of market activities into other neighborhoods, to the demarcation of dedicated areas that do not interfere with formal business and the allocation of trading space in permanent market halls, where maintenance and services are provided on a fee-for-service basis. It is worth noting here that street vendors, even though they are the ones most affected by the regulation and management of informal trade, rarely feature in decision-making processes (Bhowmik 2005). Many "integration" projects are thus still governed by an authoritative, paternalistic concept of realigning the workings of informal economic activities and making them fully compliant with the requirements of the formal economy (Chen, Rover, and Skinner 2016).

FROM COUNTERCULTURE TO GLOBAL MARKET INTEGRATION

Every Sunday, the majestic Avenida Afonso Pena in the center of Belo Horizonte is closed to traffic and transformed into one of Latin America's largest open-air markets, attracting an average of seventy thousand visitors. From the early hours onwards, workers start to assemble more than 2,500 modular tents. Groupings of uniformly colored tarpaulins form radiant blocks of red, blue, green, and yellow, which contrast with the lush tropical green of the Américo Renné Giannetti municipal park on one side and the strict lines of modernist tower blocks on the other. Twelve rows deep and 220 units long, this spectacular parade stretches along the entire southwestern edge of the park. Viewed from afar, the market's strict order and bulky lineup, along one of the city's most prominent thoroughfares, resembles a top-down, organized demonstration more than the gathering of an alternative market, as the "Hippie Fair" label might suggest.

Staging the six-hundred-meter-long fair every Sunday is an elaborate process, the study of which was the focus of local artist Lucas Dupin's six-month-long participation in the Bolsa Pampulha 2016 residency program. Amongst the multifarious materials produced during his artistic investigations is a subtly edited video piece that depicts the concerted phases and intricate interactions involved in getting the 2,500 stalls ready in time for the market to open on Sunday mornings.[4] Traders do not own or set up the tent structures themselves but rent them on a daily or monthly basis from specialist operators charging between 60 and 100 reais per day depending on the size of the stall. Involving approximately 350 people, the entire setup of the market is controlled by around thirty groups of so-called "men with a van," with the latter needed to ferry the numerous stall components from offsite storage spaces to the Avenida Afonso Pena in the city center. These storage spaces are often combined with small workshops, as most operations not only own and rent out the tent structures but also manufacture them, welding and bending the metal tubes into various shapes, sewing together differently colored tarpaulins, and adding various equipment for specialist stalls such as fridge components for food sellers or simpler items such as stools for traders.

Figure 2.1. Aerial view of the Avenida Afonso Pena and the Feira de Arte, Artesanato e Produtores de Variedades.
Peter Mörtenböck and Helge Mooshammer

Individual "men with a van" can be in charge of ten to two hundred tents, and as a result the market is divided into discrete patches that do not necessarily overlap with the official color-coded sections grouped according to different wares. Smaller patches are operated as one-person businesses while those commanding higher numbers of tents have additional "attendants" (*guardadores*) working for them, who help to set up the stalls and guard them until the handover to the traders in the morning. Usually, the first vans arrive around 11:00 p.m. on Saturdays and the helpers begin preassembling stalls on the sidewalks, before all the lanes of traffic are officially closed off between 2:00 a.m. and 3:00 a.m. on Sundays and they are allowed to move their work onto the street. As one of our key informants on these processes explains, a market attendant—who is paid 15 reais per assembled stall—can earn up to 400 reais in one night, and in the current economic climate of Brazil this work represents a highly valuable source of income that the people who have it are keen to safeguard. Similarly, those running the businesses providing the market infrastructure rigorously guard their patches with the help of male family members, who are involved in these operations from a very young age.

Focusing on these twilight aspects of market life, which are rarely acknowledged yet form an essential aspect of the market's ongoing existence, Lucas Dupin's video piece records the cyclical assembling and dismantling of the market's infrastructural skeleton, from the arrival of the vans and the off-loading of countless parts to the erection of the metal structures and the skillful throwing of the tarpaulin covers as day breaks, only to be followed by the reverse process when the market is taken down again at 6:00 p.m. on Sunday evenings. In tandem with the polyphonic soundscape of thousands of clunking metal tubes that accompanies the assembling of this massive 2,500-tent-strong fair, it becomes very tangible how the market's urban presence displays both powerful and ephemeral characteristics. The associated precariousness not only affects operations that are strongly dependent on the market, such as the tent suppliers, who recently have been seeking some measure of economic stability by forming an association, but as we will discuss later, has also been an inherent aspect of the market's existence, during which informal self-organization has been continuously exposed to often fundamentally game-changing bureaucratic interventions.

As the capital of the state of Minas Gerais and center of the eponymous mining industry, Belo Horizonte certainly has a history of monumental urban planning. The highly choreographed market setup occupies a central patch of the grandiose street plan of the city center, conceived by Aarão Reis shortly after Brazil became a republic in 1889. Reputedly inspired by the example of Washington, DC, the plan is based on a striking rhombus pattern with a four-block-wide grid of diagonal avenues placed on top of a standard perpendicular grid of blocks, allowing for long vistas and a string of prestigious squares and parade grounds at its main intersections. Oriented toward a representative display of civic pride and republican institutions, the grand layout has also engendered a highly segregated urban fabric, with workers prevented from settling within the planned inner-city districts.

Nowadays, although its official name is the Feira de Arte, Artesanato e Produtores de Variedades da Avenida Afonso Pena, locals still refer to the market as the "Hippie Fair." This colloquial name is a reference to the market's idiosyncratic beginnings in 1969 as a gathering of art students, dropouts, and other alternative thinkers on Praça da Liberdade in Belo Horizonte's main cultural quarter of Savassi. Following the Summer of Love of 1967, the hippie movement spread from US campuses to many university towns around the globe. The self-organized provision of alternative lifestyle accessories and aesthetic objects had become a common element in the hippie movement's attempt to create a holistic counterculture that not only served leisure and entertainment but also experimental terrains for autonomous livelihoods. At the time, unsolicited assemblies by members of a dissenting younger generation were met with suspicion in most places, and the situation in Belo Horizonte was certainly no different. With the country under military rule since 1964, public manifestations in any Brazilian city were the sole preserve of power. Civil liberties and legal rights had been severely restricted (most notably through the suspension of habeas corpus—the right of arrestees to be brought before a judge or into court) and students and universities became primary targets of government forces after widespread protests in 1968.

When talking to vendors who have been involved in the fair for decades, we encountered diverging claims regarding the extent to which the initial group of hippie students and a few hundred artists and artisans who began to sell their works to a predominantly middle-class clientele every Sunday actually overlapped. What arguably contributed to the long-term survival of the market was the early takeover of its organization by the municipality of Belo Horizonte. In 1973, the city officially recognized the hippie fair in a decree on the regular holding of the "Liberty Fair," laying down a whole set of conditions—repeatedly emphasizing, for instance, the prohibition on "pieces, works or productions that violate public morals and good customs"—as well as introducing yearly license fees for exhibitors (Prefeitura de Belo Horizonte 1973). To ensure ideological compliance and to confront diffuse anxieties regarding the encroachment of radical nonacademic art and an uncontrollable indigenization as well as an influx of radical modernist, nonlocal art, the decree further ordered the appointment of a technical advisory committee with members drawn from the city council and from a list of renowned artists, art critics, and cultural representatives. The granting of exhibitor licenses was thereby subject to a prior examination of artistic credentials. Artists also had to opt for a particular material classification (metals, plastics, wood, hides, precious metals, semi-precious, and precious stones, etc.) with works graded according to the material that either composed over 50 percent of their weight or represented over 50 percent of their value.

While for the municipality of Belo Horizonte—a city of considerable wealth as well as staggering social inequality—these conditions allowed for tighter direct control of the way the market functioned, it also instated a familiar instrumentalization of the arts as an appeasing cultural bond beyond conflictual class and political differences. Historically, the city's authorities have frequently utilized the popular notion of the city's outstanding artistic achievements and heritage. References range from the Pampulha complex in the north of the city (erected under Mayor Juscelino Kubitschek in the 1940s and for which a young Oscar Niemeyer was commissioned to design a series of now-iconic buildings)[5] to the city's proximity to the world cultural heritage site of Ouro Preto and the nearby contemporary arts park of Inhotim.[6] This reliance on the popular notion of Belo Horizonte as a seat of artistic richness and appreciation has framed political engagement with the fair since its inception and still informs the plane of negotiation today.

REGULATION AND MASSIFICATION

Around 1975/1976, a regular parallel fair for what was perceived as minor products was established on Thursdays. The mixed feelings around these changes are reflected in the amendment of the decree on the arts-and-crafts fair on Liberty Square from 1977, which now included, for instance, obligations "to enhance artistic and crafts research and produce highly creative works; to maintain a warm, friendly, and healthy environment; not to exhibit standardized garment products; and to refrain from imitating or copying models created by other exhibitors" (Prefeitura de Belo Horizonte 1977). In the early 1980s, a period of political favoritism reportedly corrupted the artistic foundation of the fair, with increasing numbers of licenses granted by "invitation" rather than as a result of the technical advisory committee's review process.[7] The reaction on the ground was an ever more anarchic appropriation of space. During the years of re-democratization after 1985, the alleged depredation of the historic gardens of Praça da Liberdade provided the pretext for instigating a change of venue and more tightly controlling the market. In fact, during this period many Latin American cities witnessed a so-called "fairing" of urban spaces, which began increasingly to serve as sites of subsistence work and informal trade. When the municipality of Belo Horizonte ordered the relocation of the Liberty Fair to Avenida Alonso Pena, it also shifted a number of other street markets that had sprung up on Praça Raul Soares, Rua Gonçalves Dias, and Praça Rui Barbosa to the same location—a process that cleared the inner city of Belo Horizonte of informal trading and resulted in the arts-and-crafts fair swelling to its current size.

Over the two decades since its relocation, the transformation of the market has been characterized by two main tendencies: on the one hand, an ever-stronger grip by the municipality on the market's operation and, on the other, an increased orientation toward a low-end economy. Both developments are evident in the ongoing spatial restructuring of the market. The twelve different divisions of the layout implemented in September 2013 comprise a total of 2,555 tents, of which 374 are earmarked for clothing, 204 for baby clothing, 340 for costume jewelry, 224 for bags, and 262 for shoes, but only 137 for fine art and sculpture, just a fraction above 5 percent of the total number of vending points. However, even before this, arts and crafts had literally become sidelined, with art vendors displaying their works not in tents but along the iron fence that encircles the municipal park and thus outside the main body of the market. On our visits to the market in 2012, these developments were clearly evident in the ways art vendors had been relegated to the margins of the market, their paintings fixed onto the railings of the park or placed on ad-hoc easels that could be moved quickly when required.

In official statements, there is still an insistence on the arts-and-crafts character of the market, though the inclusion of the rather diffuse classification of "producers of variety products" has opened up a considerable gray zone in terms of regulation and has in fact created a framework allowing for a continuous commercialization and takeover by manufactured goods, epitomized by the display of crude nudes and the sale of funky toilet seats. Increasing reference to the fair as *camelódromo* echoes the recognition that the market has turned into a locus of resale for *sacoleiros* shuttling in Chinese mass-produced wares from the border markets in Paraguay.[8] On paper, the regulations and bylaws are supposed to safeguard the prevalence of arts and handicrafts, for instance by limiting the power of machinery used to produce items offered for sale to five kilowatts and by forbidding the sale of third-party products. In the annual license renewal process, stallholders are required to provide the address of their workshop and authorities are supposed to check regularly for evidence of craftsmanship, such as the amount of raw material in stock, the volume of weekly production, and the knowledge and skills required for all phases of production. Furthermore, the presence of a member of the license-holder's family unit at the stalls is regularly checked to ensure that family members are replaced by an employee or agent no more than eight times a year (Prefeitura de Belo Horizonte 2010). According to regulations, the right

Figure 2.2. Adult clothing section of the Feira de Arte, Artesanato e Produtores de Variedades da Avenida Afonso Pena.
Peter Mörtenböck and Helge Mooshammer

to operate a stall at the market cannot be passed down outside the immediate family line. Not even marital partners are entitled to enter into an existing contract with the municipality. Consequently, stallholders finding that their services or range of goods do not bring in enough money have often decided to rent their pitches to more profitable businesses, even if these shadow operations bear little relationship to the arts-and-crafts tradition of the market and have helped transform its character from a middle-class playground to a weekly festival strip catering to the broad masses, be they international tourists or favela residents.

While the city authorities claim that the overall annual expenditure involved in running the market is more than double the direct intake of taxes, there is also a recognition that the fair generates and supports around fifteen to twenty thousand jobs, directly through the fair itself and indirectly through the employment of assemblers, shippers, cleaners, and inspection staff, as well as through the high numbers of out-of-town visitors it attracts (Pimentel, de Pádua Carrieri, and Leite-Da-Silva 2007). In effect, the fair has come to be understood as an event compensating for Belo Horizonte's land-locked location and lack of a beach, which in many Brazilian cities is the main site of collective leisure activities. Events in general tend to emphasize or change the routine of a group of people. They can give a new character to a particular environment and promote particular activities. Belo Horizonte's Hippie Fair is no exception to this. It has become a major center of gravity for thousands of people enjoying a great day out in the city. And yet, in recent years there has been growing concern about the lack of attention given to the fair as a leisure destination. While a wide range of national fairs and congresses regularly held in this mining city receive generous government support to boost the local economy, the Hippie Fair, as vendors often lament, suffers major infrastructural problems—inadequate sanitation, no places for people to sit and rest, and a lack of signage and policing to name but a few—that hamper not only the welfare of exhibitors but the entire urban milieu of the fair as a place for secure and pleasurable encounters between tourists, locals, and traders (de Castro Rodriguez 2008).

Moreover, a new wave of interest from economic institutions has been stimulated by the shift toward a low-end economy. While credit cooperatives such as Sicoob Divicred (a credit cooperative advertising itself as "more than a bank") (Femeart 2013) are still the major providers of microfinance for the Hippie Fair, commercial banks have begun to scour the market offering lines of microcredit and advertising what they claim are innovative credit-card schemes tailored specifically to the precarious cash flow of market vendors. To get their business started, vendors need to pay a fee for setting up shop in the fair. They also need the right inventory: a selection of well-chosen stock items, be it several sets of fashionable clothing items in different sizes or a well-curated range of handcrafted jewelry, to handle the constant shift in customer tastes. Rather than promoting the strengthening of social bonds and a culture of solidarity, commercial banks investing in these market businesses tend to focus their interest mainly on vendors catering for a more upmarket, creative, and innovation-minded clientele that holds good potential for fast business growth and high returns. Taking such risks and often making substantial investments, these vendors need to comply with the innovation paradigm of global capitalist markets. They need to be always on the lookout for new and original products so they can respond adequately to the needs and demands of discerning customers and avoid delays in loan repayments. Encouraging a general climate of entrepreneurial competition at Belo Horizonte's Hippie Fair, there is mounting pressure, not only on the part of vendors who take out a bank loan or are issued a credit card for business expansion, but also on the part of all other people engaged in the market who are equally caught up in the tension between market logic and community reality—fellow vendors, artists, manufacturers, temporary workers, service suppliers, intermediaries, or stall minders.

This shift is not occurring without support from official parties. In line with the country-wide turn toward an *Economia Popular Solidária*, numerous policy frameworks and coordinating bodies have been launched by the municipality of Belo Horizonte and the state of Minas Gerais to foster such entrepreneurial activities. The concept of an economy based on solidarity is evident, for example, in the reservation of 5 percent of vending points at the arts-and-crafts fair for philanthropic and communal initiatives, which is equal to the number of places currently allocated for the arts. In 2007 the technical advisory committee was replaced by a joint commission (Comissão Paritária) that included annually elected exhibitor representatives to consult on the running of the fair. Obtaining a license as an exhibitor is currently free of charge. However, being issued one depends on the availability of spaces and is subject to a bidding process tailored to factor in various criteria relating to social disadvantage and unfavorable socioeconomic conditions, such as illiteracy and a lack of ownership of property, land, or a vehicle.[9] The city's "right to food" program and its accompanying promotion of farmers markets further illuminates the current embrace of (street) markets as a policy device by which socioeconomic objectives are implemented in and through the urban realm. All these activities can be understood as part of a comprehensive policy catalog aimed at stimulating entrepreneurial thinking across large segments of the population to solve governance problems such as the uneven distribution of wealth and the pressures arising from economic stagnation.

Be it in Brazil or elsewhere in Latin America, creative entrepreneurship as an ideological apparatus to leverage market-oriented development is increasingly being incentivized by public- and private-sector organizations alike in the struggle for global market participation.

Despite the official discourse of inclusive policies—a widely used umbrella term under which such new political programs are implemented—the operation of the fair has not been free of conflict, as evidenced notably in February 2011, when a flawed online process of annual bidding for licenses resulted in available vending points being five times oversubscribed. This led to serious turmoil and the mobilization of the municipal guard. Tensions were eventually eased when the city reopened the bidding to existing vendors. In the summer of 2013, a new conflict arose between the vendors' association ASSEAP (Associação dos Expositores da Feira de Arte, Artesanato e Variedades da Avenida Afonso Pena) and the city authorities around the reorganization of the market's layout and fears of an unfair distribution of "good" and "bad" spots. The solution that has since been adopted, entailing groups of four tents instead of long uninterrupted rows,[10] presumably affords every vendor a corner position and equal exposure to customers. While allowing for wider traffic corridors and better emergency access as well as preventing clients from getting "lost," the imposed and strictly controlled isomorphism is also instilling an ever more invasive sense of surveillance by the authorities.

CRAFT OR COMPANY—PERFORMANCE MATTERS

Given the focus on arts and crafts, customized design, and creative talent, Belo Horizonte's original hippie fair could be understood as a precursor of today's hipster markets. There are numerous overlaps, in particular the importance of social media to creating a steady customer base attracted to the market's particular flair. The "Feira Hippie de BH" Facebook page boasts more than forty thousand likes and entices its visitors to post their photographic exploits, an endless promotion of leather bags, belts, and sandals, ceramic hens and pigs, wood-carved frogs and birds, artificial flowers, and all kinds of decorative baby accessories. However, local economic conditions and the wider geopolitical context have meant that the fair has so far gone down a different route to that commonly claimed for the urban hipster economy. Rather than heralding an economy of upmarket gentrification, the expansion of the relocated hippie fair has acted as an umbrella accommodating low-end street-market activities, which are usually frowned upon by municipal administrations as potential hives of illegality.

It is through the artisan object and the myth of genuine artistic expression that, in a paradoxical way, a hippie ideology conveyed by a privileged group of discontents has met with the interest of the political classes in promoting an authentic Brazilian culture, providing popular entertainment and serving voters with economic opportunities. Intended as a critique of capitalist consumer society, the Hippie Fair, rather than establishing an autonomous zone, has colluded with the strategies of political power to align Belo Horizonte's economy with the rhythms of global markets. The shift from underground culture to officially promoted cultural heritage has been marked by ambivalence. On the one hand, it could be argued that the fair has lost its claim to the creation of a subversive autonomous zone in the face of an influx of cheap, mass-produced imports. On the other, the fair's development can also be seen as a positive achievement in the sense that it is now reaching out to a wider section of the population and reclaiming urban space for popular entertainment and recreation in the center of the city after decades of inner-city flight that rendered former sites of civic pride such as the Parque Municipal Américo Renné Giannetti, a centerpiece of Aarão Reis's urban plan, dangerous no-go areas.

Today, the fair continues to experience a period of critical transition from a site for the exhibition for arts and crafts to a recognized terrain of economic access for the masses. This discrepancy between twenty-first-century economic policies and a cultural narrative of celebrating local artistic expression, which still constitutes the fair's legitimization in official rhetoric, produces a constant tension around the market's interaction with state governance, paradigmatic for the uneven process of global economic alignment. Brazilian organizations promoting the rise of a new entrepreneurial climate linked to artisanal production, such as SEBRAE (Brazilian Micro and Small Business Support Service), are increasingly reaching out to self-employed people, micro-entrepreneurs, and small businesses, offering training and consulting for artisan-entrepreneurs to help them better understand current market challenges. At business events, in specialized publications, and on its website, SEBRAE presents itself as a leading innovator of small business management in the field of handicrafts,[11] ready to help transform crafts into companies. Values traditionally associated with craft practices—autonomy, emancipation, self-realization—are sidelined in favor of an unbridled integration of artisan-style production into global commodity chains. Underlying these changes is a shift in commitment from originality and craftsmanship to market forces and managerialism, or in anthropological terms, the sociocultural conversion of artisans into entrepreneurs (Marquesan and de Figueiredo 2014). This naturalization of a managerialist ideology goes hand in hand with the reconfiguration of artisanal production. Symbolic traits such as pride, skill, and authenticity traditionally associated with handicrafts are being replaced by an increased demand for business innovation, one that is driven by rapidly increasing market access and which thrives on creative responses, such as those that take their lead from the arts-and-crafts traditions. However, rather than celebrating artisanal work practices and the mastery of precise techniques and skills, the new "craftsmanship" is guided by a managerial-functionalist ethos and an orientation toward profit maximization—arts-and-crafts workshops thus become business studios (Barry and Meisiek 2014).

These processes tend to trivialize the idea of handicrafts and align it to the rhythms and demands of global hypercompetition and commodification. Middle-class aspirations and the lure of symbolic and affective capital associated with the aura of time-honored craftsmanship, free-spirited contemplation, honesty, and integrity, all contributing to an alleged simplicity of life, are projected onto the complex realities that inform Belo Horizonte's Hippie Fair. Local traders often complain about Brazilian policy programs and bodies such as SEBRAE, which they see as only interfering in local know-how in order to re-signify existing practices and reclaim the arts-and-crafts mentality around the fair as an integral part of an expanding global market. Linking the Hippie Fair to international consumption circles and global venture capital, the intervention in the local fabric by such programs has put additional strain on the configuration of this social space, with less profitable and marketable productions becoming ever more marginalized and families involved in the market struggling to keep up with the demands of modernization and regulation. In-depth studies of the formation of communities and social networks around the market suggest that beyond its generation of economic value, the fair has become a theatre for producing and trading all kinds of other values (de Pádua Carrieri, Silva Saraiva, and Pimentel 2008). Over more than four decades, the fair has served as an urban site for building, consolidating, and maintaining common values among highly diverse groups of people. A mediator of extra-economic values, it has kept alive an important aspect of civic culture, namely the right to come together, regardless of economic or social status, in the city center of Belo Horizonte—a space that has increasingly turned into an exclusive urban setting for the middle-class—to dwell in the moment and celebrate life in all its richness.

What this struggle highlights are not only the tensions around traditional values connected with master craftsmanship—honesty, authenticity, integrity—and the attempt to absorb them into the circuits of rampant economic globalization, but also the necessity to understand the spatial organization linked to the fair through forms of agency, participation. and control—that is, as a significant terrain of socioeconomic negotiation rather than a predominantly functional practice. Every tent at the Hippie Fair constitutes a particular dialogue, not just an infrastructural stratification of space. Seen in this way, the fair is a case in point that demonstrates the need to open up the question of urban economic development to changing patterns of formal-informal linkages and the different policies and socioeconomic realities that inform them.

In keeping with the increasing mediatization of politics and economic reality, Belo Horizonte's local administration employs its political dexterity to manage the visual appearance of the fair and project an attractive image to the world. While on the surface this intervention emphasizes strong formal order, manifested in its rows of tents in bright assorted colors that are appealing to the media, the market's operation relies heavily on the support of an elaborate ecosystem of informal cooperation. Despite shrinking margins,[12] the fair remains a vital terrain for vendors to navigate Brazil's notoriously volatile economy. Seen in the context of a myriad of overlapping and intersecting formal-informal linkages, the challenge for vendors lies not simply in pursuing a straightforward course to obtain a trading license, secure supplies, and keep costs down, but in imagining and furnishing the market environment in such a way as to make it fit their own possibilities and to justify their participation in it. From assembling tents and displaying what is on offer, to staking out one's territory at the fair and bonding with the crowd, staging the fair is not only a project of utility and optimization but a profoundly performative occurrence that creates a common good and determines who has access to it. It is a means of achieving a right to the city and opening up the city to a multitude of inhabitations, encounters, and exchanges.

Belying the appearance of spatial formalization and economic integration, popular informal marketplaces such as Belo Horizonte's Hippie Fair are at the forefront of marking out the parameters of a new economic paradigm of speculative formal-informal linkages. In light of their inherent instability—never to be counted on, always precarious—it is indeed the formalized imagery of such hybrid economic environments that enables compatibility between the institutional demands of a regulated economy and the advantages gained from flexibilizing trade arrangements and externalizing risks through informalization. Championed as domains of grassroots creativity and innovation, popular markets like the Hippie Fair have given rise to a visual culture rich in patterns and forms that marry the skills of informal vendors and producers with policy demands for competitive marketing of cities. While this combination is emerging as a highly profitable formula in economic terms, and one that is being copied in many places around the world,[13] incidents such as recurring conflicts between vendors and the municipality about the allocation of vending spots demonstrate that more advanced political instruments have yet to be developed to negotiate the implications of formal-informal linkages on the ground. The best possible role of formal-informal linkages in this process of urban economic transformation is not to simply appropriate informal economic practices as a convenient way to access new markets but to serve as a platform to include excluded and underprivileged segments of society in these negotiations on an equal footing.

NOTES

1. In the context of Brazil, see for instance the 2003 creation of the National Secretariat of Solidarity Economy (SENAES) within the Ministry of Labour and Employment; one widely hailed regional example for these initiatives oriented toward facilitating an improvement in the working standards of informal family businesses is the Vida Melhor ("Better Life") program by the state of Bahia (Notarbartolo di Villarosa and Baddini Curralero 2016).
2. See, for instance, Meagher (2013).
3. See, for instance, International Labour Organization 2014 and Hammond et al. 2007.
4. Numerous images of the resulting installation "Paratextos" at the Museo de Arte da Pampulha in Belo Horizonte (October 15, 2016–March 12, 2017) have been posted on online platforms such as Pictaram or Imgrum, as well as on a number of art blogs. The installation housed the video inside a customized tent structure whose patchwork-like tarpaulin had been composed of all the different colors found at the Hippie Fair; see also: Maia (2016).
5. These include the casino turned art museum and the Church of São Francisco. Oscar Niemeyer later went on to work as chief architect for the design of Brazil's new capital Brasília, initiated under Juscelino Kubitschek's presidency (1956–1961). It should be noted, too, that, its architectural status notwithstanding, as a project of urban expansion, the Pampulha complex has also attracted severe criticism for its upmarket orientation and complete ignorance toward issues of social cohesion and integration.
6. This entanglement of the arts-and-crafts fair with a rich cultural history of creative production had been further underwritten by the location of its original site in Praça da Liberdade, bordered by more Niemeyer buildings, the residential Edificio Niemeyer with its iconic curved elevation and the Biblioteca Pública Estadual, as well as by the former palace of the state governor.
7. See also Pádua Carrieri et al. (2007).
8. For a more detailed analysis of these informal trade routes see, for instance, the work of Brazilian anthropologist Fernando Rabossi on the tri-border market in Ciudad del Este (e.g., Rabossi 2012).
9. The application of social criteria has since been successfully contested at court as having no relation to the original purpose of the arts-and-crafts market (see Recurso Extraordinário com Agravo 724.748 Minas Gerais. Verdict by the Federal Supreme Court. Brasilia, February 11, 2013).

10. This new layout has been in place since autumn 2013.

11. http://www.sebrae.com.br/sites/PortalSebrae/canais_adicionais/sebrae_english.

12. In 2016, for instance, vendors expressed serious concerns about their ability to make ends meet in light of the country's then-staggering inflation rate of up to 10 percent.

13. See, for instance, the instrumental use of street markets and food festivals as a key mechanism in urban regeneration programs, epitomized most starkly in the phenomenon of hipster markets (Mörtenböck and Mooshammer 2015, 472–99).

BIBLIOGRAPHY

Barry, Daved, and Stefan Meisiek. "Discovering the Business Studio." *Journal of Management Education* 39, no. 1 (2014): 162–63.

Bhowmik, Sharit K. "Street Vendors in Asia." *Economic and Political Weekly*, May-June 2005.

Chen Martha, Sally Roever, and Caroline Skinner. "Urban Livelihoods: Reframing Theory and Policies." *Environment and Urbanization* 28, no. 2 (2016).

de Castro Rodriguez, Gilda. "A Feira de Arte e Artesanato de Belo Horizonte." Paper presented at the 26th Reunião Brasileira de Antropologia, Ports Seguro, 1–4 May 2008.

de Pádua Carrieri, Alexandre, Luiz Alex Silva Saraiva, and Thiago Duarte Pimentel. "O processo de institucionalização da Feira Hippie de Belo Horizonte." Paper presented at the XXXI Encontro da ANPAD 2007, Rio de Janeiro, 22–27 September 2007.

———. "A institucionalização da Feira Hippie de Belo Horizonte." *Organizações & Sociedade* 15, no. 44 (2008): 63–79.

Evers, Clifton, and Kirsten Seale, eds. *Informal Urban Street Markets*. London: Routledge, 2015.

Femeart (Federação Mineira dos Expositores das Feiras de Arte, Artesanato e Manufaturados). *Informativo Femeart* 1, no. 1 (1913): 4.

Hammond, Allen L., William J. Kramer, Robert S. Katz, and Julia T. Tran. *The Next 4 Billion: Market Size and Business Strategy at the Base of the Pyramid.* Washington, DC: World Bank, 2007.

Hart, Keith. "Informal Income Opportunities and Urban Employment in Ghana." *Journal of Modern African Studies* 11, no. 3 (1973): 61–89.

———. "How the Informal Economy Took Over the World." In *Informal Market Worlds: The Architecture of Economic Pressure—READER*, edited by Peter Mörtenböck, Helge Mooshammer, Teddy Cruz, and Fonna Forman, 33–44. Rotterdam: nai010 publishers, 2015.

Humphrey, Caroline, and Vera Skvirskaja, eds. *Post-Cosmopolitan Cities.* New York: Berghahn Books, 2012.

International Labour Organization. *Women and Men in the Informal Economy: A Statistical Picture*, second edition. Geneva: International Labour Organization/ILO, 2013.

———. *Transitioning from the Informal to the Formal Economy*, ILO Conference, 103rd Session, Report V-1. Geneva: International Labour Organization/ILO, 2014.
Maia, Elisa. "Lucas Dupin." *Revista Dasartes Edição* 54 (November 2016): 66–67. http://dasartes.com.br/wp-content/uploads/2016/11/Revista_Dasartes_Edicao_54.pdf.
Marquesan, Fábio, Freitas Schilling, and Marina Dantas de Figueiredo. "De artesão a empreendedor: A ressignificação do trabalho artesanal como estratégia para a reprodução de relações desiguais de poder." *Revista de Administração Mackenzie* (*Mackenzie Management Review*) 15, no. 6 (2014): 87.
Meagher, Kate. "*Unlocking the Informal Economy: A Literature Review on Linkages between Formal and Informal Economies in Developing Countries*." WIEGO Working Paper no. 27, April 2013.
Mörtenböck, Peter, and Helge Mooshammer, eds. *Informal Market Worlds: The Architecture of Economic Pressure—ATLAS*. Rotterdam: nai010 publishers, 2015.
Notarbartolo di Villarosa, Francseco, and Cláudia Baddini Curralero. "How to Strengthen Urban Micro-entrepreneurs: Bahia's 'Vida Melhor' Program." WWP—World without Poverty, Brazil Learning Initiative: study case, 2016.
Perry, Guillermo E., Maloney, William F., Arias, Omar S., Fajnzylber, Pablo, Mason, Andrew D., and Jaime Saavedra-Chanduvi, eds. *Informality: Exit and Exclusion*. World Bank Latin American and Caribbean Studies. Washington, DC: World Bank, 2007.
Pimentel, Thiago Duarte, Alexandre de Pádua, and Alfredo Rodrigues Leite-Da-Silva. "Identity Ambiguities in the 'Hippie Fair'/Brazil." *Organizational Behavior and Management* 13, no. 2 (2007): 221.
Prefeitura de Belo Horizonte, Decreto No 2437, 26 October 1973.
———. Decreto No 3082, 1 July 1977.
———. Decreto No 14.245, "Aprova o Regulamento das Feiras Permanentes de Plantas e Flores Naturais, de Artes, Artesanato e Produtores de Variedades, e de Antiguidades e de Comidas e Bebidas Típicas Nacionais e Estrangeiras, da Secretaria de Administração Regional Municipal Centro-Sul de Belo Horizonte" and No 14.246 "Aprova o Regimento Interno da Feira de Artes, Artesanato e Produtores de Variedades de Belo Horizonte," 30 December 2010.
Rabossi, Fernando. "Ciudad del Este and Brazilian Circuits of Commercial Distribution." In *Globalization from Below: The World's Other Economy*, edited by Gordon Mathews, Gustavo Lins Ribeiro, and Carlos Alba Vega, 54–68. London: Routledge, 2012.
Ribeiro, Gustavo Lins. "Economic Globalization from Below." *Etnográfica* 10, no. 2 (2006).
Roy, Ananya. "Urban Informality: Toward an Epistemology of Planning." *Journal of the American Planning Association* 71, no. 2 (Spring 2005): 148.
———. *Poverty Capital: Microfinance and the Making of Development*. London: Routledge, 2010.

Chapter Three

Muraleando

Artists as Social Entrepreneurs in the Cuban Transformation Process

Natalie Göltenboth

I was walking with my friend Carlos[1] down the street in the barrio Lawton-Luyanó in Havana in May 2016 when a silver-blue Hyundai, quite new and without a scratch, drove past. New cars are an uncommon sight in the city, which still fulfills the common clichés of a postcard-Havana where old Buicks or Chevrolets of the 1950s move through the streets like heavy old animals. I asked my friend: "Who can afford to buy those cars?" I knew that only Cubans with special permission had been able to import and purchase cars since Raúl Castro's policies of opening up the Cuban economy took effect in 2011. Since 2014, everyone has been able to buy a car—subject to the condition that the prospective buyer can afford total of 25,000 to 40,000 US dollars for an ordinary secondhand vehicle. There have been some previous discourses and jokes regarding this enigmatic question, when some friends of mine had tried to figure out how many lifetimes a normal working person in Havana would need to be able to buy a car, considering that an average salary in Cuba is around 20 US dollars a month. However, to my surprise, Carlos, one of the former artisans of Muraleando, gave me a spontaneous answer right away: "Artists, for instance," he said.

This vignette offers a way into discussing the position of art and the artist as entrepreneur in the turmoil of the Cuban transformation process from socialist to a post-Soviet state, characterized by a steady opening of the economy and the integration of capitalist market policies. Based on the example of the artistic community project Muraleando, I show in this chapter that Cuban actors combine socialist and capitalist strategies rather than contrasting them. The ability to capitalize on the coexistence of both systems characterizes the successful figure of the smart new entrepreneur on Cuban soil (Brotherton 2008; Nau 2008; Widderich 2002). In the case of Muraleando, imaginaries about socialist ideals and social commitment function as selling points for the micro enterprise, which is based on artistic creativity, social ideals, and a strong entrepreneurial spirit in times of crisis.

The situation in Cuba is a unique one, as the agency of the entrepreneur willing to invest his or her ingenuity and entrepreneurial spirit in the creation of a new economy, and open the way to start a social project, is only made possible by the emergent tourism industry as a means to provide recourses for moneymaking in hard currency. Cuba's touristification started in 1991 as part of the government's strategy of saving the island's socialist system. As the tourist industry is one of the leading sources of income for the state, it allows for the government's continued commitment to basic human needs, and simultaneously is the main foundation on which private persons can build up capital.

I argue that the creation of a solidarity-based economy, or any social project in Cuba, is initially dependent upon the gains made by a capitalist endeavor—the tourist economy. This is in contrast with the theoretical discourse of the Argentinian economist José Luis Coraggio (2011), who understands the solidarity-based economy as a contraposition to the capitalist economy, which is understood as a structure superimposed by the centers of neoliberalism, particularly the United States. Cuba plays the role of a legendary pioneer in this discourse on Latin American countries who are willing to position themselves against the neoliberal US market economy. However, the transition which Coraggio and others are asking for seems to trend in the opposite direction in the stronghold of Latin American socialism. Cuba is increasingly seeing itself forced to use capitalist strategies to defend the achievements of the revolution, as Sean Brotherton (2008) argues in his work on the Cuban health-care system.

One of the declared strategies of Fidel Castro after the fall of the Soviet Union in 1991 was the construction—or better said the reconstruction—of a tourist industry, which had been rejected as a mere imperialist idea since the Cuban Revolution (Eckstein 2003). Needless to say, using capitalist market strategies is not the most conventional way to rescue the ideals of a socialist revolution. Florence E. Babb (2011) talks about her research on Cuba's tourist industry in her book *The Tourism Encounter*: "This often presents surprising contradictions, as nations that have embraced revolution now adopt practices more common to neoliberal capitalist societies" (Babb 2011, xii). Babb's "surprising contradiction" turns out to be a paradox: the touristification of Cuba and the establishment of a creative project space such as Muraleando as an example of social entrepreneurship in Cuba seem to be strongly interdependent. But that is not enough: as Babb and other researchers on tourism in postsocialist and postrevolutionary areas state, journeys to post-conflict *hot spots* with significant histories have become trendy (Babb 2011, xiii). Cultural nostalgia for the relicts and the flair of the Cuban Revolution are, in addition to other attractions such as music and Caribbean beach life, the most important highlights of the island. Therefore, Cuba has become a desirable tourist destination and is continuously increasing its touristification, regardless of its revolutionary heritage. Babb states that the tourist encounter in Cuba lends legitimacy to contradictory tendencies: enduring the socialist program of the government and advancing the market economy (Babb 2011, 38). As we will see in what follows, it also allows for the creative use of capital and the creation of a social economy for the first time, a fact that challenges Coraggio's conceptualization of the entanglements of the state and a solidarity-based economy.

In next sections, I draw a picture of how capitalist strategies manifested in the tourism industry, which is kept running by lively imaginaries of the socialist state, and how the ideas and practice of social entrepreneurship develop hand in hand based on mutual dependency in everyday life in Muraleando. With this approach, the article contributes to the discussion on postsocialist Cuba. It reflects on the special role of art and handicrafts in the Cuban transformation and the strategies of artist entrepreneurs to deal with the twofold economic system. It also draws on the theory of social economy in Latin America, highlighting the particular situation in Cuba.

I first came to know the community project in 2012, during a one-month stay in Havana. Two years later, I participated as both an artist and anthropologist in the tenth Annual Meeting of International Artists in Muraleando, conducting art workshops for children between eight and eleven years old. In addition, I had the chance to participate in the community's work by helping in the creation of a mosaic on the outside walls. These were great opportunities to get involved with the actors of Muraleando: around twenty artists, including painters, sculptors, and musicians, children and grandmothers, most of whom lived in the community, and tourists, mainly US citizens. The analysis presented in this chapter is based on ethnographic fieldwork carried out in April and May 2016 and during a brief follow-up visit in May 2018. I have been carrying out research on contemporary Cuban art since 1999; therefore, interviews with artists who are not involved in Muraleando, and visits to their studios, exhibitions, and art centers were another source through which to explore the struggles and lives of artists in Cuba.

I will first situate these processes in the context of the economic changes that characterize the Cuban transformation, with a special focus on the role of artists and art. The community project Muraleando provides a fertile terrain for examining how the new forms of capital are entangled with, and dependent on, the socialist system and its imaginaries, and how artists in Muraleando manage to create a social economy by using capitalist strategies.

ARTISTS AS ENTREPRENEURS AND EXCEPTIONAL ACTORS IN THE CUBAN TRANSFORMATION PROCESS

In 1991, three years after the fall of the Berlin Wall and the crumbling of the Soviet Union, Cuba declared that socialism was endangered. The following years were announced as a state of emergency which, under the concise motto "Special Period in Times of Peace" or *período especial*, passed into Cuban history as unforgettable years of severe penury. The dissolution of the Council for Mutual Assistance (COMECON) an economic association of the Eastern Bloc and other communist states, meant the almost sudden collapse of economic support from the Soviet Union, which, up to then, had played a dominant role in the maintenance of the Cuban economy (Nau 2008; Ritter 2004). The construction of a dual economic system was the government's coping strategy in light of the resulting severe supply bottlenecks that had affected the population. The government opened up export sectors for foreign capital to increase the economy's responsiveness to the world market (Brotherton 2008, 260). External trade was by then adjusted to US dollar-based trade relations. The creation of the CUC (*peso cubano convertible*—a local currency whose exchange rate is fixed to the US dollar), the search for foreign capital, and the opening up of the tourism industry were some of the key compromises with capitalism and its values made from 1991 onwards (Centeno and Font 1997; Eckstein 1994). At the same time, the domestic sector stuck to planned-economy principles and was based on the local *peso* currency. This dual economic system manifests itself in the double currency to this day. The very fact that the government has a hold on the specification of prices and salaries allows for a situation where the state earns in CUC but pays in *pesos* (Nau 2008, 43; Ritter 2004).

Cuban socialism has gradually moved closer to what can be called the postcommunist era (see Sullivan 2002). An ongoing transformation process and the successive introduction of reforms, many of which appear in contradiction to the ideals and principles of the revolution, characterize this period (Brotherton 2008, 260). The enactment of the law for freelancers (*trabajo por cuenta propia*) was most important for artists and, thus, also for those involved with Muraleando. Since 1993, this law had allowed personal economic initiative for some professions and activities, such as hairdressers, bed-and-breakfast offers, and taxi drivers, and has now been extended to anything that is fabricated by hand and individually, which therefore also includes handicrafts and art. As taxation and restrictions regarding artists and other freelancers have been continuously reduced during recent years, most of the so-called *cuentapropistas* (self-employed persons) are the true winners of the transformation era, as many are involved in the tourist industry or, in the case of artists, sell their artworks to foreigners or gallerists and art collectors from abroad. They benefit from strong currency movements, gaining the hard currency CUC[2] that guarantees a great profit margin, especially if one considers that the basic supply guaranteed by the Cuban government is still at their disposal (Nau 2008).[3] According to the dynamic of these laws, small or even bigger capitalist enclaves arise inside the still-communist economy of the island. Brotherton states that:

> The emergence of selective pockets of transnational capital are part of the very socialist system that encompasses them; that is to say, the socialist state has provided key spaces, similar to incubators, within contemporary Cuban society, in which a selective form of capitalism thrives. Rather than relegated to the shadows, these incubators exist to take advantage of the differential access to foreign currency that is circulating in the hands of Cubans and, ultimately, to provide the state an opportunity to tap into individual wealth accumulation. (Brotherton 2008, 268)

At the same time, the new forms of capital in Cuba's postsocialist economy are equally dependent on the socialist system for their circulation and use value (Brotherton 2008, 267). As an example, one might consider that the creation of artwork is due to the thorough knowledge and ability of the artists who have been trained in state-run art academies and art centers. Subsequently, artists can take their time to create and have enough possibilities to expose their oeuvre in state-run galleries and exhibition centers. However, as the features of socialist Cuba and its social ideals are, for many Cuba aficionados, some of the unique selling points of the island, the new forms of capital are also dependent on imaginaries of the socialist island, circulating around the globe.

Against this background, the role of artists and artisans—workers who practice a trade or handicraft—in Cuba is central. As long as they are successful, artists have access to the CUC-based economy. As no artist would ever sell their artworks for *pesos*, there is hardly any local market for art. Rather, the art market is dominated by foreigners, who pay in hard currency. The selling of just two artworks for an average price in a European or US gallery allows the artist to live a carefree life in Cuba. Cuban art is highly recognized on the global art market, especially because of the particular political situation of the island. A similar nostalgia (see Babb 2011) that shapes tourist imaginaries of the *old authentic Cuba* and its former revolutionary features stimulates the art market in search of Cuban art. Political tensions, an unsure future, and a significant past rich in symbols, relicts, and pressures is expected to produce particular artworks. Successful artists have the possibility of getting residencies abroad via exchange programs and grants, allowing them to establish transnational contacts. The idea that artists are the ones who have enough money to buy a car makes sense in terms of the Cuban transformation process, but seems puzzling for foreigners who usually associate artists with a financially squeezed existence. At the same time, this depicts an idealized image—which is far from reflective off the everyday life of most artists in Cuba but reflects very well the common image of artists on the island—of art and handicrafts as a potential means of wealth accumulation above average.

A further particular aspect of art in Cuba is that, unlike in the USSR or the German GDR, art had never been submitted to the *aesthetic dictation* of socialist realism. The freedom of fine art was respected to a high degree under the government of Fidel Castro. Cuba made itself visible in the global art world with the launching of the first Havana Biennial in 1984, making a political statement and setting up a counterpoint to the established Venice Biennial. The Havana Biennial was created as the first international platform for artists from the so-called peripheries: Latin America, Africa, and Asia. Art in Cuba has always been a *niche* by definition, where the rule of creation and the way of communicating one's own art to the outside world and the market has followed different rules than in other realms of the economy. The figure of the artist as his or her own entrepreneur, as an individual with the privilege to travel beyond the island as a global player, is not completely new in Cuban society.

The situation of the art project Muraleando, on which I will focus in the following section, is unique, as artists in this case have created a space where profits made by selling artworks are in large parts converted into a social project. The art workshops for children, teenagers, and older women have always been free. *Hard* currency is made from tourists who visit the project as an outstanding example of social commitment and socialist ideals. I will first explain some of the basic parameters of the project.

MURALEANDO: THE CREATION OF AN ARTISTIC PROJECT SPACE

A sudden break in the urban landscape will strike the eyes of the visitor when leaving the seemingly endless street of 10 de Octubre, with its ruined houses and faded facades, that connects Centro Havana to the *barrio* Lawton-Luyanó: colorful single-story houses, painted walls, and emblematic collages appear. The urban space, including houses and bus stations, has been appropriated by Muraleando members and continuously aestheticized. A sign announces: "Welcome to the community project Muraleando." The main venue is a patchwork of architecture unusual for the cityscape of Havana. Various workshops, a terrace for tourist visitors, and a shop have been constructed by project members and aficionados since 2011, based around the tall, round structure of a former water tank, *El Tanque*, which serves as the gallery of Muraleando.

Arriving at Muraleando, kids are lingering around, mothers gather in front of the entrance door to await their children from a theater workshop. Salsa music rolls from the terrace—a clear sign that the group of tourists who poured out of the big Havana Tour bus is still in attendance and receiving the special Muraleando treatment: a show, a guided tour around the project, and sometimes a dinner served on the terrace above the water tank. The sound of construction work resounds around the place. Just the usual craziness of a busy day at Muraleando.

Osvaldo, now in his fifties, bald-headed and with a strong personality, a man of action, was a successful graphic artist when he started the project in 2003. He stated that the idea of investing his energy into the community came up when he realized the increasing deterioration of his *barrio*, which had begun during the Special Period in the nineties. When the project started, the *barrio* was on its way to becoming one of the conflictive areas in Havana. People had lost the hope for a better future, children did not attend school regularly, houses were deteriorating, and garbage was thrown into the streets, something that had never happened before. According to Osvaldo's interpretation, an increased focus on the intimacy of the family during the crisis had put the "Cuban spirit of community" at stake. His idea was to break this negative circle by creating and encouraging a barrio community through artistic means. Together with his wife Misleidys and a handful of artist friends, Osvaldo started community activities, such as weekly *peñas comunitarias* or street festivals and art workshops for children and older women. These activities took place on the streets in front of his house or on the terrace. Anna, one of the founding members of Muraleando, remembers these first years as ones of constant improvisation. She is in her early fifties and a successful artist but had been working as a sweet seller before she was inspired by the artistic activities in Muraleando. Anna states that she has always been an independent woman and her economic independency is important to her. Apart from the social commitment that she feels towards Muraleando, the possibility of selling her artworks was a vital motivation for her to become involved in this project. Pedro, who is currently the tutor of the video workshop for teenagers, was one of the first children of Muraleando. He still remembers this first period when he would come home from school and want to participate immediately in the workshops that had an aura of excitement and fun for him, differing from a more educational impetus in school.

These first initial steps towards an artistic social project had a strong and unexpected impact on the community, encouraging Osvaldo and his group of artists to directly interact with the surrounding area: They cleared away the garbage deposits and transformed their useful relics into collages and artworks. Inspired by the tradition of the Mexican muralists, artists, children, and invited artists from abroad appropriated the houses and walls of the *barrio* and transformed them into colorful artworks.

Osvaldo states:

> With this action, we wanted to show that it is worthwhile taking care of the environment; that it is possible to create something even if it is made from waste. We wanted to implement the idea of recycling and care. It was also thought to be an act of education, of hope, of showing that it is better not to give up on yourself. The intention was to do something for the community.[4]

With the restoration of the water tank in 2010, the first physical venue was created. This is seen as a milestone in the history of Muraleando that, until then, had defined itself in ideational terms as a community, an idea, and an activity, but not as a concrete place. The labor carried out by artists, inhabitants of the barrio, and some associated workers has turned into a narrative

Figure 3.1. Muraleanderos waiting for the beginning of the annual show of workshop activities.
Natalie Göltenboth

which forms part of the collective memory and today serves as one of the founding myths of Muraleando. This was even expressed in a rap song. The process of place-making, understood as the art of shaping community through public art and urban design as Ronald Lee Flemming (2007) has defined it, has occurred and with it, an identification with the place has developed: "*Somos los Muraleanderos*" ("We are the people of Muraleando").

The consolidation of the *barrio* community through art was the first intention of the project, followed by the creative transformation of the place itself. Osvaldo's idea was that these arrangements were the right *medicine* against poverty in the literal sense of the word: social and material poverty.

NETWORKS AND FINANCIAL FLOWS

Muraleando has created micro-economies since its very beginning. The first opportunity for commercializing artworks was due to the networks in Havana on which the artists could rely. Osvaldo met an employee of one of the tourist offices, who was willing to bring tourists to the barrio. The same happened with the German tourist organization Aventoura. Osvaldo evokes the situation:

> They said that this is a wonderful project, but the tourists will want to take something with them—so—commercialize! commercialize!—your artwork or whatever—commercialize! Even if it is just a doll or a bracelet or something—but they should take something with them.[5]

That is how Muraleando artists commercialized their artworks: creating with the tourist in mind, smaller sizes, lighter weights, and so on. The feeling of becoming active and contributing to the improvement of the neighborhood and, consequently, also to their personal economic situation was paramount for artists such as Jorge, who together with Osvaldo is one of the managers of Muraleando. Manuel, another Muraleando artist, was able to renovate his house and buy a car with the proceeds from selling his sculptures, while Jorge, like other artists who sell in *El Tanque*, earns a living for his family. Therefore, the motivation for stimulating the community with moral and creative inputs went hand in hand with that of making money, even though only small amounts were involved at the beginning. It is important to note that from the very start, all income had to be divided: 50 percent for the project and 50 percent for the artist in the case of artworks sold, which today has changed to 30 percent for the project and 70 percent for the artist. Donations were invested entirely into the project.

A key condition for an artist's admission and, thus, the right to use the infrastructure of the gallery is the mission to conduct art workshops without any financial compensation. The willingness to participate is immense; some children are participating in up to four different workshops a week. Parents usually support their children's motivation, as Muraleando is understood not only as a space where children can be creative, but also as an opportunity to acquire new skills with which they might make money afterwards; creative professions such as art, music, filmmaking, and handicrafts are profitable freelance activities in Cuba. Usually, artworks produced by workshop consumers are not on sale. An exception are the dolls and other items sold in the little shop, which are produced in the workshop for grandmothers that is held weekly. The proceeds from sales often help to solve the very poor economic situation of the makers.[6]

Since the very beginning, Osvaldo has activated his international networks and invited artists from Germany, France, Canada, Mexico, and Argentina to participate in the project, offering workshops, creating their own project, or painting murals. Several individuals and groups of artists are permanently linked to Muraleando. They support the project with art supplies, colors, papers, and tools, as well as donations. A Canadian artist, who participates every year in the Annual Meeting of International Artists in Muraleando, told me about her strong emotional ties to the project and Osvaldo's family since 2008. In what seems to be a repeated ritual, she and Osvaldo start crying together when it comes to talking about the hardships Muraleando had to overcome in the first years and the role she played in supporting the project. The recognition of creativity, resilience, and self-empowerment against the background of material need are what motivates the Canadian artist to keep in touch and help to subsidize the project.

For artists and children, Muraleando has become a "contact zone" (Pratt 1992), a space that connects them to the world outside Cuba. To build these kinds of linkages is still almost impossible for the majority of the Cuban population and is therefore a highly privileged situation. As contacts have the potential for symbolic, social, and—not least—financial capital, they are highly valued and sought after. The gradual touristification of Muraleando has fostered the impression that Muraleando, despite being in one of the remote and non-tourist communities, is a merry-go-round not only for visitors, but also for locals. It is a place where ideas, money, and people are in constant flux; the locals emanate ideas, concepts, and artistic viewpoints, and the international tourists bring in money, enthusiasm, and esteem.

TOURISTIFYING AND IMAGINING MURALEANDO

Muraleando has increased tourist visits since 2014 due to a contract with the local travel agency Havanatur. When I visited the project in 2016, three to five busloads of international tourists, mainly US citizens, were visiting the project daily. It was intriguing to see the bus trying to find its way through the narrow streets and then stop in front of the entrance door. Tourists pour out, cameras around their necks, initially with astonished faces.

Each visit receives a warm welcome ritual, which consists of an introduction to the community's work, a guided tour, and musicians playing for them. After that kind of Cuban stimulation, visitors are supposed to enter *El Tanque*, the gallery, and experience closer contact with the artists, who position themselves behind their selling tables, and finally buy some artworks. All these activities are organized by the artists, guides, and staff of Muraleando.

In December 2014, after President Obama and his family visited Cuba, the agreements between the US and Cuban governments improved, with the result that the restrictions on individual US citizens visiting the island were eased. The United States had previously prohibited tourism to Cuba as part of the economic embargo. There were some exceptions for certain visa categories, such as religious, business, humanitarian, or journalistic, and the vaguely defined category of cultural interaction organized by People to People tours, which until then had been accessible only for tourists travelling in a group. Obama allowed individual tourists to participate in People to People activities

Figure 3.2. The community project Muraleando in the distcrict Lawton-Luyanó in Havana (2016).
Natalie Göltenboth

and enter the country with a visa for cultural interaction. The result was an increasing number of US citizens visiting the island. President Trump and his policy towards Cuba has changed this situation dramatically as he reinstalled visa restrictions from the pre-Obama times. When I visited the project in May 2018, Osvaldo, his wife Misleidys, and Jorge told me how much Muraleando was suffering from Trump's anti-Cuba policy and the lack of tourists. "There are entire days without any visits and what we earn now is not comparable to the money we made two years ago," Osvaldo complained.

People to People offers a program that includes guided tours to selected cultural or social institutions, community projects, museums, galleries, or health care providers and schools, always with the assistance of a local and a US-American guide. The program is authorized by the Cuban government and is intended to give a carefully designed image of the country, its culture, and its politics. Based on my experience, US citizens who choose this kind of program are mostly a select audience, interested in learning about the *authentic* Cuba and culture.

When I interviewed US tourists, most of them stated that they were willing to contribute to the project's economy through buying artworks and giving donations. When asked about their motivation for coming to Cuba and visiting the community project, Daniel, a fifty-four-year-old schoolteacher from Atlanta, replied:

> I always wanted to travel to Cuba and see how life is here apart from what the media are suggesting. The old Havana of Che Guevara and Fidel Castro, their fights for a better life. . . In my country, lots of things are running quite badly. I am interested in learning how life works under a socialist regime, what is it about and let me tell you: I am pretty amazed: the museum of Alphabetization, this project. . . I think they are doing much better than we thought they would.

Michael, an engineer in his early sixties, was motivated by his own family story. As the son of an American diplomat, he was born and raised in Havana. His family left Cuba after the success of the revolution in 1959. I met him on his first day in Havana; he had never returned since he was a child. He told me that one of his favorite personal souvenirs is a photograph showing his father and him, at the age of seven, with the heroes of the Cuban Revolution. For Michael, the visit to Cuba is highly emotional:

> You know, I feel like you might have felt after the fall of the Berlin Wall. We are so close, there are so many bonds, we have been separated for such a long period. I really feel happy to finally be able to come here for a visit. Now, I am curious to see how the revolution has changed the country and how it worked out. Well—how life is here.

While the US tourists I met had different backgrounds and motivations for visiting Cuba, Muraleando seemed for most of them to confirm or exceed their impression of solidarity which they had hoped for in the country, which had been presented to them by the Cuban government. These qualities were then interpreted as the direct, but nevertheless positive, result of the lack of material prosperity and a socialist regime focused on principles of equality. This became evident when I had dinner with a group of US tourists in the restaurant on top of *El Tanque* who were talking about critiques of US culture, or rather critiques of capitalism and the idea of exchange. Susan, a young medical doctor from New York who was especially interested in the health-care system, told me:

> Instead of seeing Cuba as a backward society which needs to be helped, I would prefer to see what we could learn from Cubans regarding health, education, and creativity, and then analyze how we could provide Cuba with facilities that they really want and need.

What stimulates a tourist to spend almost 5,000 US dollars for a ten-day trip to Cuba? On the one hand, there are the island's unique selling points: tourist imaginaries (Salazar 2014; MacCannell 1999) of the "authentic" Cuba, in which old Buicks and Chevrolets of the 1950s, together with Cuban music and images of Che Guevara and Fidel Castro, are welded together with the flair of the socialist state. The longing for nostalgic elements and habitus which Babb named "revolutionary heritage tourism" (Babb 2011, 30) is definitely one important motivation for travel to Cuba. However, in addition to these attractions, there are some further aspects that I noted in the discussions with US tourists on their visit to Muraleando. The imaginaries of the revolution mentioned above did not stand alone; they were often combined with more general doubts about the functioning of capitalism, as well as the values and structures it generates in society, and the wish to learn about alternative models (Richards and Hall 2000). The "exotic other" as the center of tourist attention was, in this case, interpreted as one which had developed a different model of society. It gained its importance from the doubts about one's own economic and social models.

In 2016, the government awarded Muraleando the prize for the best *proyecto comunitario* (community project) and put it on the list of projects representing the Cuban state and its achievements, mostly to US tourists and delegates. This is surprising, as Muraleando is one of the few community projects which is not state run and, consequently, had to survive without economic sponsorship from the government, even though it had received state advisory opinions and counseling from its very beginning (on Cuban community projects see Ramírez 2004). Muraleando is presented as a showcase of Cuban grassroots socialism to tourists and it seems as if the Cuban state is falsely taking all the credit. The government receives the full amount of money from the American travel agencies. The only benefits for the artists' community are the proceeds from what is sold directly in the gallery and its restaurant.

If we take a closer look at the very history of the project, it seems quite clear that Muraleando's origin does not match the idea of state control and a planned economy. More than anything else, Muraleando is based on personal initiative, and the virtues you can learn here seem to have something in common with the US "American dream": become active, get empowered, be innovative, be original, work hard, create something out of nothing, be a good networker, be smart, and be able to commercialize your ideas. However, at the same time, all these virtues are mobilized not only for the benefit of the artist entrepreneurs, but also to benefit the community. The question arises whether with Muraleando, the idea of a solidarity-based economy, in the way in which Coraggio describes it for other Latin American countries, has been realized, taking into account the basis on which it grew. More than a socialist project, Muraleando seems to be a product of the new Cuban spirit of transformation, which, in its very essence, tries to combine capitalist and socialist ideals and strategies. Asking Osvaldo for his opinion, he detailed: "I feel that we have created something unique with Muraleando that could serve as a paradigm for future projects in Cuba. It is a future-oriented project. Muraleando can contribute as a model for the actual transformation process."[7]

CORAGGIO'S IDEAS ON SOCIAL ECONOMY VIA CUBAN REALITY

I have asked the question, to what extent the concept of a solidarity-based economy might be appropriate to describe Muraleando's economic system and which elements fostered its development. In his seminal book *Economia Social y Solidaria* (2011) José Luis Coraggio argues that it is necessary for the well-being of a state, especially in Latin America, to overcome the structural separation between economy and social affairs (*lo económico y lo social*) or the productive process and the ideas of solidarity (*lo productive y lo solidario*) (Coraggio 2011, 14). As an example of the need to treat these items not only separately, but also gathered under one and the same political project, he quotes the new constitution of Ecuador, which had been drafted in 2007 to replace the text of the existing constitution from 1998. Here, a clear focus has been placed on the importance of the concept of a "good life" with its main pillar: a solidarity-based economy (Coraggio 2011, 10). In this argumentation, Coraggio understands the new constitution of Ecuador as the result of a post-developmental or post-neoliberal consciousness, which had been shaped by the experience of a capitalist economy up to 1998. It seems clear to him that a solidarity-based economy and the concept of a "good life" are to be discussed as contrapositions to a capitalist economy and politics, which is understood basically as a structure, superimposed by the centers of neoliberalism—the European Union and the United States.

> Postneoliberal. . . . This definition of a social economy makes sense. It summarizes the effort to reconstitute the element of the social in the economy, which has been practically pawned as a consequence of the neoliberal dogma. (Coraggio 2011, 15–16)[8]

The quest for a solidarity-based economy as an opposition to the free-market economy and the idea of locating it within the dichotomy of Latin America versus the US/EU was spawned with the left-wing governments of the Argentinian President Kirchner, followed by Lula in Brazil, Morales in Bolivia, and Correa in Ecuador, together with their predecessor Hugo Chavez from Venezuela. The former capitalist market economy and its effects on the societies of these countries had put the whole endeavor of neoliberalism into question.

In Cuba, as we can see with the example of Muraleando, it is the very process of transition towards a market economy that allows a project to develop which is not state run and, at the same time, works on a solidarity-based economic system with benefits for the community. If we analyze the particular situation of Cuba, we will have to consider that Cuba did not pass through the same neoliberal phase from which Kirchner and others had tried to distinguish their governments. As far as I know, there is actually no claim in Cuba for new socialist programs as catalysts to realize the concept of solidarity-based economies. On the contrary, it is the very process of a slow opening towards the market economy with the right to act and earn on *cuenta propia* (on private account), as freelancers and artists do, which has created economic niches. The latter not only stimulate economic interest, but also allow for the creative usage of resources created inside these "selective pockets of transnational capital" (Brotherton 2008, 268). It seems that in the case of Cuba, Coraggio's argumentation has been turned upside down. Whereas he is arguing for the state as the institution that is responsible for creating, introducing, and controlling the solidarity-based economy, in Cuba, it seems the other way around. It is the partial giving up of state control and the toleration of individual agency that allows for the creation of economic and cultural project spaces run by individuals, as is the case of Muraleando.

It would be worthwhile to ask whether these individuals have been shaped by the experience of solidarity in a socialist state and partly still act in accordance with the declared ideals of the state, creating a social project instead of just earning money. In the case of Muraleando, just trying to sell artworks in one of the non-tourist neighborhoods would not have worked out either, as the project only succeeds because it *combines* capitalist and social ideals and strategies. Muraleando is simultaneously the outcome and the manifestation of the actual transition process. Still, its main way of attracting capital and sales is through exactly this strategy—the solidarity-based economy or, as Coraggio explains it, the combination of "*lo social y lo productivo*" ("the social and the productive"). It is this particularity that attracts its visitors deeply, be they tourists or artists, and that works as its main advertisement.

However, as much as Muraleando might be a model for the combination of capitalist and socialist strategies, it also shows the pitfalls of this endeavor. One of these is the continuously increasing dependency on the tourism sector. This became visible on my last visit in May 2018, when artists were hanging around waiting behind their tables in the gallery for visitors. As only a small group of five people showed up, a whole structure built around entertainment and sales was going nowhere. It is also visible in the quality of the artworks, which too often show a compromise with tourist taste. The weak point of this project also appears in the continuous self-exploitation of each artist, who is a social worker, teacher, vendor, construction worker, and tourist entertainer in one and the same person, and who does not find enough time for their own creative work. Last, but not least, the dominant question of who has a hold on the distribution of money and is in the position to control the interface between the two monetary systems, pesos and CUC—a position that easily creates hierarchies and power relations—still remains to be solved. Therefore, there might be some issues that Muraleando and its staff will have to deal with in the future and which show the vulnerability of a social economy based on tourism.

CONCLUSION

Muraleando, with its twofold strategy of thinking and acting entrepreneurially via the outside world and receiving transnational funds to benefit the local community, has chosen a similar economic plan as the Cuban government: investing money earned within the tourism industry to sustain social institutions, which are gratis to the local population.[9] This constant navigation between the two systems in daily life, also manifested in the Cuban double currency of pesos and CUC, is best described with the words of Julio A. García Olivares, the former head of the Cuban Chamber of Commerce, when he talked about the logic of the recent changes in Cuban economic policies: "We have to think like capitalists but continue being socialists" (Eckstein 1994, 103). We could also change the sentence to: We need to act as entrepreneurs to produce the capital needed to be able to act according to socialist ideals and continue with social programs.

In the case of Muraleando, the combination of capitalist strategies and social engagement shows their mutual conditionality and seems to be the perfect entrepreneurial plan of action. Without the funds engendered by tourists and foreign artists, there would not be any possibility of keeping the project alive. Without the communitarian and social aspects of Muraleando, the imaginary of ideals, which functions as a counter-world to tough neoliberal practices, would not be created. These imaginaries make the project attractive and, thus, stimulate the financial influx. They are nourished by a general questioning of the ideas of neoliberalism and the capitalist system worldwide.[10]

Brotherton interpreted the combination of entrepreneurial and socialist attitudes as "internal contradictions of the state" to which the individual corresponds by incorporating informal or clandestine capitalist strategies into daily life. Emphasizing this contradiction he asks, "how many capitalist strategies can one incorporate into the local economy and still maintain the veneer of socialism?" (Brotherton 2008, 267). However the transition process underway from 2009 until now has speeded up and Cuba, instead of stigmatizing the capitalist *niches*, is now openly promoting them. The Cuban organization *Cuba Emprende* offers free coaching sessions for individual entrepreneurs and assists them in designing their own business. One of the main conditions to get this support is that the idea must show social benefit not only for the individual entrepreneur, but also for local communities.[11] In this sense, there is a clear statement in support of what we can call social entrepreneurship. The figure of the insecure or even clandestine Cuban individual negotiating between the socialist and capitalist ways of surviving in their sometimes-difficult everyday life is, thus, contrasted with the self-confident creative manager of his or her own agency. The concept has changed, even though the agency itself perhaps has not. The combination of the two opposing strategies seems to be sanctified by their effects.

In Muraleando, these effects are visible, tangible, and in the gallery of *El Tanque*, also on sale. They fill the gap and they add something to Cuban society that the state is not able to create. The acceptance of individual and, in the case of Muralenado, artistic, creative, and entrepreneurial potential may be the very essence of the Cuban transformation process that, in contrast to Coraggio's vision, is due to less state control and the partial acceptance of stimuli by the market economy.

NOTES

1. Names changed.

2. 24 pesos Cubanos = 1 CUC. Considering that a schoolteacher earns around 700 Cuban pesos a month, this might give an idea of how big the gap can be between an income in CUC and one in Cuban pesos.

3. Guaranteed basic supply ensures access to certain essentials, such as rent-free living, food ration cards, and free access to health care and education, including university.

4. Osvaldo said: "Con esta acción queríamos mostrar que vale la pena cuidar el ambiente, que es posible crear algo y si sea de la propia basura que la gente tiraba. Así implementar la idea de reciclaje y de cuidado. Era una acción de educación también, de esperanza, de no dejarse caer. Hacer algo para la comunidad."

5. "Me dijeron, es maravilloso este proyecto, pero van a querer de llevarse algo las turistas—entonces—Comercializen! Comercializen!—Sus obras de arte o lo que sea—Comercializen! Aunque sea una muñequita, una pulserita algo—para que se lleven algo."

6. An average pension in Cuba is around 200 pesos Cubanos = 8 CUC per month.

7. "Siento que con Muraleando hemos creado algo muy particular, que además puede funcionar como un ejemplo para futuros proyectos en Cuba. Es un proyecto para el futuro. Muraleando puede contribuir como modelo para el proceso de transformación."

8. "Postneoliberal [. . .] esta definición de economía social cobra sentido. Sintetizaba un esfuerzo para recuperar lo social en la economía, que había sido prácticamente hípotecado como consequencia del dogma neoliberal" (Coraggio 2011, 15–16).

9. Cuba's elaborate free health-care and educational systems, as the main pillars of the still-socialist program, are financed by state income, from its main source—the tourism industry.

10. In this way, imaginaries about the United States and about Cuba are linked in a contrasting juxtaposition which might be specified as followed: material abundance and materialism, as well as social poverty and isolation in the United States, versus a highly idealized image of material poverty, creativity, and community in Cuba.

11. The *Proyecto Cuba Emprende* is a project created by the Catholic Church of Cuba. Its mission is to offer training and advisory services to Cuban entrepreneurs who wish to start or improve small businesses so as to contribute to the development of an entrepreneurial culture and social progress, and to improve the quality of life. www.cubaemprendefoundation.org.

BIBLIOGRAPHY

Babb, Florence E. *The Tourism Encounter. Fashioning Latin American Nations and Histories.* Stanford, CA: Stanford University Press, 2011.

Brotherton, P. Sean. "'We Have to Think Like Capitalists but Continue Being Socialists': Medicalized Subjectivities, Emergent Capital, and Socialist Entrepreneurs in Post-Soviet Cuba." *American Ethnologist* 35 (2008): 259–74.

Centeno, Miguel Angel, and Mauricio Font. *Towards a New Cuba? Legacies of a Revolution*. Boulder, CO: Lynn Rienner, 1997.

Coraggio, José Luis. *Economia Social y Solidaria. El trabajo antes que el capital*, edited by Alberto Acosta y Esperanza Martínez. Quito: Ediciones Aby-Yola, 2011.

Eckstein, Susan. *Back from the Future: Cuba under Castro*. Princeton, NJ: Princeton University Press, 1994.

———. "From Communist Solidarity to Communist Solitary." In *The Cuba Reader: History, Culture, Politics*, edited by Aviva Chomsky, Barry Carr, and Pamela Smorkaloff, 607–22. Durham, NC: Duke University Press, 2003.

Flemming, Ronald Lee. *The Art of Placemaking: Interpreting Community through Public Art and Urban Design*. London: Merrell Publishers, 2007.

MacCannell, Dean. *The Tourist: A New Theory of the Leisure Class*. Berkeley: University of California Press, 1999.

Nau, Stephanie. *Lokale Akteure in der Kubanischen Transformation: Reaktionen auf den internationalen Tourismus als Faktor der Öffnung. Ein sozialgeographischer Beitrag zur aktuellen Kuba-Forschung aus emischer Perspektive*. Passau: Selbstverlag Fach Geographie Universität Passau, 2008.

Pratt, Mary Louise. *Imperial Eyes: Traveling Writing and Transculturation*. New York: Routledge, 1992.

Ramírez, Ronaldo. "Factores que contribuyen al éxito o fracas de proyectos comunitarios. Experiencias en el barrio Pogolotti, La Habana, Cuba." *Revista INVI* 19 (2004): 184–245.

Richards, Greg, and Derek Hall. "The Community: A Sustainable Concept in Tourism Development?" In *Tourism and Sustainable Community Development*, edited by Greg Richards and Derek Hall. London: Routledge, 2000.

Ritter, Archibald R. M. "The Cuban Economy in the Twenty-first Century. Recuperation or Relapse?" In *The Cuban Economy*, edited by Archibald R. M. Ritter, 3–24. Pittsburgh, PA: University of Pittsburgh Press, 2004.

Salazar, Noel S. *Tourism Imaginaries. Anthropological Approaches*, edited by Noel S. Salazar and Nelson H.H. Grabun. New York: Berghahn Books, 2014.

Sullivan, Stefan. *Marx for a Post-Communist Era: On Poverty, Corruption and Banality*. 1st edition. London: Routledge, 2002.

Widderich, Sönke. *Die sozialen Auswirkungen des kubanischen Transformationsprozesses*. Kiel: Selbstverlag des geographischen Instituts der Universität Kiel, 2002.

Part II

MATERIALITY

Chapter Four

The Making of a Proper Marketplace

The Politics of Infrastructure in the Night Market (São Paulo)

André Vereta-Nahoum

In June 2017, a Special Hearing Commission (SHC) was created at São Paulo's[1] Town Hall to investigate the conditions for granting as a private concession a large public area owned by the federal government in the neighborhood of Brás, less than two kilometers east of the city's center. Once a railroad depot allowing cargo to transfer between two of the nation's main rail lines, the area became, in 2005, a bus parking space and soon after a vast open-air marketplace for clothes and accessories with thousands of stalls operating every night but Sundays: the Night Market. It benefited from the daily arrival of thousands of shoppers from all over the country to this traditional garment shopping district of the city. At that time, the place was in its third material incarnation: a large, single-story building sprawling over forty thousand square meters divided into colored sectors of approximately four thousand stalls, often named the "New Night Market." The building was and is still surrounded every night by thousands of vendors on the adjoining streets, sidewalks, and buildings divided in small stalls, selling clothes and accessories they produce in the area or import, mainly from Southeast China.

This structure was built by the municipal government in 2014, four years after negotiating with the federal government for the right to manage the space. The local government was contractually obliged to plan, with the assistance of multiple federal government bodies, the process for granting the area as a private concession, aiming at its transformation into a "popular shopping center" well integrated with three other commercial clusters of central São Paulo. During the works by the firm holding the concession, vendors were supposed to be transferred to stalls in a temporary space, a refurbished warehouse known as "Big Yellow" due to its external colors.

The SHC's mandate included assessing the conditions in this space. Its members met weekly over the rest of the year, hearing dozens of stakeholders and inspecting the "Big Yellow." In December 2017, it concluded that numerous improvements had been made to the "Big Yellow" and the area was ready to accommodate traders.

The commission was but the last of numerous attempts of municipal officers to know, control, and improve the conditions of informal commerce in Brás, debating the appropriate infrastructure for commercial encounters over inexpensive clothes and accessories. Since the first street vendors arrived in Brás, multiple state agents have been engaged in making a proper place of exchange and defining the rightful vendors who can legitimately trade in this space, distributing levels of agency in a scattered topography of market interaction with various degrees of formality. Through its different systems of planning and control, the state has a pivotal role in assembling the Night Market and this topography.

This chapter explores the role of urban planners in the making of what they regard as a proper market of inexpensive clothes for small traders, sorting out different and contradictory claims on the formalization of this space of popular commerce in central São Paulo. It focuses on two essential tasks faced by such planners: distributing agencies and building the appropriate space of exchange. Planners include municipal officers, Town Hall representatives. and law-enforcement agencies. These planners must sort out claims by different interest groups and produce devices and agencies in accordance with their own representations of a proper "popular" market, a native category that is associated with inexpensive goods exchanged by mostly informal, low-income retailers, many of which are wholesalers and producers. The aim is to analyze how infrastructural, temporal, spatial, and legal elements aim at creating the "proper" market agents, forms of transaction, and uses of urban space.

These efforts toward formalization are met by resistance and subversion, for traders are also actively building the Night Market, trying to retain control over the space and its activities, and disputing views over how this market should be organized and who can legitimately transact there. If for the state, the construction of the Night Market is a succession of devices to sort out claims and distribute legitimate agencies, or to define a particular interactional—formal, yet "popular"—frame for exchange and the qualities of the space; for traders, many of whom are migrants, it is a process of active placemaking in which material properties are disputed for their symbolic dimension: they are creating their place in the city and its economy, no matter how informal or popular (Schiller and Çağlar 2009).

Assembling the Night Market involves a contentious politics of infrastructure that makes its physical network of material devices visible and an object of controversy (Larkin 2013). At stake is the definition of the qualities of the space (land use, cleanness, safety features, and facilities for consumers), the rules of exchange (forms of negotiation and transaction), the qualities of transacted goods (legal, tax abiding, and compliant with regulations and standards), and the legitimate agencies (agents with legal personality and permissions for trade).

This chapter retraces the political nature of material devices and the strategies mobilized by vendors and their collective actors. In so doing, I aim at rethinking informality and market devices in the urban economy. The Night Market is a case in which the state is central in the making of an informal market through planning, extortion, and exclusion. Despite common assumptions by the media, activities do not pass under the radar of the law (Aranha 2017). There is no absence or negligence, but a selective attention and intervention, in which various state agents resort to different—formal, informal, and even illegal—forms of control.

Moreover, the market devices involved in the making and operation of the Night Market deal with a different set of challenges than the ones explored in literature following Callon and Muniesa (2003). In the Night Market, devices correspond to the material configuration put in place to make it look like a proper market, and the definition of boundaries that segment agents according to their rights to operate. They distribute rightful agencies and produce relations among concerned agents, not just relations of demand and supply. To consider these to be calculative functions would be an extreme stretch.

The study presented in this chapter combines document analysis of political debates and decisions on the legislative and executive arenas, media coverage about activities and conflicts, as well as fieldwork insights into the operations of this marketplace. It scrutinizes 517 entries about the area[2] in the São Paulo Municipal Official Bulletin (*Diário Oficial de São Paulo*), a publication by the municipal government covering executive decisions, legislation, town hall debates, and until 2013, news. The Official Bulletin provides a vantage point into the crises and the tasks of sorting out claims and devising devices to assemble a proper market in the city: it is a clearly biased representation of the disputes and the problem-solving procedures. The published debates and decisions allow us to understand the forms of knowledge of agents, practices, and spaces in this area, the aspirations and intended logic of devices. They are complemented by publications from Brazil's main media outlets: two newspapers, *Estado de São Paulo* and *Folha de São Paulo*, as well as an online news website, *G1*, owned by Globo, a major communications company.

Following an ethnographic and historical description of the Night Market, I retrace the successive attempts of the municipal government to create a proper "popular" market space—an often-used category—and the proper agent. I also describe the politics of infrastructure that ensued, showing the strategies and skills developed by traders. I conclude by discussing what the case can illuminate about informality and market devices in urban economies.

MANNEQUINS, FROM ARABIC TO CHINESE

Before the arrival of thousands of small vendors, Brás was transformed in the early twentieth century by Levantine migrants into an important garment district, producing and selling wholesale fabrics and clothes for the entire country. Brazilians think of Brás as an area for bargains in clothes: the national Mecca for cheap jeans, fitness outfits, socks, underwear, clothes for neo-Protestants, wholesale inexpensive fashion, and mannequins. Thousands of shoppers from all over the country arrive daily seeking inexpensive clothes. Many, including some wholesale buyers, come to obtain the merchandise they resell in towns all over the country in shops, street markets, their homes, or the homes of clients.

Small local producers and importers started to sell in the area, taking advantage of this daily influx. Brás and its Night Market have since become the country's main distribution place for clothes, a node in the network of global flows of persons and goods (Hannerz 1997), connecting sites of production in mainland China and São Paulo, different channels of distribution, and sites of final consumption around Brazil, South America, and Angola. On the one hand, many small producers working for international brands from their homes or small shops in nearby areas saw an opportunity to use the area to increase their income by directly selling to consumers. On the other, transnational links and improved transportation channels allowed Chinese migrants to distribute goods imported from Southeast China (Silva 2014).

Every centimeter of land is disputed and, to avoid conflicts, sidewalks and curbs are painted with lines and numbers delimiting the space allocated to each vendor. Organizations that present themselves as traders' associations regularly charge for the use of small spaces on sidewalks and streets. Some sell products on a plastic canvas that can be pulled up, quickly carrying the goods away, should the police try to seize them. Alternatives are the stalls inside commercial buildings and shopping centers or the Night Market, until recently operating at the Pari Depot, an abandoned railroad facility, and now in the "Big Yellow," across the railroad lines. Each of these exchange locales has a particular temporal order: Commerce first starts on the streets, where it lasts until dawn. Sidewalks are populated in shifts by vendors from the early morning. In the depot and commercial buildings, it starts around 3:00 a.m. and continues until 4:00 p.m.

This informal market first operated during the night hours with the tolerance or extortion of law enforcement agents. In 2004, vendors first asked the manager of a large abandoned railroad depot—the Pari Depot, owned by the extinct national railway company and transformed into a parking lot for buses—if they could sell in the area. The manager organized stalls surrounding the parking spots. In 2010, following corruption allegations, the federal government granted the local government the right to control the area, with the mandate to develop a "proper" popular shopping center. The popular nature of commerce, associated with low prices and small vendors, was to be retained, but was also to be reconciled with laws and ordinances.

The boundaries of the Night Market are subject to a semantic variation that replicates regulatory boundaries. For state planners and agents, it corresponds to the activities and structure within the public land of the Pari Depot. This has been the main site of intervention by the state to construct a proper marketplace and is the focus of analysis here. For customers, the boundaries encompass a larger area, which includes the adjoining streets and commercial buildings with thousands of stalls.

MAKING A PLACE FOR A POPULAR MARKET

In this section, I retrace four waves of planning and intervention in terms of infrastructure and regulatory devices that aimed at producing the right place for market exchange. Each of these waves focused on specific situations and aspects of this space, creating particular configurations and new relations through inclusion and exclusion. In the first of such waves, the main concern was to delimit the space of activities and control the spatial conditions of trade. In the second wave, the goal was to distribute legitimate agencies and restrict the goods that could be traded within this market. In the third, the space was rebuilt to ensure its safety and new conditions for agents were defined, in an attempt to formalize them. Finally, the place was given as a concession in order to become the aspired-to "popular" shopping center, integrated with other central commercial areas of the town and operating with no political interference. For traders, Brás seemed a good place to sell inexpensive clothes in the night due to its tradition as a garment district, but traders also moved to the area after constant repression and conflicts in another central commercial street. The new location posed similar challenges. During 2005 and 2006, numerous media articles described the constant attempts by the municipal administration, with the aid of the police, to prevent the use of streets in Brás during the night. They also report that the main local square (Concord Square) had become a *camelódromo*, a gathering of peddlers. In this period, "Night Market" referred mostly to the street commerce, which became a public problem raised in media articles for the first time. The use of streets by informal vendors became a concern and object of state intervention in 2006, especially with a new mayor, Gilberto Kassab, who pledged to guarantee urban order. Operations to prevent streets vendors from setting up a "true illegal Night Market [. . .] without authorization"[3] featured on the cover of the Official Bulletin on February 14, 2006. A vast array of problems associated with street commerce are mentioned in the piece: noise, fire hazards due to irregular electrical connections, traffic, dirt, hindrances to the operation of established formal commerce, and the sale of falsified and smuggled goods. The Submunicipal Council of Mooca, in charge of overseeing and enforcing ordinances in Brás, maintained daily operations with police forces to prevent street vendors from selling goods in the street during the night from 2007 to 2010.

Irregular land use was not the only problem to be tackled: the municipality also showed a strong commitment to anti-counterfeiting and anti-smuggling measures, to which it gave great publicity, destroying merchandise in rituals created for the press.[4] The persistence of news stories about the Night Market and police actions shows that vendors resisted these devices and developed specific skills to circumvent them. Information on future police and local government operations, and negotiations and agreements with officers, including but not restricted to extortion, were ways of maintaining trade in the streets. Overall, the regulatory devices related to the goods and the use of space generated a politics of street use (Rabossi 2011). For those selling on the streets, the relationship between vendors, buyers, and the state was fundamentally mediated by the police, as is still the case. Activities are tolerated until dawn, negotiated with officers, and only at times interrupted by police raids.

Given that the main state action in the early years corresponded to an exclusion of vendors from streets—there was no place for a market in the municipal view—industrial and commercial buildings divided in stalls, as well as *bolsões* (empty plots of land used for parking) became good alternatives for vendors to escape repression. These were also condoned by municipal officers, as long as the vendors could show evidence of the provenance of goods and payment of taxes: "Initiatives with formal employment and products of known origin interest us. The use of public space to sell illegal goods does not interest us," asserted the then sub-mayor.[5]

This is the context of the emergence of the first Night Market at the railroad depot. Activities at the Pari Depot were initially organized and managed by a private firm. The municipal government, recalls Geraldo Amorim, the first "manager" of the area, asked him to provide parking spaces so as to take buses off the streets.[6] His operation relied on a dubious agreement with the Federal Railroad Network and, after this was dissolved in 2007, the Ministry of Transportation, the rightful owners of the area.[7] With the arrival of buses, street vendors asked for spaces in the area and he provided them. Other associations competed for the control of the area, also trading in stalls and charging for services such as electricity. The large area of the depot north of the rail tracks was slowly taken over by a patchwork of stalls covered with plastic canvases and surrounded by areas for bus parking.

The market at the Pari Depot first became a matter for debate and intervention by the Town Hall in 2007, through the efforts of a representative whose stronghold was in the region, Adilson Amadeu, who would also go on to be the proponent of the SHC a decade later. Adilson Amadeu took to the stand more than fifty times to criticize the situation of the Night Market. After a visit to the area in November 2007, he brought a number of goods he had purchased in the market into the debating chamber and called on the Town Hall and the mayor's office to take action against the irregular situation.[8] Amadeu believed that street trade must find adequate places for the safe exchange of legal goods, with appropriate tax collection and registered vendors. Amadeu decided to battle all the "sins" he recognized in the Night Market: the disorder, the private control of public land, and the illegal and counterfeit goods. Amadeu built on the then mayor's obsession with public law and order. At the time, the city was involved in a crusade to "clean up" the streets of São Paulo, with significant attention to violations of intellectual property rights. Amadeu called for the inclusion of the Night Market in the scope of these actions.

A year later, in late 2008, he finally succeeded in persuading different law enforcement offices to turn their attention to the area, each seeking to enforce a particular body of rules: federal and state revenue offices investigated the payment of import and sales taxes; federal police inspected the area for smuggled and counterfeit goods, together with the state police, which also investigated the specific agreements with inspectors from the local administration to maintain trade in the area and with private associations for trading stall spaces. It became important to disentangle the *agencements* (Callon 2013) of this market from spurious noneconomic—that is, political—relations with local inspectors, the Ministry of Transportation, and trade associations regarding the negotiation of space.

The actions against piracy and counterfeiting defined new boundaries for the market, excluding goods and vendors. Many returned to the streets of Brás, occupying the fringes of the market. Amorim tried to resist the increased state control of activities, claiming to have managing rights over the area and arguing that his company had always ensured a market in the area that corresponded to the moral views espoused by the city's administration.

In a letter to the Town Hall, he informs them of a set of actions he had taken and their results: the registration of traders, the prohibition on selling illegal goods, the production of formal jobs, the safety of visitors, and the promotion of entrepreneurship.[9]

This was to no avail. In November 2010, the municipal government obtained the right to manage the space. The accumulation of accusations of irregularities at the three federal levels and investigations conducted at the state and federal levels, notably regarding the profitable use of a federal plot of land by private agents, were the reasons underlying this decision. The goal was now to improve the infrastructure of the market, to regularize and regulate its activities, register its traders, and in the future, implement a project that would foster the economic and social development of the region through the creation of a shopping circuit that would connect the main central commercial streets of São Paulo.

By taking over the management of the space, the state signaled a new attitude: it would actively contribute to the configuration of the space and improve conditions there. Several municipal agencies and Town Hall representatives recognized the importance of the Night Market as a touristic destination and a commercial site. The stalls at the Pari Depot alone attracted more than thirty thousand daily visitors.

Instead of erasing trade in the area, the main objective of state action became to build a "proper" popular market. This involved enacting a number of decrees and legal acts, distributing new agencies, creating new relationships with vendors, and advancing views on the proper forms of trade, traders, and goods in the area. Several agencies received mandates to regulate activities in the market and develop a project for the new shopping circuit. These agencies were charged with registering stallholders. After an initial registration, information about traders and their goods was stored in a bar code displayed on all stalls. Each stall received an alphanumeric code as well, identifying its location, the type of goods traded, and the designated trader. In order to obtain this code, vendors had to sign a declaration stating that their goods were not illegal, smuggled, or counterfeit.[10] This was a remarkable yet simple control device that could immediately identify the irregular use of space with a fast scan.

Law enforcement and namely police forces remained important, promoting rounds of inspection. Task forces targeted illegal, smuggled, and counterfeit goods, as well as undocumented migrants.[11] At the end of the operation, an "adequacy stamp," which became known as the "green stamp" thanks to its color, was issued to all vendors who passed the inspections, creating yet another legitimating device with material attributes. Traders were required to keep the registration code and the stamp visible. As with previous devices, this had a precarious nature and the stamp could be withdrawn upon the notice of any action deemed irregular.

As a result of these actions, night trade expanded to new areas of Brás. Those excluded from the Pari Depot once more moved to the streets in a recurring trend following each intervention. But the increasing influx of consumers fostered the construction of other spaces for vendors: buildings with small stalls spread all over the neighborhood. Within the depot, changes were met with resistance by associations that were illegally trading in stalls. A battle for the *de facto* control of the space ensued, with successive attempts to exclude irregular traders from the area and repress the trade in stalls by local associations and the municipal officers acting in the area. The matter was once more under the spotlight of the press and the Town Hall representatives. In May 2011, a Special Commission of Studies and Assessment of the Formalization of the Area was created, with Amadeu as its chair.

New informal forms of organizing the market, which subverted these devices, thrived during this period. The new managing group could distribute stalls, which created new forms of extortion and corruption, amid the registration of vendors and the inspection of their goods. Members of this group acted with local associations to illegally allocate stalls and to give permissions for the construction of new stalls or works on the existing ones. A piece published in the *Estado de São Paulo* newspaper summarizes the situation at the Night Market in November 2012:[12] two years into the new, municipal administration of the area, new stalls were being built without prior authorization, and traded with interested vendors for amounts up to 500,000 Brazilian reais (approximately 250,000 US dollars, at the exchange rates of the time). Existing registered stalls were also traded, despite the fact that the permit was not transferable. The journalists also assert that, in some cases, two or even three stalls selling different sorts of goods had the same identification code. Despite the ingenuity of the system to identify stalls, vendors, and goods, its operation revealed cracks in the *agencement*, due to subversion and resistance.

New regulatory devices generated not only new relations among traders and with the state, but also new skills. Traders developed new forms of legal and public resistance to the operation of regulatory devices. The ostensive control of the space and increased attention to corruption and extortion practices required new forms of negotiation. For many associations seeking control of the area, proposing a form of joint management seemed like a possible solution. The lack of a legal framework for this, however, was always invoked by the administration to deny these claims.[13] For those excluded from the area by the operation of regulatory devices, learning how to claim rights in the judiciary also became an important skill. Vendors proposed hundreds of lawsuits and, in some cases, were successful in obtaining apprehended goods and the right to sell in the area, by showing previous registration and the regularity of their goods. They also tried to raise public awareness and earn support for their claims by demonstrating in central avenues against expulsions from the area, always appealing to the importance of the market for the subsistence of thousands of vendors.[14]

Until 2013, the material configuration of the market at the depot remained unaltered and no device targeted its infrastructural organization. But the outcry caused by a fire at a nightclub in southern Brazil provided the justification for the closure of the Market and the construction of new, safe facilities on the site. In February 2013, town halls over the country devoted significant attention to the fire safety of public areas. São Paulo was no exception and Amadeu reminded other representatives amid debates that the market was an area of higher risk, due to the large number of visitors, narrow hallways, and propane cylinders.[15] Noticing that the area did not comply with regulations, the fire department recommended the closure of the area and the government decided that works needed to be carried out to make the facilities safer.[16]

Once more, the vendors resisted and filed a class action seeking to undertake emergency works themselves while keeping the market open for business.[17] After a long judicial debate and multiple injunctions secured by the vendors, their fire prevention works were considered insufficient and the municipal government undertook a 4 million Brazilian reais (approximately 1.5 million US dollars) and eight-month-long reconstruction of the market.

The New Night Market, as it became known by the local administration, was a new infrastructural configuration of the space, with a large covered area divided into colored sectors of long, one-and-a-half-meter wide, numbered hallways with signs. The new stalls were all three square meters in size and built using brick walls. Electrical wiring was also replaced, along with all flammable material in walls and floors. Fire exits, fire-prevention doors, and extinguishers were installed and escape routes signaled.

A new inspection in January 2014 asserted that the area was compliant with regulations and allowed the market to operate. The safety of facilities became in this context a central tenet of an adequate market.

After spending considerable energy and resources reorganizing the structure and functioning of the market, the municipal government decided that a private operator would be better placed to implement a proper, legitimate market, exempt from the influence of alternative sources of authority, control, and extortion. In 2015, it finally started to work on the competition to grant the area as a concession to a private company, who would then be responsible for transforming it into a popular shopping center with set infrastructural features.

Figure 4.1. The "New Night Market" and its parallel hallways in 2016.
André Vereta-Nahoum

Planners at the federal and municipal levels continued to be intensely involved with the preparation of the concession. Whilst planning to relinquish control of the place, federal authorities and municipal officers in charge of urban planning were devoted to defining the infrastructural features of the future shopping center and making plans for its buildings. A special branch of the National Bank for Economic and Social Development in charge of projects (the Brazilian Project Company) was hired to design the facilities in consultation with municipal authorities.[18] Inquiries into the economic and urban prospects for the market, including surveys with consumers, were conducted. In this new knowledge attempt, the vices of the area were once more mentioned: "degrading," "lack of security," "impaired mobility," "precarious infrastructure," and "informality" are descriptions employed in the study.[19]

The result was a plan to reorganize the Pari Depot and integrate the area with other commercial areas of central São Paulo, mobilizing aspirations about how this popular marketplace should look and its place in the development of the area. This was the basis for the project specifications required for any bidder in the competition. The São Paulo Shopping Circuit attempts to connect the four main commercial hubs of central São Paulo, in a project to develop shopping tourism in the city. The depot is considered as a fundamental piece of infrastructure in this tourism circuit, providing parking for buses, a resting area for drivers, storage facilities, handling and expedition services, lockers, a food court, and a hotel. Yet the large area will also host office blocks, offering the concession firm the opportunity to profit from the valuable location. The new shopping center will include four thousand stalls, each five square meters in size, offered at reduced cost with preferential rights for vendors holding permissions.

A new legal battle ensued, with vendors' associations attempting to block the concession and the works. A number of judicial cases authored by vendors are still ongoing to this day, but after a battle of injunctions and adaptations to the contract, the public competition was finally held in early 2016 and a consortium gained the concession to manage the area for thirty years. Resistance to evictions from the northern side of the depot for the works, and the temporary transfer to the southern side, continued until the moment of the demolition of the municipally built New Night Market in April 2018. Police force was used to enforce the judicial decision that granted the concessionary firm the right to start the works. Many vendors who did not move to the new area went to the streets. In a demonstration of forms of alternative control and authority over the space that resist to and are fed by state action, street trade took new streets in the region. The prices for small areas of the streets soared as informal associations expanded their action into these new spaces. Even after the concession and with the municipal government refusing to issue statements on recent developments, and directing queries to the new private administration, the Town Hall has remained a site of public debate and intervention in the planning of this marketplace. The recent Special Hearing Commission and the score of recommendations it issued indicate that the place of the Night Market remains a matter of state concern and intervention.

MAKING THE RIGHTFUL AGENT

The state has been central in the making of the space and organizing the encounters of exchange taking place in this marketplace. This equally entailed distributing agencies. This does not simply involve "distributive calculative agencies," as Callon and Muniesa (2003) point out, allowing agencies to "qualculate"—qualifying goods and sorting them out in a market—but negotiating who are the legitimate agents that can offer goods in this market, sorting out claims, and defining boundaries by establishing conditions that create the rightful agent. Together with the making of the place of the market, the state interfered in making the agents of popular trade. Here we see market devices (Muniesa, Millo, and Callon 2007) and market agencing (Cochoy, Trompette, and Araujo 2016) in different roles, operating at a subjective level. Producing agents in this case is connected to attempts to formalize and distribute trading rights, but also the standards of behavior that should be observed in exchange.

As seen in the previous section, the first interventions in the Night Market focused on the repression and elimination of street vendors or of smuggled and counterfeit merchandise. The main thrust was either exclusion or setting the boundaries of which goods belonged in the market. Yet the first inspections promoted by multiple law-enforcement agencies targeted one specific agent in this setting: undocumented migrants. Many went to the streets, while others leased stalls in privately owned spaces, where documents were not required.

Even more importantly, representations concerning the "rightful" vendors and ideas about how to encourage and protect them were discussed at the Town Hall as soon as the Night Market in Brás became an issue, but more intensely after the municipal government started managing the Pari Depot with the mandate of transforming it into a popular shopping center. Some representatives, mostly from the Workers' Party, in the opposition at that time (2005–2012), condemned police raids, extortion, and other actions that prevented street vendors from working. For them, peddlers and informal traders were workers struggling to obtain income and should be recognized.

An important distinction was often voiced in these speeches: state repression attempting to organize the area should not target vendors holding Land Use Permits (LUPs).[20]

LUPs were not new to the city when vendors first took over the streets of Brás during the nights. Distributing agencies for informal and street vendors has been a concern in São Paulo since the 1990s, when the municipal government pledged to recognize and organize the work of thousands of peddlers and vendors trading on the city's sidewalks and in its squares. Under its initiative, the Town Hall passed legislation creating LUPs to be distributed by every submunicipal government's offices.[21] Since then, LUPs have been regulated by a number of specific norms.[22]

LUPs are distributed in public areas in exchange for payment of a municipal tax and can be revoked at any time by the local submunicipal government. They require compliance with multiple spatial and behavioral rules: vendors cannot use sound equipment to promote the sale of their goods, work shirtless, or gamble in the area. LUPs possess a material dimension, as permits are printed on A4-sized sheets of paper that display the category of goods they are authorized to sell, personal information, and a picture of the vendor. They must always display in the stall this piece of paper that proves their right to work.

Representatives who favored regulation and organization of this place of exchange often called on the government to use LUPs as the main instrument to control street commerce. As the main thrust of state action targeting the Night Market moved from pure repression to the organization of this marketplace, and once the municipal government took over the area in 2010, LUPs became more important and the main device distributing agencies at the Pari Depot and in the streets of the region. After the operations seizing goods and controlling the use of stalls in 2010-2011, vendors were registered and LUPs started to be distributed to vendors who had adequacy stamps. The municipal government also distributed LUPs when determined by judicial decisions recognizing the rights of excluded vendors.

Every new major intervention in the space by means of raids and closure of the marketplace was coupled with new conditions for distributing and maintaining LUPs, reconfiguring the rightful agencies in the area. At the time of the first LUP distribution, a condition was added to the previous legal requirements: legal formalization as Individual Microentrepreneurs (IMEs). The new legal form was created by the federal government in 2006 to recognize informal workers and bring them into the formal economy, allowing the state to record their activities and obtain revenues from them. With the creation of IMEs, the Brazilian state attempted to provide social-security benefits for informal workers while dealing with one of the defining features of the informal economy, tax avoidance (MacGaffey 1982; Roitman 1990). This instrument of formalization targeted informal entrepreneurs of modest revenues,[23] allowing them to register and gain legal personality in exchange for the payment of a fixed monthly sum (currently 51.65 Brazilian reais), including taxes and social-security contributions (Art. 18-A of Complementary Law 123/2006). Using the potential created by this special legislation for the first time, the municipal administration attempted to guide and support vendors at the Night Market to register as IMEs, which became another instrument with which to constitute the "proper" vendor.

Upon the opening of the "New Night Market," new regulations defined precise rules for trade and for behavioral dispositions of vendors, going as far as defining standards of personal hygiene.[24] Many stalls remained vacant at the "New Night Market" due to the increasing requirements and conflicts with and between the associations of traders that retained control of the space. Once more, the exclusionary action fostered street trade and the trend toward the division of buildings in the area into small stalls, creating shopping galleries.

At any rate, this combination of devices constituted the proper vendor: a healthy, registered microentrepreneur selling legal goods, holding only one stall—for which a permit was issued, paid, and not transferred. The submunicipal government, responsible for distributing LUPs, replaced security and law-enforcement forces as the main site of relations between vendors and the state. As having rightful vendors in a proper marketplace also implies removing all alternative sources of authority and control from the operation of this market, associations claiming to represent vendors, some of which were known for trading in stalls, were repeatedly rejected as legitimate partners in the process and their presence in the Pari Depot was prohibited.

The distribution of agencies through various devices corresponded to successive waves of formalization (Roy 2005), sorting out agentic claims with clear exclusionary effects. Not all vendors learnt to manage the simplified accounting requirements and tax system necessary to become an IME, nor the bureaucracies to obtain a LUP. The judicialization of the struggle of vendors and associations for the right to trade had equally selective effects: lawsuits depend on resources and some knowledge of the national judicial system. Those with some resources could move to galleries and shopping centers, but the operation of devices distributing agencies in the attempt to organize this marketplace was particularly harsh on new waves of migrants, notably from Haiti and Western Africa. Formalization is more costly and difficult for those who do not speak the language well or know how to navigate the bureaucracy needed to obtain a LUP. Distributing agencies is also a form of segmenting this market: without resources to claim rights, but also without important transnational networks granting preferential conditions for obtaining space or goods, these new migrants must occupy the fringes of this market in the streets, where the competition for space and trade is fiercer and the margins of gain lower.

RETHINKING INFORMALITY AND MARKET DEVICES IN THE URBAN ECONOMY: DISCUSSION AND CONCLUSION

Since its first configuration, the Night Market has constantly been a matter of public concern, state planning, and intervention as a place of exchange. Through planning, regulating, and building, state agents have fundamentally contributed to the making of the Night Market. Planning through devices constituted the place and various settings of exchange, from the depot to the streets, distributed legitimate agencies, and generated templates for practices and relations among agents in this market, materializing ideals of morally appropriate informal trade in relation to the nature of goods, vendors, and the use of space.

That is neither to say that the Night Market is the sole product of such devices, nor that the state manages to monopolize control over this place. The omnipresence of mannequins in hallways, the occasional music played through loudspeakers, the constant presence of vendors without LUPs in stalls, and the distribution of spaces on sidewalks and streets by private organizations are all evidences of resistance, subversion, and remaining alternative sources of control in this market setting. This work involves mobilizing skills and playing with devices amid the political disputes over practices prescribed by these devices (Mitchell 2007).

For those struggling for their right to transact and be considered rightful traders—especially those who were excluded by state operations—seeking new collective resources through associations, learning to navigate the scattered landscape of bureaucratic agencies acting on the area, and establishing a local economy of information and mutual care became essential. Some agents, through previous relations with state agents or associative power, can steer regulations and material configurations to their own advantage. Others, with less resources, are more often targeted by the exclusionary effects of agency-distributing devices.

Yet both the practices that correspond to the intentions of planners and those that deviate from them are related to the operation of devices and rely on state actions in the making of this market. In this sense, the Night Market allows us to reassess common conceptions and make some associated claims about the "informal economy," "low-end globalization" (Mathews and Yang 2012), or "globalization from below" (Ribeiro 2010) and the roles of market devices.

Market devices play no less of a role in the planning and design of informal markets than of formal ones. This contradicts a certain view of informality as loosely structured or defined by alternative sources of control that circumvent state regulations or are a result of their failures. Informality has been thought of in negative terms, as an exit from state regulations, involving activities that escape public records and deprive the state of tax revenues (MacGaffey 1982). It has also been considered in relation to—and as a negation of—normative assumptions about market activities. In recent times, this view has been replicated by the "globalization from below" approach, employed to describe circuits that produce settings such as the Night Market. According to this view, such circuits are promoted by alternative transnational agents who evade the normative power of nation-states (Ribeiro 2010). This state-centered view of informality fails to locate the sources of control and legitimacy of this activity (Roitman 1990; Roy 2005), as becomes evident in the case of the Night Market. This particular setting of continental distribution of inexpensive clothes is profoundly influenced by this very normative power of states, but it is also connected to formal production sites in mainland China, an aspect of informal economies that was stressed in the foundational study by Hart (1973).

It is not only that informal channels of control rely on ties with local political agents, as described by Roitman (1990), but that informality and formalization become objects of state action, which contributed to the creation of the different spaces, segments, and statuses of the Night Market. Despite common assumptions by the media, activities do not pass under the radar of the law (Aranha 2017). There is no absence or negligence, but a selective attention and intervention, in which various state agents resort to different—formal, informal, and even illegal—forms of control. In fact, informality in the Night Market thrives and is promoted, as seen here, by the actions of both urban planners that exclude agencies and local political intermediaries that tolerate them. Informal associations claiming control are either tolerated or maintained through relations with these agents.

This should suffice to enlarge conceptions about the role of market devices in the making of urban assemblages, accentuating its political nature, as suggested by Madden (2010). More than distributing calculative agencies (Callon and Muniesa 2003) and rendering transactions economic (Çalışkan and Callon 2009), they distribute recognizable agencies and define a spatially bound context of transactions, sorting out claims of inclusion and concerns regarding the features of a proper marketplace. Even the broad notion of "qualculation" espoused by Cochoy (2011) and Callon and Muniesa (2003) is not sufficient to encompass the fundamental role of market devices here. If we look beyond economists and their formulas and models and delve into the realm of urban planning, law-enforcement agencies, and municipal legislators, we see how devices are envisaged to deal with a different set of challenges. Devices also enact what Mallard (2016) recently described as containment and segmentation, describing the role of urban planners in reforming retail provisions in France. In the making of this market, the state enlists some agents, granting them LUPs and regulating their activities, while deactivating others, i.e., vendors and associations who are not recognized as legitimate participants. But excluded agents seek alternative forms of activity in different spaces, subjected to informal political relationships. Material devices distribute agencies in a scattered way, producing inequalities that reflect on the conditions of action and the worth of goods. In so doing, they display calculative properties, making objects commensurable and quantifiable, and their qualities known. After all, segments operate as a cue for classifications of goods: clothes sold at stalls located on built areas in the region, such as shopping centers and galleries, are considered of a higher quality by consumers.

NOTES

1. Research and analysis leading to this work was generously funded by FAPESP through its Post-Doctoral Grant n. 2014/13285-6. I am equally grateful to the Brazilian Center for Analysis and Planning (CEBRAP) for hosting this project during the grant.

2. The search was conducted using the online version of the Bulletin, covering the period of January 2005 until June 2018, employing the expression "Feira da Madrugada" in quotation marks. The results can be checked here: http://www.docidadesp.imprensaoficial.com.br/ResultadoBusca.aspx?PalavraChave=%22Feira%20da%20Madrugada%22&Caderno=&dtInicio=.

3. "Combate ao comércio irregular cria novas oportunidades de trabalho." DOCSP, p. I, 14/02/2006.

4. "Apreensão de produtos no Brás e de máquinas caça-níqueis em Vila Prudente." DOCSP, p. II, 18/08/2007. And "Prefeitura destri 1,5 milhão de CDs e DVDs piratas e contrabandeados." DOCSP, p. I, 18/12/2007.

5. "Combate ao comércio irregular cria novas oportunidades de trabalho." DOCSP, p. I, 14/02/2006.

6. "PR fez 'rolo compressor,' diz empresário," *Folha de São Paulo*, June 23, 2011, http://www1.folha.uol.com.br/fsp/poder/po2307201107.htm.

7. According to Law 11.483/2007, article 8.

8. DOCSP, 19/12/2008, p. 93. Speech by Mr. Agnaldo Timoteo at the 415th Ordinary Session, November 6, 2008.

9. DOCSP, 19/12/2008, p. 93. Speech of Mr. Agnaldo Timoteo at the 415th Ordinary Session, 06/11/2008.

10. PORTARIA INTERSECRETARIAL Nº 02/SMSP/SEMDET/2011.

11. DOCSP, 09/08/2011, p. 4.

12. "Propina amplia feira 'sem lei' da madrugada, em SP," *Estado de São Paulo*, November 29, 2012. http://www.estadao.com.br/noticias/geral,propina-amplia-feira-sem-lei-da-madrugada-em-sp,966846.

13. See, for example, Ofício GSJDC Nº 315/2012-SECRETARIA DA JUSTIÇA E DA DEFESA DA CIDADANIA. DOCSP, 28/06/2012, p. 6.

14. "Camelôs protestam contra restrições na Feirinha do Brás," *Estado de Sao Paulo*, November 28, 2011, http://sao-paulo.estadao.com.br/noticias/geral,camelos-protestam-contra-restricoes-na-feirinha-do-bras-imp-,672070, and "Camelôs protestam pelo quinto dia em São Paulo," *Folha de São Paulo*, November 29, 2011. http://www1.folha.uol.com.br/cotidiano/2011/10/998751-camelos-protestam-pelo-quinto-dia-em-sao-paulo.shtml.

15. DOCSP, 06/03/2013, p. 71. Speech by Mr. Adilson Amadeu at the 1st Ordinary Session, February 5, 2013.

16. PORTARIA Nº 014/2013/SDTE. DOCSP, 30/04/2013, p. 9.

17. "Justica determina que Feira da Madrugada permaneca aberta," *Estado de São Paulo*, May 8, 2013. http://sao-paulo.estadao.com.br/noticias/geral,justica-determina-que-feira-da-madrugada-permaneca-aberta,1029800.

18. "BNDES modela projeto para revitalizar polo de compras de SP e transformar camelódromo em shopping popular," BNDES, https://www.bndes.gov.br/wps/portal/site/home/imprensa/noticias/conteudo/20151204_sp.

19. São Paulo Municipal Government. Edital de Concorrência Pública no 01-B/SDTE/2014. Processo no 2013-0.363.235-3

20. DOCSP, 01/03/2008, p. 118. Speech by Mr. Jose Americo at the 312nd Ordinary Session, November 22, 2007.

21. LUPs were created by Law n. 11039/1991, proposed by the then mayor Luiza Erundina.

22. The main regulation was defined by the Decree n. 42600/2002, enacted by Marta Suplicy, who recognized its importance and was interested in regulating street trade after the public scandal involving extortion of vendors by municipal vendors.

23. The maximum gross income, defined by Art. 18-A of Complementary Law 123/2006, is currently 81,000 Brazilian reais (21,500 US dollars).

24. PORTARIA Nº 21/SMSP/2014. DOCSP,16/07/2014, p. 5.

BIBLIOGRAPHY

Aranha, Ana. "Under Cover of Darkness: Inside São Paulo's Vast Illegal Feirinha Night Market." *The Guardian*, November 28, 2017. https://www.theguardian.com/cities/2017/nov/28/sao-paulo-night-market-bras-feirinha-da-madrugada.

Çalışkan, Koray, and Michel Callon. "Economization, Part 1: Shifting Attention from the Economy towards Processes of Economization." *Economy and Society* 38, no. 3 (2009): 369–98. https://doi.org/10.1080/03085140903020580.

Callon, Michel. "Qu'est-ce qu'un agencement marchand?" In *Sociologie des Agencements Marchands (textes choisis)* edited by Michel Callon et al., 325–440. Paris: Presses des Mines, 2013.

Callon, Michel, and Fabian Muniesa. "Les marchés économiques comme dispositifs collectifs de calcul." *Réseaux* 122, no. 6 (2003): 189–233. https://doi.org/10.3917/res.122.0189.

Cochoy, Franck. "Le « calqul » économique du consommateur : ce qui s'échange autour d'un chariot." *L'Année sociologique* 61, no. 1 (2011): 71–101. https://doi.org/10.3917/anso.111.0071.

Cochoy, Franck, Pascale Trompette, and Luis Araujo. "From Market Agencements to Market Agencing: An Introduction." *Consumption Markets & Culture* 19, no. 1 (2016): 3–16. https://doi.org/10.1080/10253866.2015.1096066.

Hannerz, Ulf. "Fluxos, fronteiras, híbridos: palavras-chave da antropologia transnacional." *Mana* 3 (1997): 7–39.

Hart, Keith. "Informal Income Opportunities and Urban Employment in Ghana." *The Journal of Modern African Studies* 11, no. 1 (1973): 61–89.

Larkin, Brian. "The Politics and Poetics of Infrastructure." *Annual Review of Anthropology* 42, no. 1 (2013): 327–43. https://doi.org/10.1146/annurev-anthro-092412-155522.

MacGaffey, Janet. "How to Survive and Become Rich Amidst Devastation: The Second Economy in Zaire." *African Affairs* 82, no. 328 (1982): 351–66.

Madden, David. "Urban ANTs: A Review Essay." *Qualitative Sociology* 33 (2010): 583–89.

Mallard, Alexandre. "Concerning Urban Consumption: On the Construction of Market Agencements for Retail Trade." *Consumption Markets & Culture* 19, no. 1 (2016): 56–70. https://doi.org/10.1080/10253866.2015.1068170.

Mathews, Gordon, and Yang Yang. "How Africans Pursue Low-End Globalization in Hong Kong and Mainland China." *Journal of Current Chinese Affairs* 41, no. 2 (2012): 95–120.

Mitchell, Timothy. "The Properties of Markets." In *Do Economists Make Markets? On the Performativity of Economics,* edited by Donald MacKenzie, Fabian Muniesa, and Lucia Siu, 244–75. Princeton, NJ: Princeton University Press, 2007.

Muniesa, Fabian, Yuval Millo, and Michel Callon. "An Introduction to Market Devices." In "Market Devices," supplement, *The Sociological Review* 55, no. 2 (2007): 1–12. https://onlinelibrary.wiley.com/doi/abs/10.1111/j.1467-954X.2007.00727.x.

Rabossi, Fernando. "Negociações, associações e monopólios: A política da rua em Ciudad Del Este (Paraguai)." *Etnográfica* 15, no. 1 (2011): 83–107. https://doi.org/10.4000/etnografica.814.

Ribeiro, Gustavo Lins. "A globalização popular e o sistema mundial não hegemônico." *Revista Brasileira de Ciências Sociais* 25 (2010): 21–38.

Roitman, Janet L. "The Politics of Informal Markets in Sub-Saharan Africa." *The Journal of Modern African Studies* 28, no. 4 (1990): 671–96. https://doi.org/10.1017/S0022278X00054781.

Roy, Ananya. "Urban Informality: Toward an Epistemology of Planning." *Journal of the American Planning Association* 71, no. 2 (2005): 147–58.

Schiller, Nina Glick, and Ayse Çağlar. "Towards a Comparative Theory of Locality in Migration Studies: Migrant Incorporation and City Scale." *Journal of Ethnic and Migration Studies* 35, no. 2 (2009): 177–202. https://doi.org/10.1080/13691830802586179.

Silva, Carlos Freire da. "Das calçadas às galerias: Mercados populares do centro de São Paulo." PhD diss., University of São Paulo, 2014. http://www.teses.usp.br/teses/disponiveis/8/8132/tde-31032015-105012/pt-br.php.

Chapter Five

Formalizing through Marketizing

Interfaces of Technology, Knowledge, and Power in Popular Commerce in La Paz, Bolivia

Juliane Müller

During my initial field research at Eloy Salmón in 2013, a popular shopping precinct for electronic appliances in La Paz, Bolivia, with hundreds of traders operating side by side in sidewalk stalls and out of tiny shops, I was surprised that I was not the only person who walked from shop to shop and booth to booth to have a conversation with traders about their transactions. These interviewers were far less discreet than I was. Some carried blue vests with Samsung logos on, equipped with large notepads and questionnaires. At first sight, I considered them to be traders who were keen to wear these outfits, but they were in fact corporate employees. I was also surprised to receive vague replies from traders to my rather direct questions about their business—they would say that sales were down, or that this or the other product had good sales figures, while others were hardly selling. As I approached Sonia Quispe[1] for the first time—an experienced wholesaler who always dressed in the *pollera* skirt and boiler hat typical of market women of indigenous *Aymara* origin—she responded with a notorious one-liner "No hay venta, no hay venta" (No sales, no sales). A year later, in September 2014, when I returned to Bolivia and knew Sonia Quispe better, she told me that she had initially thought I was from LG Electronics. I had been asking similar questions as the personnel of various East Asian multinational corporations who conducted market research and reported on the wholesale and retail traders' weekly sales transactions and stocks. I was also asked by some traders if I myself was in business; it had been suggested that, in one way or another, I was an entrepreneur or was working on behalf of a larger company in the market.

These episodes from fieldwork hint at the experiences of different actors in a supposedly low-end marketplace, still considered to be part of the country's informal economy, and with a genuine popular appearance.[2] In Eloy Salmón and nearby commercial areas, the shiny surfaces of a few newly built shopping galleries with glass façades stand out in a sea of open-air street trade and amidst a colorful mosaic of single-story historical town houses, uncompleted red-brick constructions, and 1970s-style office buildings.

Contrary to what could be expected from this image, for the last twenty years, Korean, Japanese, and Chinese multinational electronics corporations, as well as department stores from the more Westernized business city of Santa Cruz, have entered the retail place of Eloy Salmón and the surrounding wholesale areas, in particular during the last decade, which has seen sustained economic growth in the country. South Korean Samsung Electronics, LG and Japanese Sony Electronics, as well as Chinese "emerging market firms" Huawei Technologies, Xiaomi, and Oppo have significantly expanded their operations in the country. In their search for new outlets, multinational corporations (MNCs) have approached popular commercial areas in La Paz and, to a lesser degree, in the other main Bolivian cities, Cochabamba and Santa Cruz. They open showrooms and back offices and employ marketing and market-research staff in the midst of popular commerce.

This chapter analyzes interactions between wholesale and retail traders, and employees of MNCs at two popular commercial areas for electronic appliances in La Paz. I conceptualize these as interfaces of technology, knowledge, and power. I am interested in the usages and effects of digital devices, marketing instruments, and material incentives in popular economies. The chapter starts from the premise that the manufacturers' practices, informed by professional merchandising, marketing, and retail chain management, are not just tools within a universe of pure social action, but constitute "a universe of possibilities that makes economic action itself" (Çalişkan 2010, 7). Technical solutions and business knowledge are, among other constituents, devices with the potential to (re)make markets (Çalişkan and Callon 2010; Callon, Millo, and Muniesa 2007).

Looking beyond purely human relations and institutions, this chapter focuses on processes of marketization of popular commerce through the seemingly minutiae of everyday material practices of MNC staff. These are no less political than sweeping claims to illegalize "piracy," but with different effects. As Çalişkan and Callon point out, we should conceive of processes of marketization in the plural, but with some recognizable common features. Marketization is understood "as the entirety of efforts aimed at describing, analysing and making intelligible the shape, constitution and dynamics of a market socio-technical arrangement" (Çalişkan and Callon 2010, 3). In this sense, the marketing instruments of corporate staff, based on technical and management knowledge, are transformative of the socio-material assemblage that constitutes popular commerce.

This focus on materiality and devices, deployed by big private actors in popular commercial areas, changes the perspective on globalization and informality in urban Latin America. While studies on Brazil (Dent 2012; Pinheiro-Machado 2013) and elsewhere in Latin America (Aguiar 2011; Galemba 2013) have focused on the politics of illegality as regards contraband and counterfeit goods in the context of the legal enforcement of intellectual property rights (IPR), my research hints at other means used by international manufacturers to regain control of the distribution and consumption of goods and services. In contemporary Bolivia, MNCs do not primarily promote their interests through claims about law enforcement within an international discourse field of combating "piracy," as could be expected from this literature. East Asian electronics corporations have found other-than-legal instruments to promote sales of original goods. They pragmatically promote their brands and "proper" market channels through the daily labor of corporate staff and the incremental usage of marketing devices, in particular market-research tools, merchandising materials, and technical applications.

The chapter is based on multi-sited ethnographic research conducted between 2013 and 2016. Fieldwork was carried out mainly at popular commercial areas in the city of La Paz, but also at the free trade zone of the Chilean port city Iquique. Interviews were conducted with Bolivian traders, resellers in Iquique, corporate employees in Bolivia and Chile, and Bolivian bureaucrats in the areas of economic policy and property rights. Direct observation of the companies was possible through a short "research internship" with one of the companies that allowed me to tour La Paz's popular markets with employees and accompany them in their daily activities. It was also possible to make use of "interface spaces" where companies represent themselves to a larger public (Ortner 2010). In my case, these events were promotional activities and business dinners offered to the Bolivian traders. I also systematically followed the national media news coverage on foreign investment and collected a range of documents about the corporations and their global outreach. I consider this kind of document analysis to be an important part of an ethnography of contemporary economies and in particular the corporate sector.

In the following, I first briefly describe the two commercial areas Eloy Salmón and Huyustus, before analyzing the different socio-material forms by which multinational manufacturers proceed to "formalize" popular commerce. To this end, I focus on the daily work and material practices of corporate employees to change shop displays and register original goods. I conclude with considerations on material devices and (in)formality.

POPULAR COMMERCE IN ELECTRONIC APPLIANCES

Bolivia has an omnipresent popular-commercial economy. Street trade that is only partly registered, small-scale retailing, and the wholesale trade of contraband items are found all over the country. Two-thirds of the active Bolivian population are said to work independently or in small units of production with fewer than five employees (Agencia AP 2010). La Paz, the seat of the Bolivian government, is a historical commercial center, located at the intersection of the routes between the Andean highlands and the Pacific coast. The densely populated area of La Paz and its twin city El Alto has about 1.6 million inhabitants. It is one of the main distribution points for electronic and digital devices in Bolivia. The commercial areas for electronic appliances are located along the street Eloy Salmón and the adjoining area, and at Huyustus, a huge fair and wholesale place. Urban residents of all social strata make almost all of their purchases of computers, home appliances, and household tools at these places in the district of Max Paredes, northwest of the city center, an area that has had a strong influx of indigenous migrants, especially those of Aymara[3] descent from the region of La Paz.

The five-hundred-meter-long Eloy Salmón has undergone continuous socio-material change over the last decades. From a place where everything from staples to manufactured goods was sold from the street, open-air stalls, and corner shops, it has evolved into a retail area mainly for consumer electronics. Street vendors have become shop owners, wholesale vendors, and importers; new traders have entered into lower levels of supply. The built environment has changed as the most successful traders have constructed *galerías* (shopping arcades). There are now about 650 traders in the area; an increasing number of them operate inside these multiple-floor galleries that have significantly expanded the retail space available. Two national department stores have opened retail spaces in Eloy Salmón. Street trade, however, continues to flourish. Shop owners rent parts of the sidewalk out to petty vendors of gadgets and accessories that complement sales of smartphones and other appliances. Parts of the street are occupied by stacked boxes and parked cars that continuously violate zoning norms, and by food vendors with and without a license.[4] As the messiness of this marketplace (Lombard 2014) coexists with its upgrading, and a practical neglect of formal-informal boundaries has persisted over the decades, global electronics companies from East Asia have abandoned their policy of working with official distributers in the city center and opened show rooms and administrative offices at Eloy Salmón with marketing and sales staff.

Eloy Salmón traders usually buy from wholesalers at Huyustus. The Huyustus street fair—it is still named a fair, although it is held seven days a week—is a bit farther away from the city center than Eloy Salmón but is still within walking distance. Traders at one end of the two-kilometer-long fair and its side streets have specialized in electronic appliances and devices. Huyustus traders buy appliances at the free trade zone of Iquique in Northern Chile and send them via informal transport agents, known as pilots (*piloteros*), to Bolivia. Supermarkets in the wealthier parts of La Paz are also part of contraband commercial circuits, as they buy the household appliances they offer directly from Huyustus. In the words of the head of LG Electronics' La Paz division: "We have no relation at all with the supermarkets in La Paz, they buy directly from the wholesalers."

By engaging with traders on a daily basis, multinational corporations tap into Bolivia's popular commerce, as other enterprises before them have. In comparison to national supermarket chains, however, they are far more interested in changing and remaking these markets over time and have more power to do so. Over the last fifteen years, they have settled in these two commercial areas in La Paz where no price tags are found, prices are haggled over, and original brands coexist with "parallel imports," copies, and stolen goods. They operate in the immediate vicinity of a street that adjoins Eloy Salmón, known as the Chinese quarter, where old and stolen gadgets and used appliances are on sale on the sidewalk and at precarious stalls.

SOCIALLY LEGITIMATE TRADING WORLDS

In Bolivia as in other countries, to make a living by the small-scale smuggling of clothes and food is considered a decent and therefore licit activity among large sectors of the population. The image of the humble native women smuggling small quantities of goods in her indigenous *aguayu* scarf remains a strong representation of subsistence-oriented "ant trade" as it persists, for example, at the Peruvian-Bolivian border in Desaguadero (Ødegaard 2016). By contrast, larger-scale contraband trade of expensive consumer electronics at the border with Chile is increasingly dismissed in the media as organized by "mafias." The state-centered MAS (Movimiento al Socialismo) government of President Evo Morales has launched severe rhetorical and physical attacks on smugglers. However, this has not lowered the markets' attractiveness to urban dwellers from all social strata. In spite of official aims to illegalize popular commerce, traders, consumers and enterprises tacitly acknowledge the legitimacy of the trade. Likewise, MNCs do not show concern at this predominant lax social attitude toward contraband and even counterfeit goods.

According to information from the Bolivian SENAPI (National Service of Intellectual Property Rights), a public institution and part of the Ministry of Productive Development and Plural Economy, there have been very few cases of infractions claims made by official representatives of global brands in recent years, and these cases were in the majority from apparel and shoe transnationals, not electronics companies. Only one report in 2013 came from a Brazilian company of household appliances. In December 2015, the police broke up two workshops in La Paz that were accused of falsifying brand logos of home appliances (La Razón 2015). When asked about the possibility of bringing lawsuits against traders for such infractions, the management staff of the corporations admitted that this had turned out to be rather a "loss of resources." Corporations woo traders to persuade them to buy from authorized intermediaries, rather than lobbying for intellectual property rights.

Even the regulating force of social institutions and networks, considered a substitute for government control (Dixit 2009)—in this case the control of traders' associations and unions—has not been invoked very often by MNCs. In some cases, corporations have succeeded in disciplining local traders this way. When one of the South Korean companies observed the circulation of false warranties, they told the president of traders' association of Eloy Salmón to put a stop to it:

> They are very organized, we sent a letter, explaining that we don't want to harm any trader, but that this was a crime, and shortly after it the false warranties disappeared.

Yet in other cases, traders' associations defended their shared interest vis-à-vis the corporation. When a rumor spread in Eloy Salmón that the same South Korean corporation had plans to work with only one big wholesaler, a boycott against the company was launched that lasted four months, as well as a protest in front of its headquarters in the city of Santa Cruz. The company withdraw from the initiative. When the other South Korean company wanted to install its own delivery service, the association of transporters protested. To rely on the coercive power of traders' unions in order to enforce "proper" market behavior has turned out to be rather risky for the corporations, as it might turn in their favor or against their interests. This shows that economic governance through persuasion of local institutions is only partially successful, as is juridical pressure. The power of social norms and legal devices has remained limited.

Despite of some success with local traders' unions, corporations downplay the importance of knockoffs[5] or the infraction of names in the area of Eloy Salmón and Huyustus. Likewise, the Eloy Salmón traders' association states that the number of knockoffs has decreased for specific types of goods (smartphones, tablets, laptops, cameras). Knockoff televisions, cameras, and cell phones can certainly be found in the side streets and narrow pathways between Eloy Salmón and nearby areas, as well as in hidden gallery spaces at both sites. This does not hinder the corporations in conducting business and materially engaging with those traders who at least partially cooperate with them, such as the retailers in one of the galleries in Eloy Salmón street, to which I now turn.

MARKETIZING POPULAR COMMERCE

One of the five-floor shopping galleries at Eloy Salmón, built by about thirty traders in the late 1990s, is *Galería Gran Poder*. The entrance is bright and welcoming; the intermediate routes are free of stalls. Gran Poder is aimed at customers who deem this to be a sign of reliability and transparency. The gallery has the highest sales rate on appliances with the manufacturers' official serial numbers and warranties. As a Samsung employee explained to me in 2013: "When Gran Poder closed for their anniversary, total registered sales were only ten whereas on a normal day they are around sixty to seventy." These high sales do not come out of a void. In fact, gallery traders have been in touch with MNCs since at least 2003 when Sony Electronics opened a showroom and back office in Eloy Salmón. High sales of products with official warranties have been reached through the ongoing material interventions of the manufacturers.

While goods made by Western manufacturers, such as Philips, Oster, and Bosch, are also sold in Eloy Salmón and Huyustus, the most prominent brands are East Asian. In contrast to their Western counterparts who work out of their regional headquarters in Miami, Samsung, Sony, and LG first came to Santiago de Chile, then established Bolivian branches, and finally became physically present in popular commercial areas. Sony was the first to arrive in Bolivia in the mid-1990s, opening in Eloy Salmón in 2003. LG and Samsung Electronics followed with showrooms and back offices in 2007 and 2012 respectively.

As is described throughout the chapter, corporate employees become socially involved with traders to gain their trust as a prerequisite to implementing marketing devices. These devices have potentially disruptive effects on popular commerce. As historical analyses have shown, merchandising, as a subcategory of marketing, is potentially a powerful management tool and market device for changing the valuation and pricing of goods (Barrey 2007). The standardized presentation of goods is inclined to supersede local forms and knowledge about the handling and sorting of foods and other things (Freidberg 2007). As a concept, merchandising first appeared in US manuals at the beginning of the twentieth century and from then on meant to formalize

Figure 5.1. Gallery Gran Poder, Eloy Salmón, La Paz.
Juliane Müller

the presentation of goods. Packaging, branding, and point-of-sale aesthetics, as will be described below, all belong to merchandising techniques. Likewise, Kjellberg (2007) analyzes structural changes in wholesale and retail trade brought about by standardized order forms and material incentives for retailers in the late 1940s and 1950s in Sweden. My analysis is also inspired by studies of contemporary commodity chains and contested forms of value creation at different points in the chain (Tsing 2015).

Banners and Banquets

There is a temporal succession of corporate interventions in popular commerce, with a continuous increase in the use of material devices. At the beginning, Sony Electronics placed corporate banners on house fronts and above gallery entrances, imitated in the following years by LG and Samsung. As a trader from the Gallery Gran Poder highlights in an interview:

> It has grown a lot. Earlier on there were not these gigantic banners of Samsung and Sony. Each gallery made their banners, according to the gallery owner. But today the very same enterprises haven given them so everything is nicer.[6]

Moreover, all manufacturers started with the organization of promotional events to inform wholesalers and retailers about novel products, technical details, and advantages. These events were planned as training sessions (*capacitaciones*) for newly launched products, but responding to traders' demands and preferences, and manufacturers' ever more ambitious marketing initiatives, they evolved into banquets for retailers and business dinners for wholesalers. During fieldwork in 2014, I tried in vain to attend these business dinners for wholesalers. MNC employees let me know that my presence was not welcomed as business secrets and higher deals were negotiated. Based on wholesalers' accounts, during these dinners, bonus payments and commissions are negotiated between MNCs, Iquique-based intermediaries, and Bolivian traders, as well as quantitative discounts for bigger purchases. Apart from extra payments for original merchandise with an official warranty, MNCs—in cooperation with the handful of official suppliers in the free trade zone of Iquique, with whom orders are placed—incentivize Bolivian traders to order in bigger quantities. In doing this, they try to influence the size and frequency of orders, which is a marketing tool to render commercial distribution more predictable (Kjellberg 2007). Discounts favor economies of scale and the concentration of market channels. Exclusive groups of only ten to fifteen distributers are invited to these dinners. A process of differentiation is put in place between those traders who are already more successful, who are then further strengthened by discounts and bonus payments, and those who receive neither of them, such that petty importers and smaller wholesalers are increasingly at a disadvantage (Müller 2018).

In contrast to the not surprising closed-door policy around business dinners, I have been able to attend various banquets for retail traders in 2013 and 2014 in La Paz and El Alto. All these events followed a similar choreography. After a few speeches and a brief oral presentation of the goods, their qualities, and their unique selling points, traders were introduced to the bonus payment scheme and then had dinner. This was sometimes followed by a raffle, and by music and entertainment: occasions when traders as Mrs. Quispe would dance with Samsung's and LG's marketing managers. An Eloy Salmón trader nostalgically remembers the days when Sony Electronics invited them to Santa Cruz and Cochabamba for seminar parties. The MNC employees frame these social interactions, and the daily socializing with traders, through a mixture of responsibility, affection, and paternalism. They told me they had to "take care" of traders' needs and concerns. They had to "be with them every day" (terms that are repeated time and again by marketing personnel), and even "spoil" them.

Promotional events were held on specific dates before Christmas, and in June and July, as bonus payments were launched for these high seasons. The extra payments to shop owners and vendors for every good sold built on already-existing conventions between shop owners and employees. Apart from a basic fixed salary, the employee usually receives a commission from the owner for every good sold and sometimes also gadgets as an additional payment.[7] This means that as corporations tried to build up a loyal base of clients and increase sales, by wooing vendors with banquets, raffles, and additional payments, they participated in the social web of popular commerce. They created trust by instrumentally adopting local practices and expectations (Müller 2018).

Part of the MNCs' responsiveness to customary practices is that traders usually do not perceive them as being intrusive. As the above-quoted trader in Gallery Gran Poder continues to explain:

> Directly, those of Samsung and Sony don't control anything. The user is the person who controls if the product is original [. . .] I don't actually know, but Sony is not sending any control, they don't say "you can't sell this."[8]

In contrast to state officers, who are perceived as trying to suppress and fine traders, corporate employees are seen as enabling and collaborative. Whereas attempts by corporations to circumvent traders in favor of a few established firms is contested by traders' associative force, as indicated above, the daily material interventions in goods and spaces are realized with the consent of traders. MNCs' work is disciplining instead of punishing. Emphasis on incentives shows a thinking rooted in economics, "directed as aligning the behavior of actors [. . .] so they will perform a desired outcome, not out of compliance with a coercive order, but simply out of self-interest" (Fourcade and Healy 2007, 302). For traders, selling goods with a serial number and an official warranty is building a reputation among middle- and upper-class customers, but it is also a prerequisite for receiving the manufacturers' bonus payments—as is an adequate positioning and display of the brand. In order to further understand the interface of knowledge and power at these commercial areas, I now focus on the daily routines of corporate employees, their practices, and their usage of materials and devices to reorder popular commerce.

In 2017, the Bolivian branch of one of the East Asian MNCs employed twenty-nine people at the "open market" (as popular commercial areas are called) in La Paz, all Bolivian young men and women in their twenties and thirties. These employees are removed from the corporation's national headquarters in the south of the city. The hiring process and all labor issues were outsourced to a Bolivian agency. Only the head of the Eloy Salmón office was in regular contact with the corporation's middle management. The opportunity I had to do ethnographic research at the open market, and the reluctance I encountered when asking for a research stay with the middle management, show the physical, symbolic, and social boundaries managers are drawing between their work and the open-market office.[9] Despite this boundary maintenance between, supposedly, the "formal" and the "informal," the information gathered locally by Eloy Salmón staff through face-to-face encounters and material practices is of primary importance for the management vis-à-vis their superiors. The managers at the headquarters rely on the open-market staff and their engagement with the messy world of popular commerce in order to generate numbers about prices and sales, clients' tastes and preferences, as well as traders' warehouse deposits. They have to deliver this data to Santiago de Chile, the responsible regional office. Without this data that produces official numbers on notoriously unregistered popular trade, the Bolivian managers would not be able to fulfill their promotional aims. Their efforts to promote the brand in Bolivia and increase sales of originals must be visualized through abstract numbers in order to be recognized within the transnational corporate structure. One Eloy Salmón employee captured this nicely, both the unacknowledged importance,[10] and the embodied material quality of their work when she mentioned to me: "We are the eyes of (. . .) [the corporation], we are gold for them. Their reports are based on the data we offer." One of her colleagues equally highlighted their situated knowledge: "Down there [the headquarters in the south of the city] they don't know anything, we tell them about prices, it is in the market where the knowledge is produced."

"We are the Eyes of the Corporation": Exhibition Spaces and Market Research

Each of the company's three product types—brown appliances (TV, audio, cameras etc.), white goods (household equipment, smaller domestic and personal appliances), and cell phones—are handled by one promoter and various merchandisers and sales assistants, all based in Eloy Salmón. These open-market employees are, as they reiterated in our conversations, responsible for "trade marketing." Trade marketing refers to initiatives that increase the demand for a good or service at the wholesaler and retailer level. For the East Asian manufacturers it means to offer trainings (as described above), to guard the brand image through merchandising material, and to engage in market research.

To reach the objectives of trade marketing in popular commercial areas, sales advisers, on the lowest hierarchical level, assist retailers directly in their shops and stalls. They engage in conversations with customers who can identify them as corporate employees. Their presence enhances the reputation and credibility of the trader vis-à-vis the client. Moreover, vendors can learn in situ how to most effectively describe and promote branded goods. Merchandisers and promoters, in comparison, go beyond a pure "selling aid" by offering point-of-sale promotion that supports the material presentation of goods. They work toward slowly changing the physical layout and aesthetic quality of traders' shops and the positioning of their brand. They monitor the presentation of goods and advise traders on their adequate display. They give away corporate-designed shelves, banners, and other advertising material. Promoters in particular have an overview of, as they called it, "the image," which means the presentation of the brand and certain novel products in the "golden zone"—international marketing jargon for those areas in plain view, first seen and approached by customers. It is the promoter who closely assists the shop owners in redesigning retail areas according to visual standards of the brands, using shelves and banners as signposts to direct customers' attention. For shops, this is normally offered for free as long as they "look after the image."[11] This means that the favors and assistance depend on a retailer's record. If a Samsung-sponsored shelf is used to display Huawei cell phones or vice versa, this puts the bonus payment in danger. If an LG commercial is played on a Samsung television and the promoter sees it, as happened in my presence, they will immediately approach the shop and politely but decisively ask the seller to change it.

As mentioned above, when the corporations first started to work in the area, they placed huge banners and screens above shops and inside galleries. These trade-marketing initiatives around the brand image—visual and aesthetic—has been followed by more meticulous work on the features and furnishings of shops and stalls, and the spatial arrangement of goods. Although traders' selling spaces are already tiny, MNCs are creating minuscular niches within these shops and stalls just for their brands, which in my interpretation is a kind of popular-market "shop-in-shop arrangement." They are trying to introduce a new form of selling, less dependent on the recommendation of vendors,[12] and more inclined toward a product that "sells on its own" through its packaging and positioning in a branded environment (Barrey 2007).

In addition to this merchandising practice, promoters, informed by merchandising business standards, are also responsible for the weekly reports sent to the national headquarters on Fridays and from there to Santiago de Chile. As the corporations do not manage or supervise logistics, basic information on stocks and orders must be arduously collected by merchandisers who tour the market and do quasi-ethnographic research through informal surveys and interviews. Traders would not tell them anything without a prior relation of trust gained through an ongoing presence. In this sense, MNC employees put emphasis on the trust relationship they had established with traders, commenting, as one merchandiser did, that as he had studied international business, he had gained traders' trust by sharing his knowledge. A comment that also hints at the mutually felt proximity between some employees and younger traders, both groups are technically savvy and often professionally trained. This proximity materializes when employees cross over to popular commerce, becoming independent retailers themselves.

Relevant data for the reports are, first of all, wholesale and retail prices. Employees reiterated that the most difficult things to know are prices and other quantities. Traders would never be precise; they would always say "unos veinte" (approximately twenty) and similar "inaccuracies." Moreover, information is also gathered about the quantities of goods sold from their own brand and those of the competition. Thus, market research, which in formalized settings is outsourced to professional agencies who realize commercial panels and market barometers (Barrey 2007), is done on the ground. In 2017, I assisted several merchandisers with their weekly tasks of gathering data on sales and stocks. One Friday in May, I sat down with a young enthusiastic white-goods merchandiser who was filling out an Excel table with data on fridges at fifty-six "selling points" (retail and wholesale shops

Figure 5.2. Popular market "shop-in-shop" arrangements: Banners and shop windows at Huyustus, La Paz.
Juliane Müller

in the area), a fixed sample of the most collaborative traders. The table accounted for twenty-five different models of the company's fridges. Only one model was exhibited to a significant degree, namely at thirty-three out of the fifty-six spots. The table also showed that the week before, this same model had been sold 786 times to importers and wholesalers based in La Paz by two official resellers at the free trade zone of Iquique. The table graphically represented three challenges for the corporation: first, traders handled a wide range of their fridges, including outdated models from previous years, which hindered the preferential display of the top fridges on promotion; second, from the range of top fridges, only one model was exposed in traders' shops in significant numbers; and third, the exhibited numbers of this model (33) represented only a minuscular portion of the fridges that, supposedly, should have reached the area lately (786).

How do the manufacturers try to narrow their huge information gap on the movement and location of fridges and other merchandise in Bolivia? I will now turn to the employees' deployment of technological devices to get an overview of traders' stocks.

Channel Specialists and Supply Chain Management

Whereas, as a promoter told me, a typical Friday is about trade marketing to "leave the market impeccable for Saturday," the day with the most customers and highest sales rates, Monday is about registering merchandise that has arrived on the weekend or that same day. The most relevant task for promoters is the timely registering of newly arrived goods. In 2017, as a visible sign that the open-market staff had moved beyond merchandising and market research to embrace wider marketing responsibilities, promoters were officially renamed "channel specialists."

Channel specialists register products upon their arrival at Huyustus and Buenos Aires; the latter is a wholesale area specialized in mobile phones, tablets, and notebooks. They visit the many importers and wholesalers at their warehouses. During the visit, they employ various material devices. First, they place an official stamp on the warranties. Only through this stamp is the warranty valid for Bolivia. Second, channel specialists also attach a bar code to the packages of goods. This bar code serves the purpose of registering the merchandise in Bolivia and storing information on its movement. It enables MNCs to know the date of arrival of the good at the market in La Paz and the date of its final sale, as the bar code is retained by retailers upon the final sale to customers. As soon as a list of bar codes is handed over, normally done once a week, the vendor and his or her boss (the shop owner) each receive a bonus payment. This commission can amount to 4 to 5 percent of the suppliers' price in the "premium category" constituted by the newest and most expensive products. From then on, products that circulate among importers, wholesalers, and retailers out of manufacturers' sight, sold unregistered through haggling, are, in the end, becoming part of a digitally trackable market channel.

"To Know the Real Numbers": Formalizing Market Channels

These material practices are part of corporate strategies to reorganize commerce in electronic appliances in Bolivia. One medium-term objective, as reiterated by both open-market staff and the corporation's middle management, is to "control all of the merchandise," which means "to know the real numbers that reach the country as well as real sales in Bolivia."

"To know the real numbers" is directly linked to the work of channel specialists as described above; that is, efforts to digitally track goods all the way from the factory (located in China or South East Asia) to the Bolivian market, passing through the hands of official providers in the free trade zone of Iquique. These efforts are intended to control the movement of goods and guarantee that the merchandise destined for Bolivia is really sold in the country. Accordingly, the market appears "without order" from the point of view of channel specialist not primarily because of knockoffs, but because of "parallel imports"[13] that come into Bolivia unauthorized, and goods for the Bolivian market that leave for neighboring countries. All merchandise that is moved in other networks that the official market channel (for example, bought at the free trade zone of Tacna and introduced via Peru)—although the product is exactly the same and the trade routes are contraband in all cases—is deemed to belong to the "informal" or "parallel" market. From the corporate perspective, the "informal market" does not refer to a spatially fixed retail site, such as the "Chinese quarter" in folk understanding, nor is it associated exclusively with certain traders, that is, those not registered properly or not tax abiding. Instead, it stands for certain transnational commercial networks that move all kinds of goods, originals for Bolivia, parallel imports, copies, and knockoffs. In contrast, an authorized and supervised market channel only moves originals for Bolivia. Whereas "formality" is constituted around a controllable commodity chain, "informality" is perceived as a vast web of trade routes, with a multiplicity of actors, spaces, and goods that are notoriously out of the manufacturers' gaze.

In addition, formalizing popular commerce also means advances in professional merchandising. The head of the branch office in Eloy Salmón expressed it this way: to "incentivize formal shops in the informal market" and "create more space for one sole brand." This is the second layer of corporate standardization and formalization: the daily work of trade-marketing and merchandising personnel, offering sales assistance, shop-in-shop arrangements, and bonus payments.

Conclusion and Discussion: Formalizing through Marketizing

This chapter has looked at the interface of multinational electronics companies such as Samsung and Sony Electronics, among the biggest corporations worldwide, and the world of popular commerce in electronic appliances, made up of several hundreds of traders. In Bolivia, where neither logistics nor market transactions are overseen by manufacturers, corporate employees engage in small talk, visit the same traders again and again to comment on the ups and downs of supply and demand, and do quasi-ethnographic surveys. These low-profile methods, however, permit managers to accumulate, unite, and compare information on prices, sales, and clients' preferences. Market research enhances the "capacity to oversee" and might reinforce an asymmetry of positions (Thévenot 2001). It aims at transferring the locus of knowledge production from the open market to the calculative centers of MNCs. Corporate employees have created durable face-to-face interactions and tapped into long-standing social networks in order to gain credibility, but they capitalize on this trust by applying merchandising techniques whose objective is to bypass the persuasive power of vendors and make the brand-name products sell themselves. Merchandising popular trade works toward a piecemeal standardization of selling spaces through product placement and selection of original brands with warranty. Through visual signs and other advertising material, manufacturers aim at interfering in customers' judgements about products (Thévenot 2001). Customers shall encounter and symbolically value products in an aestheticized, branded environment rather than guided by the vendor only. Moreover, corporations reproduce customary practices such as extra payments for traders, but they use this local convention to digitize the commodity chain and incentivize sales of their brand only. As traders open their warehouses to corporate staff, they receive commissions, but also make their merchandise legible as it is registered and enters supply-chain-management programs. All these corporate material interventions in popular commerce leave contraband trade and practices in the interstices of the law untouched. One might say that smuggling and tax evasion—in the international discursive space on illicit commerce often bundled together with counterfeiting and copying (Dent 2012, 29)—appear here as what they represent for MNCs; they are of no interest for them as long as contraband is original, with an official warranty and digitally trackable.

The formalizing efforts of MNCs do not aim at bringing economic actors and practices under fiscal and legal control—still the most common perspective on informal labor and street trade in Latin America (see the introduction to this book). Instead, for the manufacturers, informality is framed as a lack of predictability of the movement of goods, as the incomplete representation of actual sales in numbers, and as the inadequate material presentation of goods. To formalize therefore means to channel the socio-spatial movement of goods and reorder their material display. This implies processes of differentiation between authorized and unauthorized goods, between "proper" selling spaces and others, and between A, B, and C clients and traders not recognized or rewarded at all.

These processes only partially overlap with enactments of difference by state representatives. In comparison to the often broad mission of political authorities and urban planners, backed by enforceable law and discourse (Vereta-Nahoum, this book), the agency of marketing and merchandising instruments seems limited. Electronics corporations lack the devices and authority to illegalize certain trading spaces (street trade, usage of public space); they do not prohibit transactions in certain goods (smuggled and/or copied goods); they leave the ambiguous legal status of goods other than their branded goods untouched. They aim at monitoring the lives of certain products and leave others uncontrolled. Material incentives do not go hand in hand with binding contracts over exclusivity, as traders insist on their right to sell a diversity of brands and product types. These and other practices of traders and traders' associations—such as the proximity and complicity between employees and traders, or traders' opposition to more coercive corporate actions—could only briefly be touched on in this chapter. They hint at cracks in the *socio-technical agencements* advanced by MNCs. Subversion and resistance to material devices and other instruments that are perceived as restricting the agency of traders are important aspects that have not been the focus of this chapter. This shows one more time that the interface of popular economy and multinational enterprise in Latin American cities is an unstable, politically charged terrain that requires further research in order to grasp the multiple agencies involved, and the unexpected collaborations and frictions between heterogeneous actors.

NOTES

1. Name changed.
2. These episodes also hint to a general trend in market research: increased use of fieldwork techniques to understand consumer behavior and to design marketing strategies (Fisher and Downey 2006).
3. Aymara is the second largest indigenous group in Bolivia.
4. Popular traders, if importers, wholesalers, retailers, or street vendors, are in the great majority unipersonal enterprises. As such they are registered with the local

administration, and some also hold a national tax identification number. However, enterprises are often undervalued and sales transactions normally go untaxed.

5. "White goods" with the logo of a global brand attached to it.

6. "Ha crecido mucho más. Antes no había los letreros de ahora de Samsung y de Sony grandotes. Cada galería se hacía su banner, su letrero de acuerdo al dueño de la galería. Pero ahora ya las mismas empresas les han regalado para que se vea mejor."

7. Labor is largely informal with these businesses. Employees normally don't have a written contract or medical insurance. However, they claim to make more money than in other jobs. Vendors highly appreciate the material incentive in order to, what they say, force themselves to give more and "stand out" (*sobresalir*).

8. "Directamente, los de Samsung y Sony no controlan nada. El usuario es el que controla si es original. (. . .) No sé en realidad como es, pero Sony no manda control, no dicen tú no puedes vender, tú no puedes vender."

9. There are class and racialized differences that sustain this boundary maintenance. The permanent staff and middle managers at the headquarters are internationally educated, middle-class Euro-Bolivians, whereas employees at the popular market branches tend to be mestizo and lower middle-class.

10. Salaries and career prospects are relatively low for open market staff. Between 2014 and 2018, the fluctuation among them was high. More ambitious employees left either for other companies or became traders themselves. In 2018, one of the ex-employees had considerably increased his income by working as a retailer of smart phones in cooperation with two young traders he had known and became friends with through his corporate job.

11. Different from this is poster and video-animated advertisement on larger surfaces, on frontages of houses and within the shopping arcades as already mentioned. Owners of building and shopping galleries get paid for it and don't have to reciprocate.

12. Retailers are considered crucial for determining which brand clients buy. The power of persuasion of vendors is related to personalized seller-buyer relations (*casero/casera*) that involve a mutual commitment and are supposed to be long-lasting (see Buechler and Buechler 1992; Müller 2018; Tassi et al. 2013).

13. "Parallel imports" refer to the circulation of trademark protected commodities outside a geographic unit authorized by the intellectual property owner. In Latin America, as in the majority of regions and countries worldwide, parallel imports are not prohibited by state law unless the products have been modified or damaged—in other words, unless they are "materially different" (INTA 2015, 2).

BIBLIOGRAPHY

Agencia AP. "El empleo informal alcanza 74% en Bolivia." *telemetro*, December 17, 2010. http://www.telemetro.com/economia/Empleo-informal-alcanza-Bolivia_0_324267585.html.

Aguiar, José Carlos. "The Ambivalent Relation between State and Illegal Actors: Piracy Retail in Mexico." *Etnográfica* 15, no. 1 (2011): 109–125.

Barrey, Sandrine. "Struggling to be Displayed at the Point of Purchase: The Emergence of Merchandising in French Supermarkets." In *Market Devices*, edited by

Michel Callon, Yuval Millo, and Fabian Muniesa, 92–107. Malden, MA: Blackwell Publishing, 2007.

Buechler, Hans, and Judith-Maria Buechler. *Manufacturing against the Odds: Small-Scale Producers in an Andean City*. Boulder, CO: Westview Press, 1992.

Çalişkan, Kory. *Market Threads. How Cotton Farmers and Traders Create a Global Commodity*. Princeton, NJ: Princeton University Press, 2010.

Çalişkan, Kory, and Michel Callon. "Economization, Part 2: A Research Programme for the Study of Markets." *Economy and Society* 39, no.1 (2010): 1–32.

Callon, Michel, Yuval Millo, and Fabian Muniesa, eds. *Market Devices*. Malden, MA: Blackwell Publishing, 2007.

Dent, Alexander. "Piracy, Circulatory Legitimacy, and Neoliberal Subjectivity in Brazil." *Cultural Anthropology* 27, no. 1 (2012): 28–49.

Dixit, Avinash. "Governance Institutions and Economic Activity." *American Economic Review* 99, no. 1 (2009): 5–24.

Fisher, Melissa, and Greg Downey, eds. *Frontiers of Capital: Ethnographic Reflections on the New Economy*. Durham, NC: Duke University Press, 2006.

Fourcade, Marion, and Kieran Healy. "Moral Views of Market Society." *Annual Review of Sociology* 33 (2007): 285–311.

Freidberg, Susanne. "Supermarkets and Imperial Knowledge." *Cultural Geographies* 14, no. 3 (2007): 321–42.

Galemba, Rebecca B. "Illegality and Invisibility at Margins and Borders." *PoLAR: Political and Legal Anthropology Review* 36, no. 2 (2013): 274–85.

INTA. "International Trademark Association Position Paper on Parallel Imports", 2015. http://www.inta.org/Advocacy/Documents/INTAParallelImports2007.pdf.

Kjellberg, Hans. "Death of a Salesman? Reconfiguring Economic Exchange in Swedish Post-War Food Distribution." In *Market Devices*, edited by Michel Callon, Yuval Millo, and Fabian Muniesa, 65–91. Malden, MA: Blackwell Publishing, 2007.

La Razón. "Intervienen dos imprentas de stickers por alterar marcas." Bolivia: La Paz, December 24, 2015.

Lombard, Melanie. "Constructing Ordinary Places: Place-Making in Urban Informal Settlements in Mexico." *Progress in Planning* 94 (2014): 1–53.

Müller, Juliane. "Andean-Pacific Commerce and Credit: Bolivian Traders, Asian Migrant Businesses, and International Manufacturers in the Regional Economy." *Journal for Latin American and Caribbean Anthropology* 23, no. 1 (2018): 18–36.

Ødegaard, Cecilie Vindal. "Border Multiplicities: At the Cross-Roads between Improvisation and Regulation in the Andes." *Journal of Borderland Studies* 31, no. 1 (2016): 23–38.

Ortner, Sherry B. "Access: Reflections on Studying in Hollywood." *Ethnography* 11, no. 2 (2010): 211–33.

Pinheiro-Machado, Rosana. "Copied Goods and the Informal Economy in Brazil and China: Outlining a Comparison of Development Models." *Vibrant* 9, no. 1 (2013): 335–59.

Tassi, Nico, Carmen Medeiros, Antonio Rodríguez Carmona, and Giovana Ferrufino. *"Hacer plata sin plata": El desborde de los comerciantes populares en Bolivia*. La Paz: Fundación PIEB, 2013.

Thévenot, Laurent. "Organized Complexity: Conventions of Coordination and the Composition of Economic Arrangements." *European Journal of Social Theory* 4, no. 4 (2001): 405–25.

Tsing, Anna. *The Mushroom at the End of the World: On the Possibility of Life in Capitalist Ruins*. Princeton, NJ: Princeton University Press, 2015.

Part III

GENDER

Chapter Six

Culture and Economy in the Urban Global South

Braided Inequalities among Andean Migrants in Lima, Peru

Florence E. Babb

Placing my work in the shifting landscape of anthropological approaches to urban economies, I begin this chapter by tracing my gradual turn from a political-economic (if also feminist) approach to one more attuned to cultural dimensions of economies in the urban Global South. I then consider changing gender and ethnic subjectivities among Andean migrants in the urban economy of Lima, Peru, with a view to showing that an intersectional approach will enable a better understanding of differences in livelihood experiences. Much of the recent discussion on informality and urban popular sectors has overlooked the relationship between gender and race/ethnicity, thus failing to consider the heterogeneity of experience found in these sectors. An intersectional feminist approach can shed light on complex social realities and the frictions of everyday experience among the popular classes and those with whom they interact. I aim to redress some past omissions and show what such an approach can do to illuminate small-scale and urban popular economies.

My early work examined social class and gender in Andean marketplaces and the informal sector dating from the 1970s economic crisis in Peru. That period was marked by the frequent and public scapegoating of impoverished Peruvians, many of them poor women, for the expanding informal sector consisting of street vendors, domestic workers, and other service providers. By the 1980s, however, it was becoming abundantly clear that racial, class, and gender inequalities were all intertwined in the nation's dire economic problems. Moreover, deep and persistent inequalities were embedded in the political drama unfolding in the country as the extremist movement Shining Path and the military faced off in a conflict that claimed the lives of tens of thousands of rural indigenous people, and included sexual violence targeting women, between 1980 and 2000.

When my work on the economic contributions and political struggles of Andean market women in the city of Huaraz appeared thirty years ago (Babb 1998 [1989]), I had just begun to gain insights into the cultural dimensions of small-scale commerce. However, a decade later I was turning my attention more to cultural identity and commodification, and the part culture plays in the precarious lives of those making their livelihood on the margins (Babb 2001). I was finding that while cultural difference based on race, language, and social origins can lead to discrimination and exclusion, cultural resistance can often be the bulwark that fortifies individuals and communities against the incursions of neoliberalism, particularly against the extra burdens shouldered by those in the least powerful sectors. Both rural and urban women needed to defend their families against sharply rising prices, reduced employment opportunities, and declining social services. By the new millennium I had adopted a more hybrid approach to recognizing and assessing the entanglements of gender, race, culture, history, and political economy in Peru (Babb 2018).

Simultaneously with these developments in Peru, turmoil in the field of cultural anthropology leading to the postmodern turn produced a destabilizing moment which compelled anthropologists to take stock of the analytics we use to understand intersecting relations of culture and power in society. My emphasis here is on gender, race, and other forms of difference and inequality—what I refer to as "braided" inequalities (following Francke 1990)—among Lima's migrants as exemplary of experiences in Latin American cities. Illustrating with examples from two leading areas of migrants' employment in Peru's capital city, domestic work and small-scale commerce, I suggest that the forces of economic supply and demand draw disproportionately from racialized and gendered segments of the migrant stream, which serves to further entrench inequality within those groups. Women of rural and indigenous descent are typically in the most marginalized areas of urban informal and formalizing economies. Thus, I highlight their experiences in this chapter.

URBAN POPULAR ECONOMIES IN THE GLOBAL SOUTH

In the changing landscape of globalization and the transnational movement of goods, traders, and communications, there has been a notable intensification of informal economic activity on city streets in the Global South (Hansen, Little, and Milgram 2013). Scholars in the Andean region and elsewhere have noted the growing diversity of activity, from homemade pirated CDs and videos to Chinese goods sold on the Andean black market, and the increased government hostility to informal trade (Müller 2017; Ødegaard 2008). Contestations over space used by informal traders are nothing new, but the stakes are often higher now; class, race, and gender are key differences that the state may use to form a wedge among marginalized actors, if these individuals have not found ways to organize against repressive practices. In the Latin American region, sellers sometimes take advantage of multicultural neoliberalism and commodify their indigenous cultural heritage, pushing back against social exclusion as they sell artisan goods in competitive markets. If some of them "brand" and commodify themselves and their goods as "authentic"—for example artisan sellers in Antigua, Guatemala, or Cuzco, Peru—this calls for analysts to bring together political economy and cultural studies, to offer hybrid or synthetic approaches concerned with both meaning and materiality, culture and economy.

Studies of popular economies, including Lima's, must consider the politics of space and place when government clearance campaigns criminalize vendors who claim a right to sell in public areas, sweeping them from the streets in the name of securitization, beautification, hygiene, and public order. Where middle-class and elite publics and officials lack sympathy for the impoverished indigenous bodies congesting city streets, even as they can be a calling card of international tourism, we find tensions over cultural as well as economic rights. To paraphrase Saskia Sassen (1996), we might ask: whose streets are these and whose right is it to make a living on them? Furthermore, whose right is it to celebrate national patrimony in the form of indigenous bodies while at the same time demeaning the livelihood practices of these same indigenous people? The innovative and resilient responses of such individuals, including their practice of "identity management" as indigenous or cosmopolitan depending on the circumstances, may be either vilified by officials as unruly or esteemed by analysts as evidence of industriousness and resiliency.

Recent work on urban economies, poverty, and cultural politics has offered promising approaches for a more expansive consideration of Latin American popular economies. In one study of sellers in and around a Bolivian marketplace, the state's neglect and criminalization of vendors led to targeting those outside the formal marketplace, the *ambulantes*, or street vendors (Goldstein 2016); another study examined the Argentine state's complicity in the everyday interpersonal violence among the poor (Auyero and Berti 2015). Such works feature the stories of ordinary people facing extraordinary challenges as they participate in impoverished urban economies and confront unsympathetic states. They also make clear the internal differentiation within urban popular economies—those holding small shops or marketplace stalls and others selling without the benefit of stable locations on the street. As we will see, women and men in Lima's migrant population are similarly swelling the ranks of those seeking work in the city's sprawling informal, or popular, economy, and often meet with government hostility or at best indifference.

GENDER, DIFFERENCE, AND POWER IN URBAN POPULAR ECONOMIES: ANDEAN MIGRANTS IN LIMA

Since the mid-twentieth century in Peru, steady migration from the rural Andean region has contributed to vast population growth and a changing social landscape in the nation's cities, especially Lima, whose metropolitan area is now home to nearly nine million residents in a nation of some thirty million. Many scholars have examined migration in Peru (Matos Mar 2010 [1984]), the nation's racial geographies (Orlove 1993; Weismantel and Eisenman 1998), shifting meanings of being indigenous and mestizo in Peru (de la Cadena 2000), and less frequently, gender differentiation in migration (Radcliffe 1991). Contributing to the conditions that already propelled migration—the possibility of work in the proliferating informal sector of the service economy, the desire for higher education, coupled with inadequate opportunities in the rural sector—are gender differences, as fewer women inherit land to farm in the rural sector and their prospects for domestic work and petty trade in urban areas are deemed to offer greater opportunities. Even so, women migrants are exchanging one uncertain situation for another, as they often experience social marginalization and precarity in the city.

In addition to the economic motivations for migrating from the rural to the urban sector, the violence of the 1980s and 1990s instilled fear in Peru's Andean communities. Many of those living in the rural sector fled the conflict hoping to build new lives on the coast. Where I conduct research in the Ancash region, a horrific earthquake in 1970 had earlier led many survivors to leave their homes for an uncertain future on the coast, and still more migrated after 1980 as a result of the deep political unrest in the country. While those heading for Lima have tended to congregate with others from the same region, they spread out in various urban sectors depending on their social class and other differentiating factors. A good number have settled in the Cono Norte, neighborhoods to the far north of central Lima where squatters have long fought for the right to a secure place in which to live, and for urban services there. This has meant social dislocation in both the rural and urban areas of Peru, and women have often shouldered additional burdens as family caregivers.

The International Labour Organization estimates that 51 percent of all jobs in Peru are located in the informal sector, which is predominantly female—60 percent of women workers are informal ones, in domestic service, retail trade, and related employment (Asencios 2009). Women's concentration in these areas is attributed to their ability to balance informal work with the large share of family responsibilities they carry. There is a diversity of women working in street economies, but regardless of their age or marital status, the study found that a majority are heads of households. Even as Peru has been held up as an economic success story since 2000, with one of the fastest rates of growth in Latin America, women have lagged well behind men among the actively employed population (León 2010).

At a time when Peruvians are reckoning with both deep-seated racism and a desire to manifest interculturality, Lima's migrants and their cultural identity practices are reshaping contemporary urban life. The multiple and braided forms that inequality takes, and the diversity among those who are often lumped under the broad category of the marginalized popular sector, may shed light on participants in urban popular economies more generally as a heterogeneous group. Their diversity ranges from, for example, the marginal status of an indigenous migrant woman hired by the owner of a market stall to watch over the owner's small inventory, to an urban male merchant who commands the capital needed to manage four large retail stalls and half a dozen employees to work in them.

My Andean research has included work conducted in Lima since 2011, focusing on the experiences of women and men who left the Andean region for economic, political, and other reasons and now are negotiating new livelihoods and identities in the capital. Dress, language use, music, cuisine, and other cultural preferences are among the practices that may either be eroded or retained in the migration process, but here I emphasize livelihood practices as they have been adapted to the vast urban setting. Ethnographic research among migrants in Lima was conducted in such wide-ranging places as Casa de Panchita, an NGO serving household workers; Polvos Azules, a commercial center where thousands of Andean migrants now transplanted to the city find space to sell all manner of goods; and Club Ancash, a regional organization that attracts middle-class individuals wishing to retain their economic privilege as well as their cultural connections and heritage. While I discuss all three settings in what follows, I give more attention to Polvos Azules in order to underscore its importance for migrants as a site of urban popular sector economic activity.

Casa de Panchita

Women migrants who are recent arrivals in Lima often gravitate to domestic work, a vast area of the service economy that has been undergoing a degree of formalization in Peru in recent decades. Historically, there has been little protection or recourse for those seeking work in unregulated, informal domestic service. Exploitation has been the norm, with low pay, long hours, and sexual violence a common practice. Legislation now provides for a minimum pay level and basic rights, but unless household workers are aware of these legal protections, they are unlikely to find employers who are compliant.

One organization that has long provided education about these rights is Casa de Panchita, an NGO serving both household workers and employers who are seeking to hire women who have received *capacitación*. Potential employees receive several days of intensive training in skills important for the wide range of housework, childcare, and cooking responsibilities expected of workers in middle-class homes. On Sundays, workshops are directed specifically at child workers and young women from the countryside who are generally expected by employers to prioritize household work over schooling. The NGO aims to build self-esteem and empowerment among these girls and women, but they reach only a small minority of the city's vast population of household workers. In this deeply gendered and racialized sector of the economy, it is little surprise that many in domestic work aspire to leave that line of work and have more independence in the world of small-scale commerce in the city's streets and marketplaces.

Figure 6.1. Young household workers at Casa de Panchita in Lima.
Courtesy of Casa de Panchita.

Polvos Azules

For those who do not find employment in domestic work in Lima, or who wish to leave it, the main alternative is participating in small-scale trade and commerce. This work is seen as offering greater freedom than domestic work (whether live-in or live-out), particularly for women with young children (Bunster and Chaney 1985). Finding places to sell is not as easy as it was in the past, when vendors could find space as *ambulantes* in numerous streets and areas of downtown Lima. The appearance of Hernando de Soto's well-known book *El Otro Sendero* (*The Other Path*), a discourse on the "other revolution" in Peru—simultaneous with Sendero Luminoso, or Shining Path—of invading informal sector workers with evident entrepreneurial ambitions, contributed to greater efforts to manage this sector. This work, which appeared in Peru in 1986, was sold on many of Lima's street corners by the very ambulantes who were central to the book. An English edition a few years later (de Soto 1989), and translation into a number of other languages, added to the book's wide influence beyond Peru as a call to action for addressing an urban phenomenon found throughout the Global South. While de Soto argued for a reduction in the bureaucratic red tape that often prevents individuals from obtaining proper legal documentation, his neoliberal views lent support to street-clearing initiatives and efforts to contain vendors and control their activity.

Through the 1970s, it was common to observe central Lima streets filled with vendors who had migrated from the provinces in Peru. By the 1980s, with growing official efforts to control ambulant trade in prominent parts of the city, some vendors began settling behind the presidential palace in the area known as Polvos Azules. Located near the Rimac River, their numbers swelled to the thousands of vendors conducting informal trade there. Eventually however, around the time when Lima's historic center was named a UNESCO World Heritage Site, the open-air Polvos Azules was forcibly closed to informal selling and vendors were relocated once again. A number of vendors organized in the early 1990s to form the Association of Owners of the Polvos Azules Commercial Center, negotiating with the city to construct a large shopping complex in La Victoria, centrally located and occupying an entire block of Paseo de la República near the Parque de la Exposición (Vigo 2013). When construction was completed, the three-story complex accommodated several thousand vendors and became one of the city's major retail establishments. Most of the sellers are now formalized, holding licenses and paying taxes, though some are not, and much of the merchandise sold is informally produced or contraband. Many merchants accept credit cards and there is even a branch of Interbank, one of the nation's leading banks, in this vast shopping center.

My visits to today's indoor Polvos Azules for interviewing acquainted me with vendors (and in some cases their employees) selling goods ranging from meat and produce and on-the-spot meals; to clothing, shoes, and luggage; to watches and jewelry; to computers and large-screen TVs; to pirated videos and CDs; and, finally, to toys and *artesania*. This last, artesania, comprised items sought after by tourists and by those Peruvians wanting to buy gifts that would have special meaning for those coming from Cuzco, Puno, Ayacucho, Ancash, and other areas in the provinces. Spending time with these sellers of crafts and T-shirts celebrating Peru and its diversity, I often learned about vendors' experiences of migrating to Lima, how they view their experience in the city, and what economic prospects they see for their families. They have told me, for example, why Peruvians and tourists alike so often purchase T-shirts with "*marca Perú*," the trademark symbol introduced to help brand the country, explaining that Peru has a newfound sense of pride in its heritage, its cuisine, its people, and its growing economy, and this appeals to residents and foreigners alike.

The branding of Peru and all things Peruvian extends to the people themselves. This is particularly so for indigenous and rural peoples, whose physi-

Figure 6.2. The artesanía section at Polvos Azules in Lima.
Florence E. Babb

cal appearance, dress, and use of language have become commodities on the market. The iconic women of the provinces and those figuring as *cholas*, having liminal status between rural and urban and retaining traditional dress, have special purchase, as can be seen in any Peruvian market. When I ask sellers who purchase such items as "chola" dolls and why, they often respond with some ambivalence that these dolls represent women coming from the countryside who wear traditional dress and speak Quechua but are acquiring city ways; some regard the term *chola* (and the diminutive *cholita*) to be one of endearment, while others find it somewhat offensive. Young men are typically more comfortable calling each other *cholo* than are older women who have borne the brunt of hearing the word used as an epithet. Culture and economy dovetail in vendors' efforts to turn a profit on sales of cultural icons representing these ambivalent figures.

Not surprisingly, vendors frequently relate many of the social and economic challenges they experienced in coming to the city and feeling overwhelmed as they tried to find their way in the vast urban environment; many express nostalgia for their rural origins and for the security of life working on the land. Those from Ancash note the aftermath of the 1970 earthquake in the region as well as economic need and the post-1980 desire to flee violence in the Andes as factors compelling them to migrate to Lima. Many of them return to visit relatives "back home" when they can, even if infrequently. Their grown children are far less likely to do so.

There is considerable variation among the Polvos Azules vendors, who have multifarious relations within the urban economy. Clearly, some of them command far more capital and have far more control over the terms of their livelihood than others. Indeed some hire others on a full- or part-time basis to work in their stalls so that they themselves can travel to buy items for sale or engage in other activities. Their employees are participating in the informal economy, freed of some responsibility but also lacking job protection, while the stall owners pay fees and hold titles that formalize their relationship to the commercial center. Thus, I found the same heterogeneity in Lima that I had seen among Huaraz marketers in Andean Peru, where some sellers are hired by other marketers, or by shop owners wishing to diversify and benefit from the brisker sales activity in the streets.

In Lima as in Huaraz, men frequently control the larger enterprises, often with the assistance of their wives or other family members, and long-time residents of Lima appear to have a greater chance for success than recent arrivals from the provinces. One vendor from Ancash described the tensions that arise between *serranos* and *costeños* (those from the rural sierra and urban coast). Many sellers of artesania in Polvos Azules have spent long years building up their resources and their stock before acquiring a place to sell in this enormous indoor market. They feel pride in their enterprises, which might occupy as little as thirty square feet, in the same way that small shopkeepers do out on city streets. Like the streets surrounding the commercial center, the market aisles are well marked and enumerated with a grid system that shares much in common with an urban map. Many vendors present business cards with their "addresses" by aisle, block, and stall number, along with their names and phone numbers; some have detailed and catchy advertising and declare their distribution to be both national and international. These sellers enjoy their formal status but they recognize that some vendors prefer to retain their informal standing in order to avoid the high cost of market stalls and fees.

In Polvos Azules, which caters to urban consumers of many stripes, as well as in Lima's so-called Indian Market, which attracts foreign tourists and Limeños seeking Andean items, it is easy to turn conversations with highland migrants selling artesania from economic livelihood to cultural heritage. I often engage them on the subject of their items for sale, including the ubiquitous representations of cholas in paintings, tapestries, and in the form of dolls, keychains, and the like. This gives me ample opportunity to pursue the question of who is a cholo or chola, whether it is insulting or friendly to refer to someone by the term, and if the word can indeed be used to refer to Peruvians as a people, as a cholo nation. Responses, as noted earlier, are diverse, with some maintaining that the term is simply descriptive of those coming from rural to urban settings, and others saying that it could offend and therefore they would refer to a doll as a Peruanita (little Peruvian) rather than a cholita. Notwithstanding the different uses and cultural inflections of the term, it continues to signal social and economic inequality in the urban setting.

Others have written of the world of Peru's urban informal commerce, where "in the last few decades millions of new immigrants have drastically remade the national economy by turning the defiant ways of informality into the normal way of doing business" (Gandolfo 2013, 278). Ultimately, as Gandolfo notes, Lima's best efforts to formalize informal work by making it simpler for sellers to obtain licenses and become legal have been unsuccessful because of the rebellious desire of *informales* to maintain their freedom from authorities. Thus they seek to remain informal, and "prefer to inhabit a world that is strategically free from state regulation" (2013, 295). For Lima's middle-class consumers, this lack of desire to formalize and presumably improve the conditions of their trade is further evidence of vendors' "backward" ways, and is often attributed to their sierra origins. This again reveals the braided forms of prejudice and discrimination by class and race, and often gender, in Peru.

In part, vendors' efforts to remain informal are intended to conceal the increasing presence of illegal contraband and brand forgery in urban markets.

Yet, in the highland city of Arequipa another explanation for urban traders' persistent informality is given. There, migrants retain traditional Andean forms of reciprocity and morality (more akin to informality), even as they engage in extralegal commerce and embrace notions of progress and social mobility (Ødegaard 2008, 2010). In contrast, my research on Huaraz marketers in north-central Peru revealed the willingness of indoor marketers to pay for licenses and daily fees, while *ambulantes* in the surrounding streets were more apt to rebel against paying fees for what they felt, very simply, granted them precious few rights. These cases of urban marketers outside Lima show the diversity of responses to formalization, and the negotiated process by which it does or does not occur. Such negotiations of both cultural and economic forces and desires appear to be characteristic in Lima as well.

The Club Ancash

In Lima, I have been a frequent visitor to the Club Ancash, founded in 1949 by migrants from the region of Peru where I have done research over many years, who wished to retain their connections to their birthplace and their cultural identities as Ancashinos. A placard on the wall of the stately old mansion that faces the city park Campo de Marte avers that "all Ancashinos resident in the nation's capital" are welcome at the club, whose aim is to "preserve and enhance the love of their land." Frequent meetings, events, and celebrations at the club show off the "Orgullo Ancashino" (Ancash Pride) they proclaim, as does the restaurant, named Huascarán after the highest mountain peak in Ancash (the second highest in the hemisphere), that serves regional specialties to members and the public. While club members expressed the pride they had in their roots, they also lamented that the older generation of migrants to Lima might be the last to retain meaningful cultural connections and the use of Ancash Quechua along with Spanish.

The most active members are elderly men and some women (often their wives), who host events to keep alive the music, dance, and other traditions that their own children find less compelling. Recent and younger migrants are less likely to seek out the Club Ancash and avail themselves of its community connections; many would find it both elitist and outmoded. Indeed, members of the club are generally well-heeled and middle-class, in contrast to the majority of migrants coming to Lima, from Ancash and elsewhere. Nonetheless, the intergenerational differences expressed in the club regarding retention of cultural connections to members' region of birth can be found among Lima's migrants in other social contexts. Class differences are such that club members from the professions may often look down on the larger number of Ancash migrants who make their living in the urban popular economic sector—reflecting the class divisions that existed prior to these groups' migration to the coast.

NEW URBAN CULTURES AND POPULAR COMMERCE

In contrast to the generational differences in attitude that I found among members of the Club Ancash and their families, there have been new urban cultures emerging as a result of migration, including youth culture and the diverse ethnic, racial, class, and sexual identities found in a city as socially complex as Lima (Bracamonte Allaín 2001). While many rural-urban migrants attempt to shed the most obvious trappings of their indigenous or *campesino* (rural peasant) identities, a growing number embrace hybrid cultural identities as cholos, the term long used to refer to those who manifest characteristics and preferences associated with both rural and urban Peru (Quijano 1980). Associated with cholos, a hybrid *chicha* culture, expressed through dress, music, and cuisine, has proved particularly attractive among a younger population in Lima and has pervaded the popular culture (Mejía Chiang 2011; Bailón and Nicoli 2010). Chicha music blasts in Lima's markets, and trendy restaurants offer a fusion of Andean and continental items on their menus. Politically edgy T-shirts celebrate cultural diversity: cholo power, *selva* power, and *esperanza* Peru (Peru's hope) are boldly emblazoned on them, along with bright pink and green images of proud denizens of the Andes and Amazon regions.

It is fair to ask *who* exactly embraces the new hybrid identities, reclaims formerly shunned traditions, and asserts a right to be culturally different. Arguably, it is not Lima's popular classes but youth with more middle-class privilege and higher levels of education who can risk being associated with cultural traditions of the Andean and Amazonian regions that their parents or grandparents sought to leave behind when they came to the city. Those with cash on hand may buy stylish (and not inexpensive) T-shirts, shoulder bags, and caps that announce their countercultural leanings. One young woman I met on the *metropolitano*, Lima's bus system, went so far as to display a prominent tattoo around her neck reading "cholo soy" (I'm a cholo) in black lettering framed in a block of solid red. Chatting with her as we stood swaying in the crowded bus, I asked about her tattoo and why she had gotten it. She told me it was to reclaim her cultural heritage and express pride in being Peruvian, and she said confidently that she would always feel just as she does now. When I inquired why she had not chosen the feminine version, "chola soy," she replied that she was aiming for a more global sentiment, going beyond gender. She agreed that the meaning conveyed by "chola" would be different, that it might be diminished given the force of machismo (Babb 2018).

Peruvian social scientists, past and present, have looked closely at persistent inequalities based on historical legacies of colonialism that seem to lock Andeans in Lima in a position of second-class citizenship even as a small number climb their way to urban middle-class status through hard work and good fortune. Those who manage to find success, to acquire homes and property and send their children to good schools, are often resented by the older elite, *blancos* (whites) who fear their own displacement from a secure place in society's top echelon. Even progressive Limeños go to some lengths to explain their concern that the recently arrived and newly rich are causing such social dislocation that the world the old elite know might soon be overwhelmed by undeserving and aggressive newcomers. This attitude contributes to the unthinking, racialized ways in which Peruvians differentiate themselves from one another, now referred to as *choleando*, a process whereby one group looks down on another, and is subordinated by still another (Bruce 2007).

With the so-called "return of the Indian" (Albó 1991) in the Andean nations as a result of a rising consciousness of race and racial discrimination, accompanied by growing indigenous social movements, scholarship has considered the current salience of historical legacies of cultural and racial difference. In Peru, there has been less activism than in neighboring Ecuador and Bolivia and many rural Quechua-speakers regard themselves as *campesinos* rather than *indígenas* (peasants rather than indigenous people). Nonetheless, there is sufficient evidence of cultural consciousness, not to mention discrimination based on cultural attributes, to warrant greater attention to race and cultural identity among Andean people living in rural and urban areas of the country (García 2005). Peruvian public intellectuals have argued that Peruvians have failed to "decolonize their minds," referencing the damaging effects of racism in the country (Bruce 2007; Portocarrero 2009). By and large, Peruvian scholars tend toward agreement with the critical assessment of race relations set out in the classic work of historian Alberto Flores Galindo (1987) and elaborated as the "coloniality of power" by sociologist Aníbal Quijano (2000).

While there are rich possibilities for deepening understanding of the intersectional workings of discrimination by race, class, and gender in rural and urban contexts, it is striking that recent scholarship on *desigualdad* (inequality) so rarely brings gender into the conversation. Several recent works offer important analyses of the contradictions of a growing national economy in which the inequality gap persists (Cueto and Lerner 2011; Cotler and Cuenca 2011; Thorp and Paredes 2010) and systematic research findings are presented on disparities in employment opportunity, education, health care, and development. There is attention to culture, identity, democracy, and citizenship rights, as well as discrimination, social conflict, and social movements in the current context of Peru and the Andean region. These works focus particular attention on the consequences of social exclusion and inequality for the indigenous population in Peru, showing how persistent exploitation via the economy, politics, and a racialized geography result in sharply distorted social relations.

Yet only rarely does gender enter in, as when Patricia Ames (2011, 34) argues for a recognition of the interlaced ways in which racism combines with other vectors of social inequality in Peru. She comments perceptively that at the present time there may be less discrimination based on the color of one's skin, but continued discrimination against women from the high Andes (*las alturas*) who wear full Andean skirts (*polleras*), coming from zones judged to be more indigenous; the indigenous, the racial, and the ethnic are thus defined today in territorial terms, signaling the durability of social and economic inequality even as it takes new forms. It is not at all coincidental that the Andean woman in braids and pollera is the emblematic figure in the national imagination representing both a rich cultural history and the last vestiges of a "backward" and recalcitrant culture that is still on its way to extinction. My own work has emphasized the ambivalent ways in which gender, race, and cultural heritage intertwine to position Andean women as the quintessential subjects of both national pride and everyday scorn and neglect in Peru (Babb 2011). This has sharp economic consequences for migrant women in Lima as they struggle to make a living in some of the most marginalized and precarious sectors, including domestic service and small-scale commerce.

In the same vein, Marisol de la Cadena (1995; 2000) contends that rural women living in the Cuzco area are doubly stigmatized as "más indias" (or more Indian) given their subordinated racial and gender status, and shows the complex ways in which race and ethnicity have been configured in Peru over the twentieth century. More recently, Cristina Alcalde (2010) closely examined Andean women living in Lima and the stigma they bear as *serranas* (women with origins in the highlands)—suggesting that despite changes over time and place, Andean women continue to face multiple forms of discrimination, even from men of their own cultural background. The discovery of widespread domestic violence among Andean migrants in Lima echoes what some others have found in highland communities, posing a challenge to the notion of mutual respect accompanying gender complementarity (separate yet balanced gender domains and responsibilities) in Andean cultural tradition. For those migrating to the capital city, the economic consequences of disparaging serranas within their households and outside it can also be profound as they are treated as second-class citizens and workers.

POPULAR CLASSES, GENDER, AND SOCIAL MOBILIZATION

Enduring tensions may be seen between, on the one hand, forms of gender and racial inequality and, on the other hand, evidence of women's deep cultural resources enabling them to mobilize and resist discrimination and economic inequality. When, for example, rural women I met in the highland city of Huaraz overcame their reluctance to address personal experiences with discriminatory practices, I learned that some were subjected to epithets like "pollerona" (a disparaging word describing women in traditional Andean skirts). In another case, a young woman who worked in a local café catering to tourists needed to defend her right to continue wearing some elements of rural dress rather than adopt women's "modern" urban pants and hairstyles; she managed to persuade her mestiza employer that she was most comfortable wearing her hair in braids and pairing her stylish full skirt with the petticoat and bright-colored cardigan still favored by a number of young Andean women. In both cases, women are pushing back against urban perceptions of appropriate (read urban, modern) womanhood, if only by retaining forms of Andean dress, language, and livelihood practices. Among Lima's popular sectors, however, such resistance to conformity to urban norms is found less often than in the sierra—the economic and political cost would be too high, in the form of exclusion from areas in which they seek to make a living and support their families.

Recently in Peru, interculturality has found support, for example in the Ministry of Culture's advocacy for official use of Quechua in public spaces. Other examples may be seen in Lima's Club Ancash, where well-off migrants seek to retain their cultural distinction and conduct meetings in their native Quechua, and in activist organizations' efforts to teach Quechua in Lima, where the language may soon be lost among younger generations. In addition to these forms of social mobilization, a growing political movement is advocating for the recuperation of Andean biodiversity and a return to native foods as a way to produce healthy communities; the objective is to resist higher-cost manufactured foods under conditions of neoliberalism in both the sierra and the urban coast. In Lima, women and men show their resiliency in the daily act of seeking a livelihood in the sprawling Polvos Azules and in the vast Gamarra sector of city blocks where clothing is manufactured and sold at low cost—in these urban popular markets thousands of Andean migrants produce and sell an enormous array of garments and other goods.

The gendered and racialized implications of these developments are significant, as Andean women often bear special responsibilities for family well-being and for retaining cultural traditions as a critical source of livelihood and even survival in the urban popular sector. I have followed these currents of change in the Andes and in Lima, and asked whether women, especially indigenous women, have gained a degree of cultural capital and greater leverage, even as social and economic inequality persists. My reading of the evidence at hand suggests that being female and Andean may have some new purchase, yet women of rural and indigenous origins remain subject to precarity and to durable exclusionary practices. At a time when Peruvians are reckoning with both deep-seated racism and a desire to manifest interculturality, my work has considered ways in which Lima's migrants and their cultural identity practices, along with responses to those practices, are reshaping contemporary urban economic life—yet women hailing from the Andean region continue to be among the most marginalized. An intersectional approach to social differences and a recognition of braided forms of economic inequality should serve to deepen understanding of Latin American popular cultures and economies.

A robust approach to gender, class, race, and indigeneity must be capable of grappling with the culturally and economically diverse experiences of Andean people in both rural and urban settings. Using illustrations from such venues as Casa de Panchita, Polvos Azules, and Club Ancash can shed light on the different ways that migrants seek to make their livelihood and either draw on or shed the trappings of their cultural heritage to make their way in the urban setting. To advance this project and better understand the workings of gender, race, and class in the contexts of culture, economy, difference, and power, we will do well to embrace an intersectional analysis. Doing so should give us important insights into some of the most vexing urban issues, not only in Peru but in other parts of the world where disenfranchised people are staking claims to their right to gain a livelihood and to be recognized as full and creative members of society.

ACKNOWLEDGMENTS

I wish to thank Juliane Müller and Eveline Dürr, co-organizers of the conference that gave rise to this book, for their kind invitation to take part in this gathering, and all participants for the excellent discussion of our presentations in Munich. I am also grateful for the generous funding from the Anthony Harrington endowed professorship at the University of North Carolina at Chapel Hill and the Vada Allen Yeomans endowed professorship at the University of Florida, which supported my long-term research in Peru. This chapter calls on my four decades of research in Peru, and more recently, my dozen research trips totaling about fourteen months in Peru since 2006. A small portion of the material in this chapter is adapted from the introduction to my book, *Women's Place in the Andes* (Babb 2018).

BIBLIOGRAPHY

Albó, Xavier. "El retorno del indio." *Revista Andina* 9, no. 2 (1991): 299–366.

Alcalde, M. Cristina. *The Woman in the Violence: Gender, Poverty, and Resistance in Peru*. Nashville, TN: Vanderbilt University Press, 2010.

Ames, Patricia. "Discriminación, desigualdad y territorio: nuevas y viejas jerarquías en definición (Perú)." In *Desarrollo, desigualdades y conflictos sociales: una perspectiva desde los países andinos*, edited by Marcos Cueto and Adrián Lerner, 15–34. Lima: IEP Instituto de Estudios Peruanos, 2011.

Asencios, Maritza. "Peru: Women Workers Forced into Informal Economy." *Inter Press Service*, December 2, 2009. http://www.ipsnews.net/2009/12/peru-women-workers-forced-into-informal-economy/.

Auyero, Javier, and María Fernanda Berti. *In Harm's Way: The Dynamics of Urban Violence*. Princeton, NJ: Princeton University Press, 2015.

Babb, Florence E. *Between Field and Cooking Pot: The Political Economy of Market-Women in Peru*. Revised edition. Austin: University of Texas Press, 1998 [1989].

———. "Market/Places as Gendered Spaces: Market/Women's Studies over Two Decades." In *Women Traders in Cross-Cultural Perspective: Mediating Identities, Marketing Wares*, edited by Linda J. Seligmann, 229–239. Stanford, CA: Stanford University Press, 2001.

———. *The Tourism Encounter: Fashioning Latin American Nations and Histories*. Stanford, CA: Stanford University Press, 2011.

———. *Women's Place in the Andes: Engaging Decolonial Feminist Anthropology*. Berkeley: University of California Press, 2018.

Bailón, Jaime, and Alberto Nicoli. *Chicha Power: El marketing se reinventa*. Lima: Universidad de Lima, 2010.

Bracamonte Allaín, Jorge, ed. *De amores y luchas: Diversidad sexual, derechos humanos, y ciudadanía*. Lima: Centro de la Mujer Peruana Flora Tristán, 2001.

Bruce, Jorge. *Nos habíamos choleado tanto: psicoanálisis y racismo*. Lima: Universidad de San Martín de Porres, 2007.

Bunster, Ximena, and Elsa M. Chaney. *Sellers and Servants: Working Women in Lima, Peru*. New York: Praeger, 1985.

Cotler, Julio, and Ricardo Cuenca, eds. *Las desigualdades en el Perú: balances críticos*. Lima: IEP Instituto de Estudios Peruanos, 2011.

Cueto, Marcos, and Adrián Lerner, eds. *Desarrollo, desigualdades y conflictos sociales: una perspectiva desde los países andinos*. Lima: IEP Instituto de Estudios Peruanos, 2011.

de la Cadena, Marisol. "'Women Are More Indian': Ethnicity and Gender in a Community Near Cuzco." In *Ethnicity, Markets, and Migration in the Andes: At the*

Crossroads of History and Anthropology, edited by Brooke Larson and Olivia Harris, 329–343. Durham, NC: Duke University Press, 1995.

———. *Indigenous Mestizos: The Politics of Race and Culture in Cuzco, Peru, 1919–1991*. Durham, NC: Duke University Press, 2000.

de Soto, Hernando. *The Other Path: Invisible Revolution in the Third World.* New York: Harper and Row, 1989.

Flores Galindo, Alberto. *Buscando un inca: Identidad y utopia en los Andes*. Lima: Instituto de Apoyo Agrario, 1987.

Francke, Marfil. "Género, clase y etnía: la trenza de la dominación." In *Tiempos de ira y amor: Nuevos actores para viejos problemas*, edited by Carlos Iván Degregori et al. Lima: DESCO: Centro de Estudios y Promoción del Desarrollo, 1990.

Gandolfo, Daniella. "Formless: A Day at Lima's Office of Formalization." *Cultural Anthropology* 28, no. 2 (2013): 278–298.

García, María Elena. *Making Indigenous Citizens: Identity, Development, and Multicultural Activism in Peru*. Stanford: Stanford University Press, 2005.

Goldstein, Daniel M. *Owners of the Sidewalk: Security and Survival in the Informal City*. Durham, NC: Duke University Press, 2016.

Hansen, Karen Tranberg, Walter E. Little, and B. Lynne Milgram, eds. *Street Economies in the Urban Global South*. Santa Fe: School for Advanced Research Advanced Seminar Series, SAR Press, 2013.

León, Janina V. "Peruvian Women and Microenterprises." *The Canadian Foundation for the Americas (FOCAL)*, December 2010. https://www.focal.ca/en/publications/focalpoint/368-december-2010-janina-v-leon-en.

Matos Mar, José. *Desborde popular y crisis del estado: Veinte años después*. Lima: Fondo Editorial del Congreso del Perú, 2010 [1984].

Mejía Chiang, César. *Cultura popular limeña y prensa chicha*. Lima: Grupo Editorial Mesa Redonda, 2011.

Müller, Juliane. "Travelling Against the Odds." *Anthropology News Website*, September 8, 2017. doi: 10.1111/AN.606.

Ødegaard, Cecilie Vindal. "Informal Trade, *Contrabando* and Prosperous Socialities in Arequipa, Peru." *Ethnos* 73, no. 2 (2008): 241–266.

———. *Mobility, Markets and Indigenous Socialities: Contemporary Migration in the Peruvian Andes*. Burlington, VT: Ashgate, 2010.

Orlove, Benjamin S. "Putting Race in Its Place: Order in Colonial and Postcolonial Peruvian Geography." *Social Research* 69 (1993): 301–336.

Portocarrero, Gonzalo. *Racismo y mestizaje y otros ensayos*. Lima: Fondo Editorial del Congreso del Perú, 2009.

Quijano, Anibal. *Dominación cultura: Lo cholo y el conflict cultural en el Perú*. Lima: Mosca azul editors, 1980.

———. "Coloniality of Power, Eurocentrism and Latin America." *Nepantla: Views from South* 1, no. 3 (2000): 533–80.

Radcliffe, Sarah A. "The Role of Gender in Peasant Migration: Conceptual Issues from the Peruvian Andes." *Review of Radical Political Economics* 23, no. 3–4 (1991): 129–147.

Sassen, Saskia. "Whose City Is It? Globalization and the Formation of New Claims," *Public Culture* 8, no. 2 (1996): 205–223.

Thorp, Rosemary, and Maritza Paredes. *Ethnicity and the Persistence of Inequality: The Case of Peru*. New York: Palgrave Macmillan, 2010.

Vigo, Manuel. "Beneath Its Polished Surface, a Black-Market Shopping Center Thrives." *The Rockefeller Foundation's Informal City Dialogues*. January 29, 2013. https://nextcity.org/informalcity/entry/polvos-azules-black-market-retail-destination-cleans-up-its-act

Weismantel, Mary, and Stephen F. Eisenman. "Race in the Andes: Global Movements and Popular Ontologies." *Bulletin of Latin American Research* 17, no. 2 (1998): 121–142.

Chapter Seven

Relational Autonomy, Reproduction, and Popular Trade

Mobility Trajectories and Appropriation of Space among Female Street Vendors in Quito, Ecuador

Cristina Vega and Magali Marega

RETHINKING POPULAR STREET TRADE

Today, approaches to the economy from the perspective of common life are using new formulations that place a focus onto the transactions and commercial exchanges in the city (Narotzky 2015). Along these same lines, the shift from the focus on informality to one on the popular economy enables us to consider a series of processes that, up to now, seemed scarcely relevant. New perspectives are being used to examine the relationship between economy, culture, and everyday life, between exchange, reciprocity, and affection, between global and ordinary transactions, or between work in the public sphere and the work of family reproduction and care that it is interwoven with. The study of street and market trade related to transnational connections in purchase-sale exchanges, ongoing mobilities between the countryside and urban settlements, and the recreation of ethnicity, gender, and community in the midst of commercial networks, everyday cooperation, and competition is taking centerstage in this body of work. Shifts in analysis with regard to informality, survival, poverty, exclusion, marginality, and illegality are accompanied by other innovations in methodological terms that reveal the dynamic meanings constructed by actors in the confluence of precariousness, creativity, and autonomy. As Susana Narotzky suggests, there is a need to "get to the bottom of how this ordinary knowledge and practice questions the theories we employ to understand reality and how they need to be transformed" (2015, 68). Relations with the state, and claims for rights and citizenship, assume a new dimension. This recognizes that modernization, instead of having a linear and progressive history, generates heterogeneous, complex, and often ambivalent spaces and links where "citizen" demands cannot always be assimilated into normative standards of integration. Identities and relations of gender and ethnicity are important dimensions of people's lives that need to enter into these reconceptualizations.

This chapter[1] analyses popular trajectories and interactions in the context of urban transformations and political reorientations during the period of the progressive government of the Citizens' Revolution in Ecuador. As an entry point, we look at the life and work trajectories of female vendors who settle in the city, seeking to find a suitable location for their trade and appropriate space through family ties. Their reproduction strategies reveal the framework in which popular existence takes place and the way it intersects with the visions and regulations implemented by the municipality. Removed from "indigenous popular overflow" (Tassi et al. 2013), which is anchored to the vigorous global networks that may be seen in other Andean urban environments, the sale of food and clothing in the south of Quito highlights relations and negotiations of proximity. These express a precarious urban environment in which, nevertheless, there is affirmation of intergenerational commercial traditions learned and transmitted through a history of mobility to and around the city, and of female work for the household and neighborhood settlement. The affirmation of a "sense of autonomy" (Millar 2014) accounts for the women's self-understandings rooted in their work on the streets of Quito. The political demands made by these women express a legitimate right to work in the city under specific parameters, thereby challenging the recent cycle of modernization. In permanent tension with the latter, this affirms a reproductive autonomy that is anchored to a family tradition of selling and of spatial mobility.

Methodologically, the analysis is based on interviews with organized female vendors and municipal and neighborhood actors, as well as observations of commercial activity on the streets of a neighborhood in southern Quito. We conducted in-depth interviews with over twenty retail traders and made observations on sales work by accompanying them. The interviews sought to cover the retailers' trajectories, the advantages and difficulties that surround them, and their spatial and social strategies. In addition, we conducted another twelve interviews with guild leaders, municipal government officials, and residents of the neighborhood who became organizers. Fieldwork was conducted in various stages, from late 2015 to early 2017.

The chapter is organized as follows: Firstly, we map out the main outlines of the shift from informality to gender and the popular economy. Secondly, we present a set of dynamics that are key to understanding the urban context in Quito and street trade, together with the continuities and changes introduced by the Citizens' Revolution government. Finally, we develop the most relevant findings on the relational autonomy of female traders, family reproduction, and the appropriation and negotiation of selling spaces.

IN THE INTERSTICES: POPULAR ECONOMY, TRADE, AND STREET LIFE

The focus on informality has important antecedents in the linear and normative vision of modernization that was disseminated in Latin America during the 1950s and 1960s. The idea that industry would put an end to "underdevelopment" and the "traditional" world through a mixture of "acculturation" and social control soon proved to be counterfactual; city migration and structural unemployment increased the labor reserve and with it the universe of those integrated in a precarious manner. The link between the informal world and the development of peripheral capitalism implied therefore a double reference: that of the "reserve army of labor," available at low cost according to demand, and that of the "marginal mass," the population who were not functional for the system that renders them surplus (Nun 2001). The Marxist perspective of dependency considered the international dynamics that perpetuated economic inequality between centers and peripheries, as well as the national political elements that made it possible. Small-scale economic activities outside the state's purview were not only maintained by ceasing to be a "marginal" manner of integration but were also becoming stabilized and expanding their scope of action in the following decades.[2]

The critical concept of informality, developed by Keith Hart (1973) and popularized by the International Labour Organization and the Regional Employment Programme for Latin America and the Caribbean (PREALC) between the 1970s and the 1990s, was seen by social scientists as key to explaining competitive labor pressure (Tokman 1982). It was associated with the new international division of labor, subcontracting chains, and capital accumulation processes in general (Portes, Castells, and Benton 1989). Studies were conducted into its precarious nature, which was feminized and unrelated to social rights and protection (Benería and Roldán 1992), and consideration was given to its importance in the generalization of work vulnerability (Antunes, 2015).

In the following years, the vision of the informal being linked to poverty, exclusion, and lack of resources of all kinds gave way to a series of studies that boasted extensive experience in the field of history and anthropology. These highlighted the internal heterogeneity of the informal, its colonial roots, and the challenges it posed to urban modernity based on the "paradigm of separation" (Barragán 1990; Kingman 2006; Tassi et al. 2013). Its deployment in theoretical and analytical terms revealed forms of production, circulation, and consumption that were closely linked to capitalism through more extensive territorial frameworks, sometimes global ones, as well as the expanded (and transnational) reproduction of families and communities.

The idea of popular sectors as being dispossessed, on the edge of biological survival, not modern, disconnected from any fiscal and financial relationship, or lacking in their own strategies, has been losing ground (Giraldo 2017). The role of saving and indebtedness, unproductive expenditure (parties, games, luxury consumption), complex social and trans-local networks, or organizational modalities have revealed specific, vigorous, and expansive references and practices. These could be considered in relation to the critique of Marx's political economy, to E. P. Thompson and Scott's moral economy, to Polanyi's social and economic concept of embeddedness. It could also be related to the recreation of ethnicity raised by critical studies of race in Latin America, or as we propose here, to the reproduction perspective developed by Marxist feminism by authors such as Lise Vogel and Silvia Federici, who were increasingly inclined toward an intersectional approach. All this departed, in any case, from the degraded, anti-political conception of the *lumpenproletariat* (Denning 2011) by adopting a powerful vision of alternative economic frameworks.

Informality was then replaced by other formulations such as "globalization from below" or "non-hegemonic globalization" (Portes, Guarnizo, and Landolt 2003; Ribeiro 2012).[3] The borders between formality and informality or between legality and illegality were shown to be diffuse or porous, both in the examination of capital flows, and of work and migration (Sassen 2007). Precarization, the popularization of consumption, and the creativity of those who operate in the cracks by satisfying local demand took the lead, both in terms of structural approaches and those that highlighted the practices (not necessarily resistant) of those seeking out opportunities. This generated socioeconomic regulations on the margins of the state.

The popular nature of these economies refers, as indicated by Ribeiro (2012, 21–22), citing Canclini, to the participation in and unequal appropriation of general economic and cultural resources of the globalized world by subaltern sectors. The popular economy is a contemporary updating of the colonial and republican asymmetries that propitiated the indigenous economic and political spaces and structures, removed and segregated from the official world of work and citizenship rights reserved for white elites, who paradoxically required this parallel institutionality for the provision and circulation of labor and basic supplies. The tension between reproducing these structures and functionalizing them has continued to this day. Their recreation in trade and markets highlights the ability of the popular, indigenous, and mestizo sectors to adapt and proliferate on their own terms, generating supplies, consumption, and ways of life that are completely "modern" (Kingman 2006) and often ambivalent with regard to liberal and subsequent neoliberal logics (Gago 2015).

The focus on popular economy, encouraged by the examination of colonial continuity, highlights the role of gender, ethnicity, and migratory history. The reproduction perspective, whose epicenter is the analysis of production and social reproduction processes, according to Marxist political economy, is key to understanding the recreation of popular economies (Vogel 1983; Bhattacharya 2017; Federici 2014). As a family activity subject to conditions of uncertainty and vulnerability, street trade relates to "life without wages" (Denning 2011) and its impact on women, whose experiences are located in the periphery of the formal, regulated, and moral integration of wage work. As Kathleen Millar (2014) shows with regard to the *catadoras* (female recyclers) of Rio de Janeiro's peripheries, and taking into account the restrictions and constant contingencies in favela life, women yearn for the formal world. However, they end up opting for the flexibility and autonomy that daily income through recycling provides, adapting their work to the demands of family reproduction and daily contingencies. Unlike the self-employed entrepreneur who sets out to operate under instrumental and maximizing principles, these women affirm a sense of "relational autonomy" (Millar 2014, 35–36). While this is often described as "pure suffering," stigmatization, and sacrifice, it also appears as a safe resource and refuge from the abuses and rigidities of the formal world ("there's no end to rubbish"). These women decide how much and when to work. Without falling into the trap of idealizing the popular economy or assimilating it into a social, caring, or feminist economy (Coraggio 2016), it should be emphasized that street transactions are guided by a "reproductive rationality" (Quiroga 2015). This rationality places domestic units in the foreground by transcending the classic public/private separation, by hybridizing resources of different sorts, and by instituting rights (to space, rubbish, income, ties, irrigation water, loans, recognition, and political representation) independent of labor and the social systems of the formal world. This become clear when considering trade union practice, as in Denning's work (2011) on associations of the self-employed in India. What these women bring into play are transversal, multiple demands related to working spaces, housing and the provision of food, family care, safety, and the ability to interact with state agents. This is, without doubt, an assertion of the right to work in the city.

QUITO: URBAN DYNAMICS AND THE SPATIALIZATION OF STREET TRADE

Markets and mercantile exchanges structured the Andean popular economy in the pre-Hispanic, colonial, and republican periods.[4] In the late nineteenth and early twentieth century, a process that Eduardo Kingman (2006) has called "first modernity" operated in Ecuador. This had distinctive features, since it was viewed more as civility and separation than as a construction of citizenship. In Quito, during the early decades of the twentieth century and until the 1950s, urban reforms in social hygiene and street furniture were carried out, while "an attempt was made to build a city of progress based on notions of beauty, order and hygiene" (Granja 2010, 37).

The agrarian reforms of 1964 and 1973 substantively fueled the new characteristics that the city has adopted since then. The reforms led to a destructuring of the landlord regime that consisted of a model of "private administration of communities" (Guerrero 2010), promoting processes of mobility and sometimes of the proletarization of the indigenous peasant family. As a result, there was an increase of migratory flows to intermediate urban centers and then to Quito and Guayaquil. The historical trend of interregional highland-coast mobility that generated the primary productive export matrix began to lose its predominance, as revealed by new intra-regional and intra-provincial migrations (Ortiz and Martinez 1999). The literature captures the way in which this was interwoven with a history both of segregation and racism, and of proximity and interaction (Kingman 2006; Hollenstein 2009).

As a result of this process, Quito underwent a major transformation in the 1960s. This was seen in the increase in population that coincided with the division into lots of the grand estates located on the urban perimeter. The city "grew longitudinally until the 60s" and by the 80s had multiple centers of growth" (Ortiz and Martínez 1999). The city's historical center became a major receiver of migrants who were engaged in street trade.

With the growth in population, the Urban Planning Plan was created in 1967. This began to promote policies to conserve the city's heritage, a process that led UNESCO to declare Quito a World Heritage Site in 1978 (Granja 2010). In the 1990s, from the governmental perspective promoted by the media, one of the major problems afflicting the city (especially the historic center) was informal trading, and this was invariably reported as being interwoven with urban criminality. International organizations and international cooperation agencies intervened with the municipal governments in matters of territorial organization and heritage conservation policies with the intention of promoting national and international tourism. To finance a recovery plan for the historic center of Quito, the mayor's office received a loan from the IDB in 1992 and created the Historic Center Company to administer it. The eviction of itinerant traders and vendors from the historic center acquired extreme characteristics in 1999 with a modernization project that sought to relocate traders from the Historic Center of Quito (Granja 2010), whereby the municipality attempted to "relocate" over eight thousand vendors, mostly through violent means (Valdivieso, 2009).

At the end of the first decade of the 2000s, a new modernizing momentum promoted by the municipal government of the Citizens' Revolution signified the formation of new *urban centralities and subcentralities* around the strategic capacity to concentrate businesses, large surface areas, and new consumption.[5] The regulation of retail trade was key in such configurations, although, as we shall see, the momentum did not achieve the goals set by the administration with regard to concentrating trade in an orderly way and deploying it for particular ends. Popular trade continued to appropriate spaces, both in the historic center and more obviously in the suburbs, which had better conditions of entry.

POPULAR TRADE DURING THE CITIZENS' REVOLUTION AND ITS MARK ON THE SOUTH

Martha Bucaram is the name of the avenue that runs through seventeen neighborhoods belonging to the Ciudadela Ibarra in the parish of La Ecuatoriana in the southwest of Quito. Its first inhabitants were mostly rural migrants and former *huasipungueros* who had turned into "sub-proletarians" (small traders, itinerant vendors, female domestic workers, construction workers, small-scale craftspeople). These inhabitants formed the housing cooperative, the Quito Autonomous Workers Union (UTAQ), at the end of the 1970s. As a result of collective organization, they were able to bring about the purchase and division into lots of the land belonging to the old Ibarra Estate during the government of Jaime Roldós Aguilera (1979–1981).[6]

Since the 2000s, the area of Martha Bucaram Avenue has experienced a commercial boom generated by the displacements from the historic center produced by the planning measures mentioned above. By mapping this information, we have concluded that the area has become a strategic space for small traders. The reasons for this are: its location at the intersection of several expanding neighborhoods, easy supply for vendors due to the proximity of the Solanda wholesale market, the avenue's breadth and easy access, and, of prime importance, the scarce police persecution.

In 2009, control of Quito City Council was won by Augusto Barrera of the Alianza PAÍS, a political movement that two years earlier had also won power nationally under Rafael Correa, giving rise to the so-called *Revolución Ciudadana* (Citizens' Revolution). Barrera's political proposal sought to combine the "right to work" with the "right to the city," which meant new guidelines for the organization and regulation of retail trade and autonomous work in the city. This distanced itself, at least rhetorically, from the preceding "criminalizing" approach. It also pointed to the need to organize the activity within the framework of a decentralized understanding of the city.

In parallel, the new momentum, articulated by the Secretariat of the Popular and Solidarity Economy, failed to convince this sector of traders, who felt that their status was threatened. This modernization, conceived from above, implied limitations and new strategies for space management. Regularization required training, the use of a regulatory uniform, the issuing of identification cards, the payment of royalties, and tax and fiscal formalization. According to the female traders we interviewed, these requisites were too demanding. In the case of Martha Bucaram Avenue, these regulations were also accompanied by tight police control and by an initiative to move the traders to a platform (at the beginning of the avenue), a proposal that was actively resisted by the association's female vendors.

In 2012, when both the presence of traders and the control and persecution by the police had grown significant in the area, a group of vendors took the initiative and convened an assembly in order to organize themselves as a guild. This gave rise to the Martha Bucaram Association (AMB), which was aimed at confronting the police raids in which merchandise and other items essential to people's work were confiscated. At present, the AMB has approximately one hundred members who work between streets 6 and 10 on the avenue. It comprises mostly mestizo and indigenous women, although its management has been predominantly made up of men since its foundation. The AMB[7] acts as an intermediary for obtaining street occupation and trading licenses from the Quitumbe Zonal Administration, an entity that governs the sector's spatial regulation. This link has been changing in recent years due to the change in municipal government.

The capacity of the AMB to negotiate with the administration has been based on the legitimacies and links created on the street. It has also been key in mediating interactions between traders with regard to the use of space. Since public policies attempted to regulate "from above" mobility in and occupation of the area, the strategy of becoming an association operated as a way of affirming traders as citizens and making them valid actors. The use of institutional language and codes, while mobilizing practices that were typical of street trade, aimed to maintain the possibility of organizing by retaining a relative autonomy. Characteristic of the popular economy, this would guarantee traders the reproduction of business and family.

SPATIAL TRAJECTORIES AND REPRODUCTIVE STRATEGIES: AFFIRMING RELATIONAL AUTONOMY

Kinship, community, and neighborhood networks that permanently link rural areas with locations in the city represent a central characteristic of the popular dynamic that has continued under new configurations up to the present. Family migration and the networks built around it operate as a nucleus of meaning that supports the historical experience surrounding the work of the female traders of Martha Bucaram Avenue. The trajectories of these women with regard to their family reproduction strategies are linked to a history of mobility, settlement, and appropriation of space. The very management of time and space becomes a centerpiece of the relational autonomy characteristic of retail work.

María Estela,[8] forty-nine, sets up her vegetables on the avenue two or three times a week. She places a canvas sheet on the ground and, on it, a bag containing potatoes and another containing peas. She lives in the Camal Metropolitano, although she travels to her place of origin very often: "I live a bit here and a bit in the Carchi [province of the northern highlands located 180 kilometers from Quito]" (Interview with María Estela, August 7, 2015). Since she was twelve, she has worked in the "potato business." She sows, harvests, and sells potatoes in the markets of the northern and central towns in Ecuador, accompanied by her family.

Like María Estela, several of the interviewees come from families with a long history of trading. Susana, twenty-nine, sells clothes every day on the pavement. Her parents, originally from Riobamba in the central highlands of Ecuador, were also itinerant vendors; they sold wooden Christ figures. "My parents sold those figures; we sold them everywhere. We did not have set places, we were always moving around with my parents" (Interview with Susana, August 7, 2015). While her parents travelled around the region, Susana took care of her four brothers and sisters. "On Fridays, Saturdays, and Sundays we all went to work," she said. In the late 1990s, the family left Riobamba to go to Martha Bucaram Avenue. From the age of thirteen, Susana supplemented her selling by doing paid domestic work in the city. It was her father who taught her the "trade":

> My father showed us how to move around, to work. [. . .] We would go out, then it was in the north, around the airport [north of the city of Quito]. He took us to Machachi [a town to the south of the province of Pichincha], then he took us to

> Ambato [a town in the central highlands]. We were used to moving around with my father [. . .] Always selling Christ figures.

At the age of fifteen Susana got married and together with her husband she began to sell clothing in an itinerant manner and on her own. They separated years later and he "took everything." She asked for a loan and now she has a set place in Martha Bucaram Avenue, which she "looks after," as well as her children aged thirteen, eleven, eight, and three. In 2013, Susana decided to join the Association because "the municipal police kept coming and taking our things so we ran out of merchandise. As we were members (of the AMB), by being united they didn't take our things away, that is, by standing together" (Interview with Susana, August 7, 2015). The AMB has started applying for licenses for its female members and this enables them to be better placed to negotiate with police officers. Susana said that "they carry out raids all over the place but here it's not like that." In contrast, another vendor and member of the AMB, Adriana, reports that "we were assured by the woman from the municipality that by paying the charge and following the rules, as she told us, they would help us with the licenses. But, as we've seen, they haven't helped us at all" (Interview with Adriana, July 18, 2015).

Like Susana and Adriana, half of the women interviewed said that they began selling at a very early age with their families of origin; while they have continued trading, merchandise and places have changed. Each of these changes implies undertaking a "new" business and building and rebuilding the connections that make it possible. The other half spoke of previous jobs in agriculture or urban activities of a strongly subservient and racist nature, such as domestic work, which they tried to escape as fast as possible in order to assert their autonomy and respond to their family needs. Both began working when they were between eight and twelve years old.

Many women come from family trajectories linked to the retail trade, with specific know-how: knowing the where, when, how, and what of selling is a skill they have learned since they were girls. Others explained, however, how motherhood, marriage, separation or violence in their homes of origin, and accidents or unexpected events motivated them to start selling as an activity that was accessible. For some, being on the street and selling on the street are part of the same story.

Approximately half of these women reside in the Martha Bucaram neighborhood or in the Ciudadela Ibarra. Hardly any of them said that they have lived in the neighborhood since the formation of the UTAQ, although some considered themselves to be initiators of that process, recalled the *minga* associations and the organizational processes that developed at the time, and said that they feel a solid sense of belonging. Most spoke of how they arrived in the past decade, a time when the area increased in value and retail sales expanded. The rest live in different rural parishes in the south of Quito (Buenaventura, Camal Metropolitano, Guamaní).

Some women may be found each day on the avenue; others, however, are only there one day per week, on public holidays, on weekends, or in particular seasons, after having previously been granted a set place. There are some who travel several kilometers a day as itinerant vendors in different commercial circuits that include the avenue; they move through the streets and sidewalks or take a bus. Others, most of the members, set up a spot in certain locations and maintain fixed stalls and storage sites. They sell clothing, processed foods, cakes, fruits and vegetables, sweets, meats, fish, and other goods that, as they said, form "their business."

These two types of trajectory—a family history of selling or selling brought about by some kind of accidental event in the life cycle—impact on the creative strategies of family reproduction, which are fundamentally linked to the creation of support networks and to mobility and remaining in the space.

Sometimes, family history in selling and responding to life's contingencies, particularly separation processes, are combined. This is the case for Olga, who has a spot on the avenue where she sells vegetables. She has been selling since she was twelve, encouraged by her grandparents, also itinerant vendors. Beginning when she was fifteen, she worked for a year and a half in a food parlor. However, when she became pregnant she decided to devote herself to selling in order "to get by."

> At that time, the basic wage was 160 (dollars), just that, [. . .] and, the truth was that 160 a month didn't get me anywhere at all, because my son was still in nappies, he was still small. He was still in nappies and it wasn't enough because I had to do the shopping for the house, the rent. But here though, for example, today I make 20 dollars and I can buy nappies, if another day I get 30, I save it and if I can pay the rent, then I do so. So, little by little, you get by. (Interview with Olga, 7 August 2015)

Income in the salaried jobs that these women are able to access does not vary significantly from that provided by street trade. However, the perception is very different. Olga said that she currently earns between 150 and 200 dollars a month for her work as a retailer. The sense of female relational autonomy, to which we referred previously, seeks to evade the subordination involved in some jobs and respond to the needs associated with rearing children, while constituting a strategy for appropriating spaces and taking care of "their businesses" in the face of the transformations in municipal urban planning policies described above. It is from this sense that the initiative to both occupy the city and have an occupation in it is affirmed. The need both for money every day and to be able to manage for themselves when and where they work makes selling a highly attractive occupation, despite the precariousness in which it takes place. This vision is reinforced when compared to women's recollection of exploitation in other precarious jobs.

> It's calm here because when you work as an employee, you get shouted at, to do this, to do that. That's how they talk to us and if possible, they want to hit us. But here though, nobody says anything, nobody, because you're working on your own. And if I want to work, I work, and if I don't, I don't; it's my problem. Nobody tells me what to do. On the other hand, working as an employee is hard; if you don't do something, they tell you off, insult you, take money off what you earn each month for the hours you are late. (Interview with Olga, August 7, 2015)

Olga now lives in Buenaventura, a rural parish in the south of the city. She has been selling on the avenue every day for eight years. It began gradually, a few days a week, until she managed to get established. In an interview, she said:

> I started bringing the things one by one. But, you know, one tomato, a box of tomatoes, a box of *paiteñas* (onions), as well as peppers, and any little thing. I started little by little. From there I started to bring potatoes, corn, like that. You start little by little and then you get going . . . (Interview with Olga, August 7, 2015)

The combination of selling and caring for the family in the same place and its surroundings is a central element in the maneuvering by women that coexists with the uncertainties of daily income and those generated by other dynamics characteristic of unequal gender relations. Veronica is thirty-one years old and sells clothes on the street. The possibility of "managing her time" to take care of her children was one of the main motivations behind devoting herself to selling after spending several years working in jobs in the service sector and paid domestic work.

On our successive visits to the Martha Bucaram neighborhood, making contacts and talking to the women on the street, we observed this combination of selling and caring for children and grandchildren. Some did this individually; others received the support of relatives, friends, neighbors, or older daughters. Cooperative support for caring is a key resource among women, something whose workings are starting to be studied more closely in the specialized literature (Vega, Martínez, and Paredes 2018). Street work is a strategy for care: to socialize children in the activity, to create links, and also to receive support from one's own sons and daughters. As reported by Prieto and Miranda (2018), for the indigenous vendors working in markets and with a strong connection with their communities of origin, boys and girls are there to be shared.

Blanca, thirty, leaves home each day to sell shoes with her two sons. One is ten and the other fifteen. "I get up at six in the morning, with my children, and then I go out to work, to sell." Her husband too; "when he hasn't got any building work, he comes to help me here" (Interview with Blanca, August 23, 2015). The chance to not have to abandon care tasks, combined with the important help that she receives from her children, from other relatives, and from neighbors, reinforces this idea of relational autonomy; something that for our colleague Lucrecia Saltzmann (2016) is associated with subsumed autonomy. Blanca said: "[I'm a trader] because I spend more time with my children and I do not leave them behind in the house." This also enables her "not to be a slave to others. Here as an independent trader, I have the advantage, for example . . . let's say for example my son gets sick, I can stay with him at home" (Interview with Blanca, November 23, 2015).

Other vendors justify their decision to devote themselves to selling "because they had no other option." Another element reiterated by the interviewees refers to the impossibility of getting a good education. María said that, in her family, her brothers were able to study, while the women were forbidden to do so. "By studying, my brothers are now on fixed wages. Meanwhile, I have to suffer to get money; there are days when you sell

Figure 7.1. Female vendor with her family, taking care of her selling place, on Martha Bucaram Avenue.
Cristina Vega and Magali Marega

things and there are days that you don't sell anything" (Interview with María, July 18, 2015).

The trajectories of these women reveal levels of precariousness and vulnerabilities connected to their gender, class, ethnic identity, and "living for the day." However, they also highlight the range of family reproduction strategies that are linked to family socialization of knowledge, resources for survival and supporting oneself, as well as with links (particularly among women) aimed at attending to care needs while affirming the capacity to manage daily life. "Reproductive rationality" (Quiroga 2015), a real driving force for the recreation of popular transactions, lies at the heart of a female dynamic that, as we shall see, establishes demands and negotiation in the urban space.

STREET TRADING: AGREEMENTS AND APPROPRIATION OF SPACE

On Martha Bucaram Avenue, there are commercial spaces of all kinds (hairdressers, shops, hardware stores, restaurants, pharmacies, supermarkets) and some state services (day-care centers and schools). Active commercial and neighborhood life is concentrated on the avenue, both in the morning and in the afternoon, a time of day when prepared food is sold around the sports fields. The weekends are another time for commercial and neighborhood activity. Between streets 6 and 10, the female members of the AMB set up their fixed, semi-fixed, and itinerant selling places; these vendors connect with the above establishments and with a wide range of actors who order and shape the public space each day. "Remaining on the street" is the basic principle that sustains popular trade and family reproduction. This reflects the way in which the relationships between producers, suppliers, vendors, and consumers are structured, organized around a singular retail culture that is based on the demand for everything to be "on hand." It expresses the unevenness with which popular politics takes place in negotiations and disputes about the measures introduced by the municipal government.

Persistence and mobility have their rules and implicit codes, which are established habitually through existing networks and the constant practice of agreement, cooperation, and conflict. The legitimacy to remain and move through the space comes from socially-shared codes and values. Any woman who intends to take over a certain space may do so as long as she does not take the place of another female colleague, does not impede access to an establishment and has its approval, and respects the spatial distribution and diversity in job classifications. It is vital for these women to know how to negotiate and manage relationships with neighbors, home and shop owners, as well as with passers-by and institutional actors. These interactions reveal the "moral economy" of which E. P. Thompson spoke: a form of legitimate social organization that is based on common customs. Failure to comply with these regulations entails moral sanctions, in addition to expulsion or latent conflict. Much of the legitimacy is gained from the action of "taking care" of the selling place, the space and the link, and to do so a sustained, regular presence is vital. A salesman on the avenue, a former head of the Association, described the organization process for the allocation of places as follows:

> They have priority, obviously, because they *mark* the spot. [. . .] If you come, you work only [. . .] two, three days and then nothing, and after two or three years you come back and say, "my place was there," but now another woman is there already, working every day, all the feast days of the year. So who has priority? The one who works, the one who's there. (Interview with Gerardo, former leader, February 12, 2017)

As we have said, in addition to daily occupation, there are those who come to sell only on the weekend, on public holidays (Valentine's Day, Mother's Day, etc.), or even in particular seasons. Even in these cases, regularity and the maintaining of relations with neighbors and traders, constructed as appropriate, enable sellers to update their right to be there.

Another strategy that we identified refers to the expansion of family networks in the occupation of space. A member of the family takes over a specific location; this might be a corner, an intermediate sector, on the curb, or in the avenue itself; it might be in the best sites, where there is greater affluence and better material conditions, or in a marginal location. Once the woman has taken over a space, she requests the help of other family members, who in this way can gain access to other adjoining locations. María has a place on one of the most sought-after corners where she can sell vegetables; she managed to negotiate this after an arduous battle with the grocery store that is right on the opposite sidewalk. Her daughter started a small point of sale adjacent to hers, also with vegetables. Maria's brother then moved in, with fruit in this case. On the opposite corner, in the afternoons her son brings out a cart with prepared foods. Everyone must "take care" of their positions, in addition to contributing in different ways to feeding the networks that support and protect them. The clothes vendor, Susana, formerly of the wooden Christ figures that we mentioned above, travels several kilometers to stock up on clothing. "I go shopping in Tejar [Quito's historic center] or sometimes in Otavalo [a town in the northern highlands, ninety kilometers from Quito] and sometimes the *fantasy stuff*[9] we make ourselves."

The notion of relational autonomy also lies behind the sense of "family business" that is affirmed in traditions and "common customs." Alejandra is thirty-seven years old and sells pork in Martha Bucaram Avenue on Sundays. From Monday to Saturday, she is employed as a stewardess on the integrated trolleybus system. Her interview shows that "taking care of business" is not only linked to territorial appropriation, but it also constitutes a practice that is maintained over time through cooperation networks between women.

> Traditionally we are people from the countryside, we are business people. My grandma also sold pork in the markets in Machachi, in Latacunga. Then, I came here after some years and we decided to buy and sell animals for breeding. Seeing the businesses of my mum, my aunts, my family, I also started selling animals. We went to the villages, to the fairs, like Latacunga, Saquisilí, Ambato, Salcedo. We came back with animals for breeding. (Interview with Alejandra, August 23, 2015)

The accounts obtained in the fieldwork show the existence of circuits that reach up to two hundred kilometers away; kinship, both biological and ritual, and a sustained commercial relationship are vital. It is necessary to work on not just kinship relations, but also those that form the base of the commercial circuits of supply (wholesalers, but especially retailers), both neighborhood and regional, from which traders draw their strength.

In the nearest environment, the avenue is integrated into a sales and supply circuit consisting of the markets or fairs of Las Cuadras, La Aurora, Guamaní, La Ecuatoriana, La Arcadia, and La Argelia, which are rural parishes in southern Quito.[10] Other more extensive concentric circuits, linked to the supply, production, and marketing of manufactured articles, can be detected through the interviewees' accounts. Some female vendors of agricultural products (vegetables, tubers, and pig, cow, and sheep meat) are also supplied by their families and places of origin, which are located in the rural areas of the central-northern highlands of Ecuador. More than vast global networks, in the case of these food retailers, the activity centers on the relationship between countryside and city or between towns, together with medium and small suppliers located in the same city. Despite the expansion and impact of supermarket chains, both in terms of marketing and consumption and when imposing conditions on their suppliers, these transactions continue to be of huge economic, social, and cultural importance (Arrazola et al. 2016). Accordingly, it should be noted that tension continues between the new modernizing project to create subcentralities, based on the concentration of types of commercial activity, and the popular "on hand" sales culture.

Regulatory activity over the period has sought to control and contain this type of selling. In the face of the appropriation (and hoarding) of space by the family networks described, the municipality chose to limit their capacity through the "purging of lists." Censuses, created by the association and dis-

Figure 7.2. Female fruit vendor serves a customer.
Cristina Vega and Magali Marega

cussed with the Zonal Administration, served as the basis for limiting access to positions by members of the same family, a measure that was supported by the previous leadership. The ex-president of the AMB said: "This is common, but in the Municipality they were trying to put a stop to it because a kind of monopoly is being created. I take a spot, and my son then grows up, he takes another one; and my son has children and they grow and there goes another. So the same family becomes the owner of the whole fair. And the municipality does not want that." (Interview with Gerardo, former leader of AMB, February 12, 2017). He told us how the mechanism for the purging of lists works.

> We have the municipal registry and we give a list with our full names, ID numbers, things about us. Then they put the information in the database and take a look at them. In alphabetical order, if my name is Moreno, or Silva, and I have my parents, my nephews and nieces, my uncles and aunts, there are about fifty Silvas there and they look. My descendants are going to have the same surname. But in the case of Silva Meneses for example, there will be about twenty. Then they realize that this one is his son, this one is his nephew. So they remove them. They say no, we only give two places per family. (Interview with G., former AMB leader, February 12, 2017)

Negotiations and permanent disputes about the right to remain and mobilize in the space are expressed in various institutions and highlight the complexity of dialogue with the state agents. They involve the daily lives of tens of thousands of female retail traders who maneuver to reproduce their families by creating and asserting networks, especially through the family and the different locations that are woven into the latter.

CONCLUSIONS

Understanding the popular in today's popular economy requires a close examination of the relational component of popular economies from a gender perspective. It is also necessary to weave this further into the analysis of ethnicity. Such an analysis highlights both the role of family reproduction and the relational elements mobilized by women to move into and establish themselves in the street and in urban space in general. A reproductive logic and relational autonomy hint at the consideration of the relations and entanglements of female vendors, both with each other and in their negotiations with the authorities.

This chapter has highlighted different dynamics in order to understand the recent past. First, it demonstrated continuities in the transfer of knowledge and dispositions that encourage women to start selling and the way in which trading is linked to family histories and life cycles. Second, it highlighted the continuities between the countryside and the city, as well as the networks of proximity in which popular trade continues to exist today. The promotion of sub-centralities by the municipality (governed by Alianza PAÍS) and its regulatory management has not restricted the thrust of this process, which has grown even further since the weakening of the Citizens' Revolution project. Third, it showed how women traders have articulated associative responses to resist the new regulations and be recognized by the administration. They have been negotiating and managing their own places and expanded their sense of spatial appropriation. Other elements—such as fiestas, elections, political work, party forces, and the dialogue with the municipality—are also important and ought to be looked at from the perspective of gender relations and identities, but we have not been able to address them here. All these, just as the reproductive dynamics that have provided our focus, promise to advance toward a bottom-up understanding of the complexity of popular transactions in the city.

NOTES

1. This text is based on research carried out as part of the project *Promoting the Economic Empowerment of Women through Better Policies*, coordinated by the Interdisciplinary Centre of Development Studies-Uruguay (CIEDUR) and funded by

the International Development Research Centre (IDRC). The Ecuadorean team also included Lucrecia Saltzmann and Héctor Fabio Bermúdez from the Study Group on Work of Facultad Latinoamericana de Ciencias Sociales, FLACSO-Ecuador. Other findings are reported in Vega et al. (2016) and Saltzmann (2016).

2. In Latin America, in 2015, the informal non-agricultural unemployment rate rose to 46.8 percent (International Labour Organization, Labour Outlook, 2016). In Ecuador, in June 2017, of those in employment, 47.9 percent worked in the formal sector, while 45 percent worked in the informal sector (INEC 2017).

3. It is the differential of power and the taking advantage of the interstices of state regulations and political structures that characterize the actors of "globalization from below" (Tassi et al. 2013, 38–39). The "hegemonic" system, which expresses the institutional and operational logic of the state and private capital, and the "non-hegemonic" are intertwined (Ribeiro 2012). An emblematic example of the latter is the cross-border trade in counterfeit products that are distributed from China through a series of hubs and ultimately reach smaller fairs in Latin America.

4. According to various studies (Salomon 1980; Del Pino y Marín de Terán 2005; Granja 2010), Hoya de Guayllabamba (where the present city of Quito is located) can be seen as a center where inter-regional trade routes converge.

5. Rather than subcentralities promoted by globalized capital accumulation processes in the peripheries, territorial hierarchization in Martha Bucaram could be considered as a process toward "popular subcentralities" (Beuf 2011), with a preponderance of small-scale sectors and activities.

6. The neighborhood, the avenue, and the association of retail traders took the name of Martha Bucaram in honor of the wife of former President Roldós (1979–1981).

7. The AMB, which is constituted as a primary organization, is affiliated to the Federation of Retail Traders of Pichincha (FEDECOMIP) and, nationally, to the Unified Confederation of Retail Traders and Autonomous Workers of Ecuador (CUCOMITAE). The capacity of these organizations was reinforced in the 1990s at a time of major political upheaval and growing social precarization. Since then, its local bases have been weakened, although it has also been present in the emergence of new associations, which, like the AMB, were born in the context of new urban policies.

8. All names have been changed.

9. Necklaces, bracelets, and other imitation jewelry products.

10. Several of these neighborhoods in the south of Quito resulted from the division into lots of former estates in the years following the agrarian reforms. Solanda, for example, was the property of the Marquesses of Solanda. According to the testimony of the former butler of the La Argelia estate, the landowner Augusto Saá owned several estates in this area (Castañeda 2013, 28).

BIBLIOGRAPHY

Antunes, Ricardo. "Los modos de ser de la informalidad: ¿hacia una nueva era de la precarización estructural del trabajo?" (Tema central). *Ecuador Debate*, 94 (2015): 69–79.

Arrazola, Iñigo, Nataly Pinto Alvaro, Johanna Renckens, Héctor Ballesteros, and Patric Hollenstein. *The Role of Private Actors in the Quito Metropolitan District Food System*. Quito: VECO Andino and RUAF Foundation, 2016.

Bhattacharya, Tithi. *Social Reproduction Theory: Remapping Class, Recentering Oppression*. London: Pluto Press, 2017.

Barragán, Rossana. *Espacio urbano y dinámica étnica: La Paz en el siglo XIX*. La Paz: Hisbol, 1990.

Benería, Lourdes, and Marta Roldán. *Las encrucijadas de clase y género*. México: Fondo de Cultura Económica, 1992.

Beuf, Alice. "Las centralidades urbanas como espacios concebidos: referentes técnicos e ideológicos de los modelos territoriales del plan de ordenamiento territorial (POT) de Bogotá (Colombia)." *Cuadernos de Geografía: Revista Colombiana de Geografía* 25, no. 2 (2016): 199–219.

Castañeda, Cesar Iván. "La ruta de la memoria: revalorización simbólica del Qhapac Ñan, camino ancestral del sur de Quito: el caso del barrio oriente quiteño." Master thesis, FLACSO-Ecuador, 2013.

Coraggio, José Luis, ed. *Economía social y solidaria en movimiento*. Buenos Aires: UNGS, 2016.

Del Pino, Inés, and Luis Marín de Terán. "Algunas reflexiones sobre el Ecuador prehispánico y la ciudad inca de Quito. Quito-Sevilla: Junta de Andalucía, Municipio de Quito, Embajada de España y Pontificia Universidad Católica del Ecuador. 2005.

Denning, Michael. "La vida sin salario." *New Left Review* 66 (2011): 77–94.

Federici, Silvia. *Revolución en punto cero. Trabajo doméstico, reproducción y luchas feministas*. Madrid: Traficantes de Sueños, 2014.

Gago, Verónica. *La razón neoliberal. Economías barrocas y pragmática popular*. Buenos Aires, Tinta Limón / Madrid: Traficantes de sueños, 2015.

Giraldo, César, ed. *Economía popular desde abajo*. Bogotá: Ediciones desde abajo, 2017.

Granja, Ángeles. "Análisis de la situación de los comerciantes informales del Centro Histórico de Quito, después de su reubicación en los Centros Comerciales del Ahorro, vista desde la perspectiva de los propios comerciantes." Master thesis, FLACSO-Ecuador, 2010.

Guerrero, Andrés. *Administración de poblaciones, ventriloquia y transescritura. Análisis históricos: estudios teóricos*. Lima: IEP, FLACSO-Ecuador, 2010.

Hart, Keith. "Informal Income Opportunities and Urban Employment in Ghana." *Journal of Modern African Studies* 11, no. 3 (1973): 61–89.

Hollenstein, Patric. *La reproducción de la dominación racial: experiencias de una familia indígena en Quito*. Quito: FLACSO-Ecuador—Abya-Yala, 2009.

Instituto Nacional de Estadística y Censos de Ecuador. *Encuesta Nacional de Empleo y Subempleo*. Quito: INEC, 2017.

International Labour Organization. *World Employment and Social Outlook: Trends 2016*. Geneva: International Labour Office-ILO, 2016.

Kingman, Eduardo. *La ciudad y los otros: Quito 1860–1940*. Quito: FLACSO-Ecuador, 2006.

Millar, Kathleen. "The Precarious Present: Wageless Labor and Disruptive Life in Rio de Janeiro, Brazil." *Cultural Anthropology* 29, no. 1 (2014): 32–53.

Narotzky, Susana. "Economías ordinarias: valores escondidos. Otra antropología de la crisis desde el sur de Europa." *Antrópica. Revista de Ciencias sociales y Humanidades* 1, no. 2 (2015): 67–76.

Nun, José. *Marginalidad y exclusión social*. Buenos Aires: Fondo de Cultura Económica, 2001.

Ortiz, Santiago, and Elvira Martinez. "La propiedad, un sueño realizado: relato oral de los pobladores de La Argelia." In *Antigua Modernidad y Memoria del Presente. Culturas urbanas e identidad*, edited by Ton Salman and Eduardo Kingman. Quito: FLACSO, 1999.

Prieto, Mercedes, and Maria Isabel Miranda. "Travesías del cuidado de la niñez indígena en Quito y en el medio rural de Ecuador." In *Cuidado, común y comunidad. Experiencias cooperativas en el sostenimiento de la vida en América Latina y el sur de Europa*, edited by Cristina Vega, Raquel Martínez Buján and Myriam Paredes. Madrid: Traficantes de Sueños, 2018.

Portes, Alejandro, Luis Guarnizo, and Patricia Landolt. *La globalización desde abajo: transnacionalismo inmigrante y desarrollo. La experiencia de Estados Unidos y América Latina*. México City: FLACSO-México-Miguel Ángel Porrúa, 2003.

Portes, Alejandro, Manuel Castells, and Lauren Benton. *The Informal Economy: Studies in Advanced and Less Developed Countries*. Baltimore, MD: The John Hopkins University Press, 1989.

Quiroga, Natalia. 2015. "Decolonial Feminist Economics: A Necessary View for Strengthening Social and Popular Economy." *Viewpoint Magazine* 5. https://www.viewpointmag.com/2015/10/31/decolonial-feminist-economics-a-necessary-view-for-strengthening-social-and-popular-economy/.

Ribeiro, Gustavo Lins. "La globalización popular y el sistema mundial no hegemónico." *Revista Nueva Sociedad* 241 (2012): 36–62.

Salomon, Frank. *Los señores étnicos de Quito en la época de los Incas*. Otavalo: Banco Central del Ecuador, 1980.

Saltzmann, Lucrecia. "Trabajo autónomo en la ciudad de Quito: Sentidos y trayectorias de trabajo de las comerciantes minoristas organizadas en la Asociación Martha Bucaram." Master thesis, FLACSO-Ecuador, 2016.

Sassen, Saskia. *Una sociología de la globalización,* Buenos Aires: Ed. Katz, 2007.

Tassi, Nico, Antonio Rodriguez, Carmen Medeiros, and Giovana Ferrufino. *Hacer plata sin plata: el desborde de los comerciantes populares en Bolivia*. La Paz: PIEB, 2013.

Tokman, Victor. "El imperativo de actuar. El sector informal hoy." *Nueva Sociedad* 90 (1982): 93–105.

Valdivieso, Nancy. "Reubicación del comercio informal en el Centro Histórico de Quito. Conflicto y resolución." Master thesis, FLACSO-Ecuador, 2009.

Vega, Cristina. "Rutas de la reproducción y el cuidado por América Latina. Apropiación, valorización colectiva y política." In *Comunalidad, tramas comunitarias y producción de lo común*, edited by Raquel Gutiérrez. Puebla: Pez en el Árbol, 2018.

Vega, Cristina, Raquel Martínez Buján, and Myriam Paredes, eds. *Cuidado, común y comunidad. Experiencias cooperativas en el sostenimiento de la vida en América Latina y el sur de Europa*. Madrid: Traficantes de Sueños, 2018.

Vega, Cristina, Alison Vásconez, Magali Marega, Héctor Bermúdez, and Lucrecia Saltzmann. *Ecuador: Mujeres, Empoderamiento y Trabajo Informal en Ecuador Diversidad de Regímenes y Restricción de Derechos*. IDRC, CIEDUR, CEDLAS, 2016.

Vogel, Lise. *Marxism and the Oppression of Women: Toward a Unitary Theory*. New Brunswick, NJ: Rutgers University Press, 1983.

Afterword

Guillermina Rico's Family: Four Generations of Street Vendor Leaders in Mexico City

Carlos Alba Vega

Guillermina Rico, a lemon peddler who bargained her way to wealth and power as the head of a political machine she forged from the ranks of Mexico City's itinerant vendors, died on Wednesday of a cerebral hemorrhage. She was sixty-three. In the market stalls and side streets she was known as *La Jefa*, the boss, and at her death her office walls were adorned with photos of the curly-haired matriarch, often wearing a trademark white apron, with senators, mayors, police chiefs and every Mexican president since Jose Lopez Portillo took office in 1976. [. . .] In a forty-year career, Mrs. Rico led thousands of market peddlers through cycles of street war and peace with successive Mexico City mayors, who have repeatedly sought to clear the streets of the informal merchants who block sidewalks in front of tax-paying businesses. Sometimes the vendors have been removed to suburban markets, but always they have returned. The vendors, whose ranks swelled during years of economic crisis as farmers lost their land and factory workers were dismissed, hawk everything from tortillas to tires to pirated American music tapes. Today Mexico City's central market is among the largest outlets in the world for contraband. In 1946, Mrs. Rico joined the governing Institutional Revolutionary Party, known as the PRI, and eventually she organized the vendors into a powerful bloc that cast thousands of ballots for the governing party. During the early years, Mrs. Rico's leadership was informal, but in 1965 she organized 500 merchants into the Civic Union of Street Vendors of Old Merced. Twenty years later, the union's ranks had swelled to 3,000, and by 1985 it stood at 7,000. Mrs. Rico gained the power to assign the choicest market stalls, for which she charged a quota, and those and other revenues made her wealthy. The Chamber of Commerce estimate in 1988 that Mrs. Rico and other union leaders collected about $1 million annually. She funneled vast sums into the pockets of city authorities, partly to forestall their periodic threats to remove the vendors. Some of her riches she channeled into

> social work, and she once responded to a reporter's question about what she had done for Mexico: Ask the priests in the downtown churches who is the one that helps them. Go to the shelters. Ask the drug addicts and the alcoholics undergoing rehabilitation. (Dillon 1996)

This acknowledgment of Guillermina Rico's death in the *New York Times* (Dillon 1996) points to the political power and economic activities of a female leader in an "informal" street market in Mexico City. It reveals her enormous influence in seemingly diverse, but inextricable, interlinked spheres, such as trading contraband, social work, and political engagement. In this epilogue, I take this obituary in a renowned newspaper as a starting point to give voice to Guillermina Rico and Silvia Sánchez Rico, her daughter and successor.[1] In what follows, they narrate their personal trajectories and experiences, first as street vendors and then as the heads of the most important vendor organization which they presided over in the Historic Center of Mexico City. Located in the east of the Historic Center, the Merced market (*La Merced*) was the most important wholesale and retail food market in Mexico City. In 1957, it was expanded and remodeled, but the city's demographic and economic growth, as well as the traffic this caused, led to the creation of the Central Market (Central de Abastos) in 1982, in the current municipality (*alcaldía*) of Iztapalapa. The Merced market, which still exists, was one of the centers from which street commerce radiated out in Mexico City, and in this same neighborhood the vendor organization led by Guillermina Rico, and later her descendants, started. Drawing on their accounts, it is possible to reconstruct the family leadership trajectory passed down over four generations spanning almost a century: from Susana González in the 1930s, followed by Guillermina Rico, then by her daughter Silvia Sánchez Rico, and, finally, by Julio Ramos Sánchez Rico, the current leader.

"My grandfather drank a lot and my grandmother Susanita suffered a lot because of that. My grandfather died because of the alcohol when Guillermina was six years old."

My grandmother, Susanita González Díaz, was born in San Juan del Río, Querétaro, and arrived in Mexico City very young, during the time of the Spanish flu, because she was orphaned and her stepfather treated her very badly. She and her sister were six and nine years old and were *arrimadas*[2] in a house where they worked as maids. When she was twelve, she married Manuel Rico Mejía of Metepec, near Toluca, in the State of Mexico, and they lived in a huge *vecindad*.[3] Later they moved to another *vecindad*

Figure 8.1. Guillermina Rico with her husband, Salvador Sánchez; her mother, Susana; and other members of her family, Metepec, State of Mexico, circa 1955.
Archive Sánchez Ricos' family

located at Talavera number 14, where my uncles were born. Manuel worked in construction and as a baker; later he worked in commerce: he sold ice cream and fruit drinks. Susanita had her first child when she was thirteen, her son Vicente. Then came Fernando, Cándido, and Manuel. Lastly came Guillermina, my mother. My grandfather drank a lot and my grandmother suffered a lot because of that. He was in the military and went to fight in the Cristero War.[4] He died as a result of the alcohol when Guillermina was six years old. My grandmother Susanita was on her own, but two other children were given to her: María and Francisco Rico González, who were orphans, and she took them in. Later there were more, in total she raised nine. She suffered a lot and earned a living selling fruit in baskets. "She sometimes didn't even have tortillas to make us *chilaquiles*," Guillermina would say. All my uncles worked in commerce: they made and sold ice cream; they were *boleros* and *chicleros*.[5] Finally, they sold fruit in the old Merced market. My grandma went to sell fruit in the Zócalo, next to the National Palace, but she said that the soldiers would *malorear*[6] her, they grabbed her and everything. Therefore, she went to sell *tamales*[7] and *atole*[8] in the Merced. Later, in the 1930s, they were given their places here, and wooden stands with metal roofs were made for them. Here she sold on Corregidora and Roldán Streets. My grandmother Susanita was also a leader of the vendors in the area of Manzanares Street.

"My mother Guillermina started working at eight years of age"

My mother Guillermina was born on February 10, 1934, at Roldán Street number 40, in the heart of the Merced, and my father was born in 1932. She started working at eight years of age; they unloaded the fruits and vegetables close to her house. She and her brothers picked up what was left on the street, they washed it and sold it. Some time later, the leader provided her with her first wooden stand with a metal roof on Roldán Street. My grandmother also sent my mother out to sell lemons from the time she was eight years old. She sold everything—lemons, oranges—or she would go on buses to sell gum, newspapers or magazines—*Prensa, Pepín, Chamaco.*

She only studied until the third grade at the school called 18 de Marzo, and she also had to support her siblings, who were all boys. My grandmother did not want them to become pot-heads, thieves, or addicts. They stayed at home and the women went out to work. It was true what my Mom said, she had to maintain her brothers.

My father, Salvador Sánchez Velázquez, is from Texcoco. He always sold bananas, it was his specialty: plantains, or Dominico or Tabasco bananas, here in the middle of the street. That is how my mother met him, watching him. She got married at twenty-one, and she soon became interested in the defense of the interests of street vendors.

In one interview, Guillermina states:

> Since I was little I liked to get involved in politics, as they say. From the time I was a girl I got involved in that mess. My mother paid a quota of 20 cents to the legislator Manuel Ávila, but there were also several leaders of a union here they called the "Union of the Four." [. . .] There were arguments sometimes and the leaders fought to see who would support each of them; we were with two men, Salgado and Velázquez. Mr. Salgado had an ice cream shop right at the corner of Corregidora and Jesús María, and Mr. Velázquez had his poultry shop around the corner from the ice cream shop; those were the true leaders at that time. . . . So, I stopped going to school and started going everywhere with those leaders. That's when I learned a lot, that's why I stuck to them, because they went to get the permits [to sell in the streets]; I hung onto the arms of the ladies so I could hear what they were saying . . . and they always convinced the authorities to let us sell. The only thing they didn't want was for us to block the passageways of the stores. But from that whole time, the thing I remember most is that we suffered a lot; we really suffered. . . . The hardest time was with Mr. Uruchurtu [Regent of Mexico City] and Mr. Ruiz Cortines [President of Mexico]; they really went after us, they set the riot police on us

because they didn't want a single street vendor in these plazas. . . The life of the street vendor is sad and full of suffering. You work out in the cold, out of doors, and the kids get sick, because sometimes we didn't even have a place to wash our hands, and if you were breastfeeding you had to do it without washing up or anything. [. . .] When they took the old Merced market from us, there were very few of us selling in the street. They set the riot police on us, they sent police after us, they sent inspectors, and they couldn't finish us off. (Rimada Ovideo 1994, 14, 15, 18)

Silvia recalls: From the time she started to live with my father unmarried and until now, we never saw any separation between them. My father was working in his business and she had hers. He let her defend the people. She would say to him, "Let me do it Salvador, the people are in need." "Yes," he would say, "but let them be, they have to do it for themselves." "No," my mom would answer, "the people believe in me, I have to be there." When he started to see that she had that leadership, he said: "Do what you want, but take your daughters with you." At that time the three of us were very little. My mom had to *jalarse* (go) with the three of us. Guillermina observes:

My husband was an energetic man and he set the pace for me. I suffered a lot with my husband because, as they say, when you love a person you suffer and when you don't, the separation comes soon. Everything you sold had to be handed over to the man and if you didn't present your accounts properly, you got hit. I already lived with my man, and before they rented to us there, it was a "hotel" and the place was full of *mujeres galantes* (prostitutes). . . Then after some time my eyes were opened. I opened my eyes a little and we went our separate ways my husband and I, as they say: he had his things and I had mine, and we separated, and it's hard because of the love one feels, but that's how I could support my children and teach them to work and forge ahead, but with respect for their father" (Rimada Oviedo 1994, 19).

My mom started to have influence and people followed her even before she got married. With regard to her experience as alternate legislator, she affirmed:

I was in [political] campaigns, running up and down, without caring about anything or anyone else, all just for the campaigns, and I became alternate [legislator] for Mr. Juan Araiza Cabrales; but I never knew what it meant to be alternate, I was never called to the Chamber of Deputies; I thought they would call me and say, "you have to be here and you have to do this," but there was nothing. That's why I said no when they asked me if I wanted to be a legislator, because frankly I think I can help my companions more from the streets than from "inside." (Rimada Oviedo 1994, 29)

Commerce has always taken place in the streets, where people circulate . . . and these streets have always been busy; for example, there were vendors on Corregidora Street, not just now, but many years ago. . . . Trade takes place out of necessity, because there are people who are "elderly" and they can't get work, or they are made to retire. (Rimada Oviedo 1994, 17)

"She had charisma, but the important thing was: she spoke the truth"

My mom liked to be on the corners, she couldn't stand to see an injustice. She had that gift to be able to say: "I'll go help them out." How many vendors did she bring together? At the beginning, a relationship developed between about sixty people in 1963. They were from the Merced area, all sold fruit, there were a lot of men, but the majority were women. "The first to start the organization with me," says Guillermina Rico, "were the folks from Anillo de Circunvalación [Avenue]; those people had been selling for 35 or 40 years; then all the people from Corregidora, Manzanares, also joined in" (Rimada Oviedo 1994, 26).

At that time, we had been "picked up" [forcibly taken off the streets]. An organization or relationship was developed, but it wasn't [formally or legally] established. The formal organization was created in the early 1970s: it was called the Civic Union of Street Vendors of Mexico City, and we later changed it to the Civic Union of Street Vendors of the Antigua Merced, and it is registered with Notary Public number 28. This was the first official organization. I later represented the organization.

My mother's main qualities, as a leader, were that she had charisma, but the important thing was: she spoke the truth; that created trust. Kindness was another; also, as we say here in Mexico: you had to have guts to defend the people. She went knocking on doors until someone listened; she reached the level of the president. She spoke to a lot of presidents; she also spoke to the one with the ears, what's his name, with Carlos Salinas de Gortari. He invited all of us women to eat at Los Pinos [the residence of the President]. I also went there with my mother and saw Los Pinos. That was before they gave us the plazas [shopping centers]; we were invited in about 1990. We were all scared because they had expropriated [buildings and lands]. In that conversation, the only thing discussed was that they wanted a different historic center, modern, pretty, without removing the colonial homes. In situations like that, Guillermina Rico said: "I believe in a pretty Mexico . . . but we have to eat . . . since I'm not God, I can't speak of what will come . . . I was born here and, where else can I go? If I go elsewhere, I won't know anyone; but here it's a family . . . we've been through everything together: sad times, nice times, and happy times" (Rimada Oviedo 1994, 5).

My mom represented up to ten thousand people. There were groups that joined this organization. It was a social and democratic organization; everything that Guille did was with helping other people in mind, helping our companions; in earning our daily bread. She didn't run things as a business. Because a lot of people say: if there are ten thousand vendors, at so much [she receives] from each one . . . she makes a lot of money. No. Suffice it to say that nothing was even charged for office expenses; that tells you all you need to know. It was a democratic organization, it was there to help.

The organization grew because people started to hear that there was support and protection in this organization; there were groups from other streets, from other neighborhoods, from other markets that started to come to the organization. If there were no permits for a market, we went to support them, to negotiate with authorities and there were positive responses from them. And in this way, the authorities let others sell.

In order to lead these ten thousand people, there were "delegates" in each zone. She would see how things were going in each zone, if there were any problems or not. She had up to thirty or forty delegates. The authorities lend us the streets, because they belong to the citizens, they belong to all Mexicans. Are we as vendors owners of the streets? No. There are a lot of people in this country.

There were more women delegates than men. Women are predominant because we're stronger. They see us as the weak sex, but we're tougher. We're

Figure 8.2. Guillermina Rico and her daughter, Silvia Sanchez Rico, selling fruit before the opening of the economy and the arrival of Chinese merchandise.
Archive Sánchez Ricos' family

the ones who pamper the husband, and the children; we're the ones who say: "yes, we're going to suffer, we're going to fight." Sometimes the man doesn't want to suffer, he doesn't want things to cost him a little. He says: "I do it for pride's sake." We women like to suffer, to be fearless, we like to defend our families.

Doña Guille (Guillermina) also dealt with people's family and personal matters. She'd have to get the husband out [of jail] because he'd been imprisoned; she'd go and see how to fix the problem if a husband had hit his wife; if a child was being beaten at home, all those sorts of problems. Or if someone's son was on a bad path and had been arrested . . . and if we let him be taken to the reformatory or to jail, if he were over eighteen, maybe he'd turn bad. That's why we'd go and *Doña* Guille would lend a hand. She'd say: "I'll lend you money. And hopefully he'll get out with an *amparo* (injunction)."

"I didn't register for junior high because my dad said no, women should only study until sixth grade, and know how to read and write"

I [Silvia] was born in 1957, at Manzanares Street number 24, in the city center. My mom lived there with my sisters and me. The children of Guillermina Rico are Margarita, Silvia (me), Chabela (Isabel), Salvador, and then the other two siblings who were given to my mother. I started working outside my home from the time I was six years old; I sold my piles of lemons as well as gum at Roldán number 16, outside *el cafeto*. When I wasn't selling anything, I'd go on the buses. I started selling there. Even the buses drivers knew me; they found it funny; at first they wouldn't let me on the buses because I was young and short. If I was six years old, I looked four. They let me on, and I sold. And it wasn't out of necessity, or because I was being exploited by my mom or my grandmother, no. It was because I wanted to, because I wanted to earn my own money. That money was mine, I kept it.

My father set me up selling in the warehouse he rented. Later I bought it, in 1985. We sold peanuts and bananas year round; then there were the seasonal fruits: cantaloupe, mango, guava. He also sold replacement parts for machines, oil, fan belts, and to one side I had my fruit. I sold everything: haberdashery. I started to sell *fayuca*[9] in the 1970s and 1980s: cosmetics, Dove soap, bubblegum, the perfume with the little pineapple, Sirena, Giovanni. My spot was at the corner of Corregidora and Correo Mayor [Streets], on the east side.

From the time we had a small restaurant, my sister Isabel started to drink beer, from when she was ten and none of us realized. She saw the *macheteros*[10] unloading and how they enjoyed their beer. She was a real alcoholic. She was a lot of fun. Very pretty, with big, made-up eyes; she got really dolled up. She was younger than me.

I went to the school here, Cristóbal Colón, which is around the corner, next to the alley; I only studied until sixth grade. Then I didn't register for junior high because my dad said no, women should only study until sixth grade, and know how to read and write. He was really macho. And he didn't let me continue studying. I wanted to get my degree in law. But it wasn't possible. Also, I got married very young, I had my son. And then later, I got into Secondary School Number 6, on the corner of Carmen and Guatemala, where only women go in the afternoon. I left my son Julio there with the caretaker, when he was young. But once one of the people from the store called me to go and pay for the merchandise my husband had ordered one season. And since he knew my husband, he'd lent to him. So I had to pay what he owed. I left the secondary school because I had to pay. I said: "if I don't pay, then this man won't lend to me. And so I can't continue studying." That's why I didn't keep studying. Because I did have time, but I really enjoyed selling, I liked working. Then I worked as a *fayuquera* [trading *fayuca*]. At that time I was about seventeen; and until I was twenty-five years old we still had our cases with gum, our sandals from China, blouses with baubles, all of the *fayuca* that was around at that time. I brought it in from Laredo. I'd go by bus. The plane wasn't worth it, we'd bring two or three small suitcases. When I changed my line of business and started selling clothes made in Mexico, then I'd buy here from the Jews. I also sold dresses on Correo Mayor Street, dress suits for women. That's how things changed. I sold shoes made here, from Guadalajara and from León. It changed every season. In December, I sold my ornaments and my garlands, my pilgrims [nativity scenes with the Holy Family]. I'd go to Guadalajara and there was a lady who'd lend me all the nativity figures. Once the season was over, I'd pay her. The same with the person for the garlands and for the tree decorations.

Every year, from the time I became independent of my parents when I was fourteen, I went off with my husband, and we married in a civil ceremony. His name is Julio Ramos García; the father of my children is still alive. I have four boys and a girl. The eldest is Julio Cesar Ramos Sánchez Rico and I had him when I was fifteen; next is Juan Francisco, who was born when I was seventeen; then came Pedro and later Raymundo and the girl, Silvia. The oldest two are married now, and each one works on their own in commerce. Julio has been a vendor since he was a kid. He was a really hardworking kid, because he was the oldest he was the one we expected a lot of: "here son, do this." And "bring me this and bring me that." He was the one who helped me the most. Or if he wasn't helping me, I'd say: "stay with your brothers and sisters, make them soup, and then come to the stand with me." Then comes Paco. There's a ten-year age difference between the rest of them. All of them studied until high school, but then didn't want to study more. They preferred selling. If as a parent you work in commerce, sometimes it's our fault, but we don't have the means to have them at home and just studying. For me, as a woman, it was difficult. There was no one to be sitting down with them doing homework, motivating them. So, a lot of times children also need their mom to help them be motivated for school. I would have liked my mom there to motivate me, but since she worked all her life, and in all honesty she always gave us the opportunity to study, but we didn't want to keep studying. But that's where the problem is: we need the mom or dad to be there helping them, lending a hand to motivate them. It really is true what the commercials say: if we don't motivate a son, we can't make him a great man. Now I see that. I needed their dad around, even if just to be checking that they did their homework, not to maintain me, I knew how to get things done; I knew how to work. I tell all the women: "don't give up on your husbands; tough it out. Because if the first one treated you badly, the second one will treat you worse." That's the truth. Men go to see their kids, but they're not going to see the ones they had before. Well, not all of them, but that's the reality of life. That's why when I see a woman who wants to separate, I give her advice: "no, don't leave him; look, deal with him, put up with him, don't be jealous, don't throw him aside. Team up. Take care of him." But I'm divorced and I ended up in this situation to be able to do my own work. My husband said to me: "it´s either your mother or me." And I told him I chose my mother. Because I helped her out: I went to make purchases, to supply the stands, I helped her out when she was trying to get them to let us work.

"There are a lot of women vendors who are on their own. The husband just knocks them up and then leaves them"

There are a lot of women vendors who are on their own. The husband just knocks them up and then leaves them. Once they've given birth, they come back, they get them pregnant again, and then they take off again. I had friends who I took into my home—fellow vendors—because I know what it's like to be alone. Why not lend a hand to others? Women in Mexico were left on their own, now we are braver. Now we're not afraid [when we're asked] what are we going to do, who is going to support us, who is going to feed my kids. Now women are taking on a new attitude. I know that there was a woman president in Argentina, who led the women. I didn't think a woman would be able to become president. As a woman I feel proud. I was with my mother all the time, from the time I was little, I always had the gift for giving orders, the ability to say to someone else: "do this for me because this has to be done this way; this is the way to sweep, this is the way to set up, this is the proper arrangement." I feel that I've been a leader since that time. I was never a "delegate" for my mom. I was her right-hand man. I had my own business, but I had to split my time, to work at my mom's stand. My mom was a great vendor. She sold her tacos. We're very proud of our work in commerce. I wasn't a delegate because I was more interested in selling than in being a delegate, because I had my kids and I had to help out my mom. My mom also acknowledged the roles of the other people who were representatives [delegates]. She was so fair, she didn't place us above other people just because we were her daughters. She was very respectful, very upright and loyal.

But when the organizations was established at the official level, from then on I was the organization's treasurer, starting in around 1972. We were always in the struggle. For the struggle, the daughters were on the front line. We went together, to the demonstrations, not to protest but to support them. We never went to one to protest, it wasn't necessary. There was always dialogue with the authorities and a positive response. We were in the National Confederation of Popular Organizations (*Confederación Nacional de Organizaciones Populares*, CNOP), but since the year 2000 I don't support the PRI (*Partido Revolucionario Institucional*) or any other party. Now, in the situation we're living in, it's better to wait for when it's our moment. They say that times are good and you have to wait for them.

When my mom was alive, there was respect among the leaders, they respected one another's areas: "I won't go into your area and you don't go into mine." The areas were specialized according to product. There were a lot of Spaniards in the stores; they went to the Central Market (*mercado de abastos*) even before the Merced market changed location. I knew at that time that changes were coming and that the street vendors were going to be relocated. And that what the Mexico City government had bought was to make the shopping centers for us. My mother was supposed to enter into the [relocation] program, because she had to obey the authorities. And they wanted a better historic center. That's the way a politician is, they look for solutions for their people. She believed in that project, up to that time. Here we have the Roldán shopping center; I think it's a good project, but it requires modifications.

All the presidents helped us out; at that time no one took us off [the streets]. When someone takes care of us, we can't be ungrateful. She was always grateful. It wasn't that she was a PRI supporter through and through. At the time we didn't know any other political party. There wasn't, as they say, democracy. There wasn't anything to choose from.

I didn't participate in the negotiations with Uruchurtu, the city regent in the 1950s and 1960s, because I was very young, but I imagine that it was the same as things were at that time. Although I know that he was very tough, very rigid, he was the toughest; he didn't want anything. But like all people, he let the people *torear*[11]; but there weren't a lot of us.

The difference between male and female leaders is that there are still a lot of chauvinist men. There really are. They don't want to be women's helpers, they don't want to be led by them. They call them the weak sex. I see it among the young men as well; they are still macho, although they say they are modern.

If his woman is wearing a miniskirt, he wants to put pants on her. Meanwhile we, as women, don't care if the helper is a man or a woman.

People need to be proactive. But my mom took people into consideration [when making changes in the organization]. It was the people who had the final word. If people didn't say anything, then it wasn't my mother's fault. If something was going wrong, there were changes. Thank God there weren't many changes [in delegates]. And those were because she didn't like to see [the delegates] taking advantage of people. She didn't like locations to be sold[12] to the highest bidder, as they say now. *Doña* Guille didn't like that. She said: "the authorities didn't sell them to me"; she said to me: "the street is there, set up your people from the organization." She never charged a peso [for a location]. And I never said it costs this or that for the location, because the authorities never asked me for a cent. Now things are handled differently. When my mother was around, or when I was there, I didn't allow it; it wasn't allowed because the authorities never asked us for money. The location was given and people didn't have to pay for it.

"Since my incarceration, now all the delegates who worked with my mother have their own organizations"

Doña Guille died in 1996. On her death, everyone agreed that I should be the general secretary of the Civic Union of Street Vendors of the Antigua Merced. My mom told everyone: "when I die, I want you to support my daughter." She told a lot of people. But that's not why I did it or wanted it. As in every organization, there was a board of directors; everyone was called to a general assembly and they voted for me to be the general secretary, just as *Doña* Guille, who was always general secretary but never president of the organization. Then there was the treasurer and the board members. That's how *Doña* Guille did things, and that was best for her, and I continued to respect that. People voted for me. At that time, more than twelve thousand people voted, many more, but I only took 7,500 signatures to the Notary Public. I still have them stored away. From the time the PRD (*Partido de la Revolución Democrática*) arrived, they [my mother's delegates, the so-called *comadres*[13]] tricked people by saying that I had sent them, and that when I got out of jail, they would be delegates again. I was in jail from March 1999 to March 2000, for one day short of a year. My incarceration was planned by the government.[14]

The organization [of Guillermina Rico] didn't do it for money, but for political reasons. To have more union members in order to have . . . At that time people said: "they belong to the PRI . . . so, they wanted to break up the organization." But they were wrong; because times change, people change, everyone has different ideologies. I always told the people: "vote for whoever you want." No one here was forced or no one was told, because we already saw what was coming; we saw the strength of the PRD. In a way I wasn't the threat, the threat was that the organization was strong. That's why they started to attract people and the *comadres*. Dolores organized meetings. Now I find out. There are people who told me: "yes, Silvia, we were called and they made an offer for us to become the representatives of streets." Yes, they betrayed me.

The organization has never disappeared and I've never shut it down. We have the shopping center at Roldán, the one on Venustiano Carranza, on La Soledad; there are nine centers that they handed over to the Civic Union of Street Vendors of the Antigua Merced. I am the joint guarantor of these shopping centers and all these people are still part of the organization. Those are the union members we have. Right now I don't represent anyone from the street. But if people come and seek me out, we go to knock on doors and we'll respect the authorities.

Now that all the vendors are in the shopping centers, sales in these centers have been very low. It's hard because everyone has to provide food for their homes. But anyhow, those who were clever, those who were sharp, who didn't sell or transfer ownership of their location in the street, they were the smart ones. Because now they go home with the *persinada*,[15] because the "bullfight" is tough. Now a lot of people say: "it's a good thing I didn't sell my premises, that I still have it, that I paid for it."

I do agree with a lot of things. I want a pretty historic center, where I can walk and I know all my neighbors. The government's project isn't new, it's been around for years, and they've been tweaking it. We'll have some opportunity. Because I don't think there'll be an end to commerce in the street; there'll always be the person selling candies, or the person selling seeds [pumpkin seeds] or gum. They will always be around. Because a person who sells gum or packets of seeds is not going to set up in a shopping center or market. There are a lot of opportunities for all of us to be okay. Not to affect others or be affected. We all want to pay taxes, but it has to be fair. That he who has more pays more. If we're going to pay for water and they're going to charge us three times what we paid, that isn't fair. If we're going to pay for electricity and we get a bill as high as if it were a residence, that's unfair. And while they get around to fixing the meters, in the meantime you have to pay or they cut off service. That forces people to [illegally] connect to electricity cables in the street.

"We had to all create a common front, shoulder to shoulder"

How we were able to maintain order when there were so many of us in the organization? There was respect and people knew that this organization fought so that everyone would have space; and that we all had to create a common front, shoulder to shoulder. If someone came from outside to attack us, it wasn't allowed, they were thrown out. If a companion assaulted a fellow vendor, they were given a penalty of a day or two, depending on the nature of the assault, because there was a leader and there was respect. You can't go and say to one of your fellow vendors: "get rid of that." No, that's why there's a leader, a representative, to resolve problems. *Doña* Guille was one of those who would say: "okay, here you have to have respect, you have to line up the stand in line with your companion. Otherwise you'll have to pack up." Why? Because in the bylaws of the organization it states what can and cannot be done. Every organization has bylaws. Those bylaws granted the authority to be able to say: "you have to keep your location clean, your space; pick up your garbage when you leave; sweep the area that corresponds to you." There was order. The delegates were responsible for making sure that order was respected. All the people respected it. From 1999 onwards, there has been disorder. We all have rights, but order is needed. If I'm blocking a sidewalk with four rows of vendors, then I'm even affecting the other street vendors, because they're not going to sell [the same amount] as if they were in one line. What is divided up into three, can be taken by just one row. Street commerce is totally out of control. But, well, that's how it is. There are more of us Mexicans, so we have to be alert in order to help all other citizens. It's true, there are doctors here, architects, professionals. There is a lot of unemployment. They have no other option but to get out there and sell.

On the topic of health. If a person was sick and had no money for a doctor, the organization helped them out. But to really dig deep and find out people's needs, no leader has that information, because that's not our work. We need to seek advice to figure out how we can help the people we represent and the government. That's a serious health problem that the local government isn't addressing. Before, you couldn't get involved in other spheres. Why? "The person who makes a move won't show up in the photo." What are you as a street vendor leader doing involved in that? Now, since we're in a democracy, we do have to think about how we can help our fellow vendors. But I need to have more information. I need to know how we can help our companions.

I showed you guys all the photos I have [three to four photos]. I showed you the *comadres* and the authorities. I also have photos of Cuauhtémoc Cárdenas. He presented me with the shopping center on Venustiano Carranza. He was mayor, he had to hand it over to me, although the agreement existed since 1993. I asked Cárdenas to start charging us a year later . . . so that we wouldn't have to pay interest, because we didn't want to have an overdue loan like everyone else. He did me that honor. We started paying a year later, but if we didn't pay, we were charged 15 percent interest. Thank God we were able to pay. So, tell me if I was a good leader or not. No other leader did that!

FINAL COMMENTS

The narrative of Silvia Sánchez Rico, intermingled with some comments from her mother, Guillermina, provides insight into the construction of female leadership, and allows us to distinguish the characteristics that are recognized in a leader who is entrusted with the representation of the interests of others. It also reveals the challenges involved in taking on the role of a leader in popular commerce, such as the role of the extended family, which, despite the poverty experienced during the early stages of this leadership, accommodates adopted children and later spills over into social actions vis-à-vis homeless, destitute, and marginalized people. In case of extended family, commercial activities encompass all members of the family—this can be seen as an opportunity, or it can occur because family members do not see other options. In the world of street vendors, it is therefore common for all family members to be vendors and the formation of new couples takes place among the young people working in commerce.

The female life stories further reveal that once women become key actors in production and social reproduction, their life as a couple, commenced in adolescence, at times weakens and ends with the dilemma of having to choose just one option: husband or work. Once women become involved in commercial activities, they fully embrace them, yet that does not imply they are no longer responsible for all domestic tasks and childcare. These "invisibilized" tasks denote a pronounced inequality of work between men and women.

This account also points to the social organization and the prominent role of *compradrazgo*. This system of "elected kinship," which is considered "sacred," bolsters a social and religious union that is reproduced not only through traditional *compadrazgo*—which is based on the married couple—but through the bond almost exclusively among women. The women, many of them single mothers, sometimes end up working as street vendors as it is their only alternative for survival and they create their own sphere of legitimacy and autonomy; through their work and struggle they have earned the respect of their families and companions, and they become the vanguard for hundreds or thousands of vendors.

At the same time, it is important to note the participation of children in commerce from a very early age. Besides the material needs and precarious situations which lead them to work, there is social and cultural pressure signaling that everyone should provide for him or herself from a young age. That is also why new families begin their cycle just after adolescence and women especially abandon school early.

The story of the Rico family allows us to appreciate the multiplicity of products sold by each person over the course of a year and a lifetime, which vary according to the cycles of rites and ceremonies of civil and religious holidays, fashion trends, and the rhythm of the schools. But the merchandise also changes for other reasons, which are more linked to technological, economic, and commercial transformations, driven by international political decisions, for instance by liberalizing trade. Thus, commerce in the street is tied into the local, national, and international economy. There are periods when vendors purchase merchandise from established merchants, who in turn buy products made in Mexico, and other times when they bring in *fayuca* products or small-scale contraband from the United States and, since the 1990s, increasingly from China.

Silvia Sánchez Rico's narration offers us also a window into the relationships, agreements, and clashes with the world of politics, ranging from street politics to politics at the highest level, as street vendors are essential bases of support for campaigns and elections. Her story reveals the reasons, both economic and political, that lead certain local authorities to tolerate and promote street commerce. She states confidently: "The authorities lend us the streets because they belong to the citizens, they belong to all Mexicans."

NOTES

1. The narrations stem from various interviews conducted in Spanish by Carlos Alba and Pascal Labazée at El Colegio de México on October 16, 2007, when Silvia Sánchez Rico agreed to participate in a roundtable with students and other leaders of street vendors; the second interview took place on the same day in a restaurant; the third was recorded at her street stall on November 3, 2007; the fourth interview was recorded by Carlos Alba and Hélène Rivière d´Arc in a restaurant near La Merced market. The interviews were translated into English by the author.
2. In this case, *arrimada* refers to domestic workers.
3. A *vecindad* is a one- or two-story building made up of several small homes where several poor families live, generally in one room with a kitchen, and with a shared patio and shared services, such as bathrooms and laundry facilities.
4. The Cristero War refers to an uprising in central-western Mexican states against the secular Mexican government from 1926 to 1929.
5. In Mexico, *boleros* and *chicleros* are people who work shining shoes and selling gum.
6. *Malorear* probably means to do bad things to her or touch her inappropriately.
7. A steamed corn dish, often served in a banana leaf.
8. A hot beverage, based on corn.
9. *Fayuca* is the term used in Mexico to refer to any trade bringing in contraband from the United States.
10. *Cargadores* are people loading and unloading merchandises from the trucks.

11. *Torear* literally means to "bullfight"; in the language of street vendors, it means not having a fixed stand in the street but to continually move to evade the police.

12. Some organizations "sell" the right to use areas in public spaces to the vendors and also charge rent for "use rights." This rent differs depending on the location; it can vary from a few pesos to 100 pesos (5 US dollars) per day.

13. *El compadrazgo* is a form of social parentship which is not necessarily based on consanguine kinship. When a child is baptized, the parents—or the mother of the child should she be single—choose a couple (similar to godparents/sponsorship) as *compadre/comadre* and establish a close social relationship with them. In the popular economic realm, there are many single mothers who are referred to as *madrinas* to emphasize that this relationship exists only with the women but not with a couple with the women only.

14. It is important to note the process of fragmentation undergone in the city's most powerful street-vendor organization when the party in power in the city government changed in 1997, shifting from PRI to PRD, and when, in this context, street vendors supporting the PRI became the opposition. Some members of the new political class in power created incentives for those who were second in command to or delegates of the leaders who controlled the streets—Guillermina Rico's *comadres*—to accept the trade-off offered to them by the politicians. For different reasons, the main leaders of the street vendors affiliated with the PRI were jailed, in this case, those of the Civic Union of Street Vendors of the Antigua Merced. The new government achieved its goal to weaken the leadership, without completely eradicating it.

15. The *persinada* is a vendor's first sale of the day, with which they make the sign of the cross to give and ask for thanks.

BIBLIOGRAPHY

Dillon, Sam. "Guillermina Rico, Boss of Mexico Vendors, 63." *New York Times*, September 6, 1996.

Rimada Oviedo, Antonio. "Interview Antonio Rimada Oviedo with Guillermina Rico in 1991." *SUMMA,* November 18–23, 1994. Revisited in *¡Si hablaran estas calles de la Merced! Memorias de Guillermina Rico González*, 17. México: Autoridad del Centro Histórico, 2010.

Index

About the Authors

Carlos Alba Vega is a professor in social and economic development at El Colegio de México. He has taught and has been visiting fellow and professor at universities in Mexico, France, Germany, and the United States. He has been editor of the journal *Foro Internacional* (Center of International Studies of El Colegio de México), is a member of the editorial board of *Tempo Social* (University of São Paulo, Brazil), *Sociétés Contemporaines* (France), and *Frontera Norte*, and was a member of the editorial boards of *Revista Mexicana de Sociología* (Institute of Social Studies, UNAM, México), and *Perfiles Latinoamericanos* (Facultad Latinoamericana de Ciencias Sociales, FLACSO, México). His last book, edited with Gordon Mathews and Gustavo Lins Ribeiro, is *Globalization from Below: The World's Other Economy* (London: Routledge, 2012). His next book, with Marianne Braig, is *Las voces del Centro Histórico: La lucha por el espacio en la Ciudad de México* (El Colegio de México and Freie Universität Berlin, forthcoming).

Florence E. Babb is the Anthony Harrington Distinguished Professor of Anthropology at the University of North Carolina at Chapel Hill. She is the author of *Between Field and Cooking Pot: The Political Economy of Marketwomen in Peru* (University of Texas Press, 1998 [1989]), *After Revolution: Mapping Gender and Cultural Politics in Neoliberal Nicaragua* (University of Texas Press, 2001), and *The Tourism Encounter: Fashioning Latin American Nations and Histories* (Stanford University Press, 2011). She has recently published *Women's Place in the Andes: Engaging Decolonial Feminist Anthropology* (University of California Press, 2018).

Rudi Colloredo-Mansfeld is professor and senior associate dean for social sciences and global programs in the College of Arts and Sciences at the University of North Carolina, Chapel Hill. He has written and taught about community economies and cultural change in the context of globalization since 1991. His recent books include *Fighting Like a Community: Andean Civil Society in an Era of Indigenous Uprisings* (University of Chicago Press, 2009) and *Fast, Easy and In Cash: Artisan Hardship and Hope in the Global Economy* (with Jason Antrosio, University of Chicago Press, 2015).

Eveline Dürr is a professor at the Institute of Social and Cultural Anthropology, Ludwig-Maximilians-Universität in Munich. Previously, she held a position as associate professor at the Auckland University of Technology in New Zealand. She received her PhD and venia legendi (Habilitation) from the University of Freiburg, Germany. She has conducted fieldwork in Mexico, New Zealand, the United States, and Germany. Her research projects include urban anthropology, spatiality, tourism, mobilities, globalization, and human-environmental relations, and take into consideration the historical trajectories and power imbalances that have formed present conditions. She published widely on urban issues, including a monograph on identity and meaning of urban space *Identitäten und Sinnbezüge in der Stadt. Hispanics im Südwesten der USA* (Münster, Lit, 2005), and edited with Rivke Jaffe, *Urban Pollution: Cultural Meanings, Social Practices* (Oxford: Berghahn, 2014 [2010]).

Natalie Göltenboth holds a PhD in social anthropology with a specialization in urban issues, arts, and religion in the Caribbean and the Mediterranean. She is a lecturer at the Institute of Social and Cultural Anthropology at Ludwig-Maximilians-Universität in Munich and at the Venice International University, Venice. She is also an artist, freelance author, and editor working in the interface of anthropology and contemporary arts, and is engaged in outreach projects on aesthetics, politics, and anthropology. Her current research focuses on contemporary arts, urban transformation, and economies in Havana, Cuba. She is author, among author publications, of *Art and Cult in Cuba* (Berlin: Reimer, 2006).

Magali Marega is a PhD student at the Center for Research and Advanced Studies in Social Anthropology (CIESAS)-Mexico in Mexico City. Her lines of research are related to the anthropology and sociology of labor, trade unionism, informal work, and gender.

Peter Mörtenböck is professor of visual culture at TU Wien, director of the Centre for Global Architecture, and research fellow at Goldsmiths College,

University of London. His current work focuses on urban speculation, global resource consumption and new data publics. He is also developing new research around the notion of "Building Capital"—how architecture's capacity to both materialize and signify the production of value is being enlisted in the creation of new geographies of investment. Mörtenböck's most recent books include *Visual Cultures as Opportunity* (2016) and *Informal Market Worlds* (2015). Together with Helge Mooshammer, he is currently working on three major book publications—the edited volumes *Data Publics* and *Incorporating Informality*, as well as the monograph *Building Capital: Urban Speculation and the Architecture of Finance*.

Helge Mooshammer is an urban and cultural theorist based at TU Wien, Director of the Centre for Global Architecture and Research Fellow in the Department of Visual Cultures at Goldsmiths College, University of London. He has initiated numerous international research projects around questions of (post-)capitalist economies and urban informality. Mooshammer's most recent books include *Visual Cultures as Opportunity* (2016) and *Informal Market Worlds* (2015). Together with Peter Mörtenböck, he is currently working on three major book publications—the edited volumes *Data Publics* and *Incorporating Informality* as well as the monograph *Building Capital: Urban Speculation and the Architecture of Finance*.

Juliane Müller is a lecturer at the Institute of Social and Cultural Anthropology at the University of Munich (LMU). She received her doctorate from Martin-Luther University Halle (Germany) and has been a postdoctoral scholar at the University of North Carolina at Chapel Hill. She specializes on the anthropology of trade and markets, migration and mobility, community organization, and sports. Recent publications include "Entrepreneurship, Artisans, and Traders. The Remaking of China-Latin America Economies" (Special Dossier, *Journal for Latin American and Caribbean Anthropology* 23(1): 9–93, 2018, co-edited with Rudi Colloredo-Mansfeld), "Place-Based (In)Formalization: A Bolivian Marketplace for Consumer Electronics and Global Brands" (*Latin American Research Review* 52(3): 393–404), and "Plurale Ökonomie anders denken: Populärer Handel im Plurinationalen Staat Bolivien" [Rethinking the Plural Economy: Popular Commerce in Pluri-National Bolivia] (*Psychosozial* 145(39): 95–109, 2016).

Cristina Vega is a professor at the Department of Sociology and Gender Studies of FLACSO-Ecuador and part of the research group "Transactions, Economy and Common Life" of FLACSO-Ecuador. Her research addresses processes of feminization, informalization, and precarious labor. She has done extensive research on reproductive and care work. Current projects address retail sales in Quito and strategies of post-earthquake production and reproduction at the Ecuadorian Pacific. Her latest publications are: "Rutas de la reproducción y el cuidado en América Latina. Apropiación, valorización colectiva y política" in Raquel Gutiérrez Aguilar (Ed.), *Comunalidad, tramas comunitarias y producción de lo común*, Pez en el Arbol, 2018; "Explorando el lugar de lo comunitario en los Estudios de Género sobre sostenibilidad, reproducción y cuidados" *Quaderns-e*, 2017; and "Más allá del mito del emprendedor. Estrategias económicas, familiares y afectivas de los retornados a Ecuador desde España" *Papers*, 2016. She has coordinated the book *Cuidado, comunidad, común. Experiencias cooperativas en el sostenimiento de la vida en América Latina y el sur de Europa* (Madrid: Traficantes de Sueños, 2018).

André Vereta-Nahoum is professor of sociology at the University of São Paulo, associate researcher at the Brazilian Center for Analysis and Planning (CEBRAP), and at the Research Group on Culture and Economy (NUCEC) at the Federal University of Rio de Janeiro. He holds a PhD in sociology from the University of São Paulo and the Max-Planck-Institute for the Study of Societies (Cologne, Germany). His research currently deals with the role of experts' discourses and practices in the making of markets and economic realities. His most recent paper is "Conversões da dívida entre os Yawanawá Um modelo de análise dos fundamentos culturais, sociais epolíticos da troca" (Tempo Social, Revista de Sociologia da USP 29,1).

www.ingramcontent.com/pod-product-compliance
Ingram Content Group UK Ltd.
Pitfield, Milton Keynes, MK11 3LW, UK
UKHW020210290926
15470UKWH00001B/109

9 781498 572392